BOOKS *of the* BIBLE

A Survey of the Old and New Testaments

John H. Hayes and Keith Schoville

ABINGDON PRESS
Nashville

About the Writers

Dr. John H. Hayes wrote the text portion of BOOKS OF THE BIBLE: A SURVEY OF THE OLD AND NEW TESTAMENTS. Dr. Hayes is Professor of Old Testament at Candler School of Theology, Emory University.

Dr. Hayes has authored a number of books, including *Introduction to the Bible, Understanding the Psalms,* and *An Introduction to Old Testament Study.*

Dr. Keith Schoville, the writer of the workbook portions of this study, is professor emeritus in the Department of Hebrew and Semitic Studies at the University of Wisconsin-Madison. He is the author of *Biblical Archaeology in Focus,* an introduction to archaeology, and numerous articles in dictionaries and journals on archaeology and the biblical world.

Dr. Schoville has excavated at Tel Dan in northern Israel, Tel Lachish in the south-central region of the country, and Tel Aroer in the southern region. He is also president of the Near East Archaeology Society.

BOOKS OF THE BIBLE: A SURVEY OF THE OLD AND NEW TESTAMENTS
New Edition,
Copyright © 1983 by Graded Press
Third Edition,
Copyright © 1998 by Abingdon Press

ISBN 0-687-05519-9

This book is printed on acid-free paper.

MANUFACTURED IN THE UNITED STATES OF AMERICA.

03 04 05 06 07—10 9 8 7

TABLE OF CONTENTS

EDITOR'S INTRODUCTION

BOOKS OF THE BIBLE: A SURVEY OF THE OLD AND NEW TESTAMENTS is a study for adults of all ages who want to be better informed about the Bible. This study unit takes six months of weekly one-hour sessions to complete. The contents of the Bible are divided into twenty-six parts.

In these twenty-six lessons, you will learn about all sixty-six books of the Bible in the order in which they appear. At the end of this study, you will have paged through the whole Bible, from Genesis through Revelation. And, you will also have learned something about the content of each book in the Bible. Writing answers in this workbook will help you commit to memory some of the contents of the Bible. What follows will tell you how to use this workbook.

- During the previous week you will read selected portions of Scripture in order to have a general idea of the content of the upcoming lesson.
- In each session you will complete the sections in the workbook.
- After the group completes the workbook, you will take a few minutes to recall the highlights of the Scripture studied in that lesson. Try to commit these highlights to memory for future reference.
- Then you will check your workbook answers and raise questions about answers you do not understand.
- You will use the remainder of your class time to discuss the questions at the end of each lesson.

We hope that after finishing this six-month Bible survey, you will be acquainted in a general way with the content of each biblical book.

DAILY READINGS FOR GENESIS

Day 1: Genesis 1:1–2:3
Day 2: Genesis 11:1-9
Day 3: Genesis 12:1-7
Day 4: Genesis 18:1-15
Day 5: Genesis 28:10-22
Day 6: Genesis 32:22-32
Day 7: Genesis 41:1-57

THE PENTATEUCH

INTRODUCTION

The first five books of our Bible are called the *Pentateuch*. The word is of Greek origin and means "five books." The Pentateuch was written on a single scroll by Jews who called it the *Torah*. The word *Torah* means "law," or "moral instruction," and the references to "the Law" in the New Testament apparently refer to the Pentateuch. The five books contain a variety of stories, poems, and legal texts that have been combined by a writer or editor into a unified work in a five-part sequence.

THE STRUCTURE OF THE PENTATEUCH

The five books tell the story of God's people from the call of Abraham to the death of Moses. The call of Abraham is recorded in Genesis 12:1-7, and the death of Moses is found in Deuteronomy 34. The time span covered by the story is from about 2100 to 1250 B.C.

The first eleven chapters of Genesis set the stage for the call of Abraham. The stories in this prologue go back into prehistory, answering questions each generation wants to know about how things came to be the way they are. The stories point to the moral degradation of humankind. They set the stage for Abraham, a man who believed God and whose faith was counted as righteousness.

Abraham, his son Isaac, and grandson Jacob are known as the *patriarchs*. Their stories and the stories of Jacob's sons make up the remainder of Genesis. At the close of the book, the descendants of faithful Abraham are in Egypt, rather than the land of Canaan. From a small group of seventy persons in Egypt, the descendants of Israel, as Jacob is called, multiply until their numbers threaten the security of the Egyptians. This initial fulfillment of a part of God's promise to Abraham sets the stage for the story of the Exodus.

Exodus recounts how God raised up Moses to deliver the people of Israel from slavery and to lead them to the Promised Land. With difficulty, but with God's help, Moses leads the people out of Egypt to the base of Mount Sinai. At Sinai, the people enter into a covenant to be God's people, while the Lord agrees to be their God.

Leviticus provides detailed instructions for the priests and people on living carefully with a holy and jealous God. The Book of Numbers records the travels of Israel to the border of the land of Canaan. However, they were destined to wander in the wilderness for forty years rather than to take possession of the land immediately. The book describes the trek to the eastern side of the Jordan Valley. Deuteronomy describes how, before he dies, their leader, Moses, repeats the rules and regulations they are to obey when they cross the Jordan under his successor, Joshua, and take possession of the Promised Land.

The Pentateuch thus ends on a note of expectation. The promises of God to Abraham have been only partially fulfilled. The possession of the land and the blessings to the families of the earth await fulfillment in the future.

THE AUTHORSHIP OF THE PENTATEUCH

Jewish and Christian tradition held that Moses was the writer of the Pentateuch, except for the last few verses that tell of his death. However, in the modern period many scholars have questioned the authenticity of the tradition. An alternative theory was developed in the nineteenth century. According to this theory, the Pentateuch contains different literary and oral traditions. Careful analysis suggested four main documents that had been welded together by editors over the centuries. Abbreviations for the names scholars gave to these theoretical documents give us the title, the "JEDP" or "Documentary" Hypothesis.

IMPORTANT THEMES IN THE PENTATEUCH

God's call of particular individuals and then of a particular people to fulfill God's purposes is a major idea in the Pentateuch. We call this idea *election*. However, election is not for selfish enjoyment but for service to God. In this way, God's ultimate purposes will bless all humankind.

God established special relationships with individuals and with the people of Israel by means of covenants. God initiated covenants with Noah, Abraham, and Israel (at Sinai). God's covenants were connected with new revelations about the divine nature. They imposed moral and ritual demands on the participants. These covenants provide a background for understanding the new covenant under which Christians live.

The idea of law is another theme in the Pentateuch. Jeremiah (31:31) looked to the time when God's law would be written on the hearts of his people, as Christians believe it is through the presence of the Holy Spirit.

The Exodus is the last major theme we will mention. The Exodus is often referred to in the Bible. During the Exile in Babylon, the Jews looked for a new Exodus to restore them to their land. And when Jesus came, his work was described in the language of the Exodus. (See Luke 9:30-31.)

GENESIS

Mimi Forsyth

In this lesson we will study the first book of the Bible, Genesis. This name comes from the Greek word that means "origin" or "source." The book describes the origin of the world as well as the origin of the ancestors of Israel, the chosen people. The Hebrew name for the book is *bereshith,* which means "in the beginning." This title comes from the first word in the book. In the ancient world, books were often called after their opening words.

The Book of Genesis covers the time from Creation until the death of Joseph. That's a lot of history to cover in only fifty chapters! The book ends after setting the scene for the work of Moses, which the Book of Exodus narrates.

The Book of Genesis has two main parts. The first part, Genesis 1 through 11,

describes the creation and early history of humankind. The second part is Genesis 12 through 50, which provides narratives about the patriarchs of Israel—Abraham, Isaac, Jacob, and Jacob's sons.

THE CALL OF ABRAHAM

The call of Abraham in Genesis 12:1-3 is the dividing point between the two parts of Genesis. If the Book of Genesis were a seesaw, then the call of Abraham would be the support on which the seesaw rests. The first part of Genesis focuses on all humanity. In the second part, the focus narrows to the time of Abraham and his descendants.

Read Genesis 12:1-7.

God commands Abraham, here called Abram, to leave his native land and migrate to another. In addition to this command,

God promises Abraham several things. Read Genesis 12:1-7. Then answer the questions below.

a. God commands Abraham to migrate from Haran to Canaan. Locate these places on the map on page 12. How many miles did Abraham and his family walk? Underline your estimate.

(200) (400) (600) (800)

b. God promised to make of Abraham a great nation (12:2). Read Genesis 11:30; then explain in your own words why this was a special promise.

c. In Genesis 12:3 whom does God promise to bless?

d. In the New Testament we are told that "by faith Abraham obeyed when he was called to set out for a place that he was to receive as an inheritance; and he set out, not knowing where he was going" (Hebrews 11:8). Which verse in Genesis 12:1-7 shows the faith of Abraham?

GENESIS 1–3

Genesis 12 through 50 describes what happens to Abraham in the new land and how God fulfills these promises. So the call of Abraham looks toward the future and the realization of the promises. How then does Genesis 1 through 11 relate to the call of Abraham and the rest of the Book of Genesis? The answer is this: Genesis 1 through 11 is the backdrop against which we view the call of Abraham and the origin of Israel as a people.

THE CREATION

The first eleven chapters of Genesis describe the creation of the world, humankind's disobedience, God's judgment, and God's grace. Genesis 1 through 11 contains stories and genealogies. The stories narrate early human history and thus provide the historical background for the call of Abraham. The genealogies trace the various branches of the human family, giving the ethnic background for the call of a chosen people represented in Abraham.

The worship of many gods is called *polytheism.* Israel's neighbors associated various phenomena in nature with various gods. This is a fragmented view of the universe. In contrast to this view, Genesis 1 and 2 present God as apart from the universe. What God has created is not to be feared by humankind, but to be subdued by humankind. And God called the creation good. There is only one God, the Creator.

Genesis 1 and 2 give the biblical account of Creation. In fact, we have two Creation stories in these chapters. Each comes from a different time in Israel's history. In the first account, Genesis 1:1–2:4, God creates the world in six days; and God's final act is the creation of human beings. Read Genesis 1:26-28.

In the second Creation story, which begins with the second half of Genesis 2, verse 4, God first creates a man and places him in the garden of Eden. Then God creates trees, animals, birds, and finally a woman. If we read Genesis 2:24, we see that one purpose of this account of Creation is to explain why the sexual bond is so strong.

Chapter 3 tells the story of Adam and Eve. They refuse to live within God's limits by eating the fruit of the tree in the midst of the garden. So God punishes them and expels them from the garden.

1. The Creation stories taught the Israelites about the nature of God and humankind. What does Genesis 1:26-28 tell us about God?

2. What do these verses tell us about humankind?

3. The author of Genesis 3 wants to explain why certain conditions exist. The union of man and woman is described in Genesis 2:24. What three conditions does God's speech in 3:14-19 explain?

a. (3:14)

b. (3:16)

c. (3:17)

GENESIS 4–6

Genesis 4 tells how Cain kills his brother Abel after a disagreement about offering sacrifices to God. After God punishes Cain, we read that many of the elements of civilization develop from Cain's descendants. These elements include the building of cities, the making of musical instruments, and the working of metals.

Chapter 5 begins with a genealogy that traces the human family from Adam to the time of Noah. This chapter tells us that many of Adam's descendants lived more than 900 years!

Genesis 6 through 9 records the Flood story. Chapter 6 describes the reason for the Flood. It also tells about the building of the ark.

1. The descendants of Cain developed elements of civilization. Read Genesis 4:17-22. What point do you think the writer of Genesis is making here?

2. What human characteristic grieved God and brought on the Flood? (6:1)

3. What does Genesis 6:11 teach us about the nature of God?

GENESIS 7–22

Chapters 7 and 8 tell about the Flood. At the end of this account God promises to restore the natural order in the future and to never destroy the world by water again. In Genesis 9, we read about Noah and his sons Shem, Ham, and Japheth. Also we learn that the rainbow symbolizes God's covenant with Noah.

Like Chapter 5, Chapter 10 is a genealogy. This genealogy lists the nations of the world according to whether they descended from Shem (the Semites), Ham (the Egyptian-Hamitic groups), or Japheth (the Indo-European peoples).

The story of the tower of Babel in Genesis 11:1-9 describes how humanity tries to exceed its limits and glorify itself by building a tower to the heavens. God then confuses their speech. These verses are ancient Israel's way of explaining why persons speak different languages and so have difficulty cooperating with one another. Our use of the word *babble* to describe

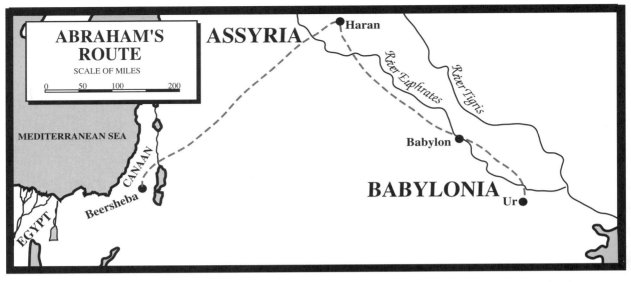

ABRAHAM'S ROUTE

SCALE OF MILES

0   50   100   200

ASSYRIA

Haran

River Euphrates

River Tigris

Babylon

BABYLONIA

Ur

MEDITERRANEAN SEA

CANAAN

Beersheba

EGYPT

meaningless language comes from this Old Testament story.

We find another genealogy in Genesis 11:10-32 where the writer traces Shem's descendants as far as Abram and Sarai (later changed by God to Abraham and Sarah). This genealogy of Shem sets the scene for the call of Abraham in the following chapter.

With Chapter 12 we begin the second part of Genesis, which focuses on the patriarchs and ancestors of Israel. Genesis 12 through 50 contains four main collections of ancestral stories. In each collection, one of the ancestors appears as the primary personality. These four collections revolve around Abraham, Isaac, Jacob, and Joseph and usually their wives.

Genesis 12 through 25 tells the story of Abraham. In Genesis 12:4-9 this ancestor of Israel leaves his homeland and journeys about 400 miles to Canaan. In verses 10 through 20, Abraham goes to Egypt when a famine strikes. There Sarah spends some time in the pharaoh's house. Chapter 13 tells how Abraham and his nephew, Lot, divide the land of Canaan. Lot chose the Jordan Valley, leaving Abraham the hill country. Like most of the Abraham stories, this story in Genesis 13 emphasizes God's promise to Abraham. Read Genesis 13:14-17.

Genesis 14 describes how Abraham and his followers defeat four neighboring kings who invade Canaan. Notice that this chapter is the only one that describes Abraham as a warrior rather than a shepherd.

In Genesis 15 God renews the covenant with Abraham. Although Abraham is childless, God promises him many descendants. Imagine Abraham's reaction to this promise since he was about eighty-five years old! Chapter 16 relates the attempt of Abraham and Sarah to have children. Abraham fathers a child by Sarah's maid, Hagar.

Chapter 17 explains how the rite of circumcision becomes part of the covenant. The destruction of the sinful cities of Sodom and Gomorrah and Lot's escape are the subjects of Genesis 18 and 19. In Chapters 20 and 21, Sarah gives birth to Isaac, and Abraham and Sarah expel Hagar and her son, Ishmael.

Genesis 22 is the famous story of God's test of Abraham's faith. God demands that Abraham sacrifice Isaac and thus end the hope of having descendants. However, God spares Isaac and renews the promise of many offspring.

1. Genesis 14 also tells how Abraham paid tithes to Melchizedek. Who was this man? (14:8)

2. Read 19:36-38. Besides telling why the cities of Sodom and Gomorrah were

destroyed, what else does Genesis 19 explain?

3. Because Abraham obeyed God and offered his son, Isaac, what four things did God promise?

a. (22:17)

b. (22:17)

c. (22:17)

d. (22:18)

GENESIS 23–50

Genesis 23 describes Sarah's death. In Chapters 24 and 25, Abraham sends a servant to his homeland to get a wife for Isaac. Then Abraham remarries and fathers more children. He dies "in a good old age" at 175 years, and his sons bury him with Sarah.

Isaac's wife, Rebekah, gives birth to twin sons, Esau and Jacob. The struggle between these two sons is the central theme of Genesis 27 through 36. Jacob buys the right of the first-born from Esau, and then in Chapter 27 tricks the aging Isaac into blessing him. Jacob then goes to Haran, a city in Mesopotamia, to secure a wife. On the way, the Lord comes to him in a dream at Bethel. Chapter 28 describes this dream.

Chapters 29 and 30 tell how Jacob secures his wives, Leah and Rachel, and has many offspring. In Chapter 31, before

returning to Canaan, Jacob tricks his father-in-law and flees with many possessions. In Chapters 32 and 33, Jacob finally returns home to a friendly encounter with his brother.

After some stories about how Jacob's sons destroy Shechem, in Chapter 34; how Jacob returns to Bethel, in Chapter 35; and a list of the descendants of Esau, in Chapter 36; the Bible's attention shifts to Joseph. Chapter 38 is the only one of the remaining chapters that does not deal with Joseph. Chapter 38 is about Judah, the older brother of Joseph.

Chapter 37 tells how the jealous brothers of Joseph sell him into slavery. In Chapters 39 through 41 we see that Joseph is a successful servant to Potiphar until he refuses the sexual favors of his master's wife who then charges him with sexual assault. Potiphar throws Joseph into prison, but releases him after he interprets the pharaoh's dream. The ruler then makes Joseph prime minister over the land of Egypt.

When Jacob's ten sons come to buy grain because of the famine, they unknowingly deal with Joseph. Joseph then tests his brothers in several episodes before revealing his true identity in a touching reunion scene. Chapters 42 through 45 narrate these events.

In Chapters 46 and 47, Jacob and all his descendants settle in Egypt where "they gained possessions in it, and were fruitful and multiplied exceedingly." The last three chapters of the book, Chapters 48 through 50, narrate the deaths of both Jacob and Joseph in the land of Egypt.

Read aloud Genesis 50:22-26. These last words of Genesis alert the reader to a coming exodus of the descendants of Abraham from Egypt. This event is not realized until the Book of Exodus. But even that book does not fulfill the promise of God to Abraham, that his descendants would possess the land of Canaan. We think of the first five books in the Bible as separate books. Actually they are like chapters in a story, one leading into another. The Jews treat them as one complete work, the Torah, from Genesis through Deuteronomy.

1. Read Genesis 26:1-4 and 28:10-15. To whom was the promise of Abraham repeated?

2. Read Genesis 45:4-9. Who was behind the events in Joseph's life?

3. Read Genesis 50:24-26. After Joseph's death, how were the Israelites in Egypt reminded of God's promise to the patriarchs?

SUMMARY

Many of the stories in Genesis are familiar to us. These episodes are not only well known, they are important events in the history of the world and of God's chosen people. Six familiar stories found in Genesis are listed here.

(1) How God created the world and people (Genesis 1–2)
(2) The expulsion of Adam and Eve from the garden (Genesis 3)
(3) Noah and the Flood (Genesis 6–9)
(4) God's call of Abraham (Genesis 12)
(5) Abraham's offering of Isaac (Genesis 22)
(6) The story of Joseph and his brothers (Genesis 37–50)

QUESTIONS FOR DISCUSSION

1. The pagan neighbors of Israel thought that the earth was made from half the body of a god. The heavens were made of the other half. The god was slain in a battle of the gods. To these ancient people, trees, stones, springs, and the forces of nature were really the work of separate gods. How do the stories in Genesis 1 and 2 oppose these ideas?

2. What do you think God meant by telling Abraham that "in you all the families of the earth shall be blessed"? It may mean that as a result of Abraham's faithful obedience all peoples on the earth would benefit. Christ was a descendant of Abraham, and through him the blessings of salvation from sin are made available to all peoples. How has the Christian tradition come to understand the promise? What does God's promise to Abraham mean for your life?

3. A number of genealogies are found in Genesis. (See Genesis 5; 10; 11.) The genealogies help to bind together the long period from Creation to the descent into Egypt. Some of these events are before recorded history. The lists of people help give the sequence of events the flavor of history. They lead from time immemorial to the time of Abraham, Isaac, and Jacob. The lists seem to fit a specific historical period. What role do these lists play in a story that begins with Creation and ends with the people of the promise in Egypt?

4. A book generally has a well-defined beginning and an ending. How does the end of Genesis leave you expecting more?

DAILY READINGS FOR EXODUS AND LEVITICUS

Day 1: Exodus 1:1-14
Day 2: Exodus 2:1-10
Day 3: Exodus 3:1-14
Day 4: Exodus 14:19-31
Day 5: Exodus 19:1-9
Day 6: Exodus 20:1-17
Day 7: Leviticus 26:1-13

EXODUS LEVITICUS

Sixth-century mosaic of the ark of the covenant

The story of Israel's ancestors, which began in the Book of Genesis, continues in the books of Exodus and Leviticus. The names of these two books tell their central themes. Exodus tells the story of the Hebrews' departure from Egypt, and Leviticus contains laws about priestly or levitical matters. The term *levitical* comes from the name *Levi*, the ancestor of the Hebrew priests.

Let's recall some of the last lesson. Genesis closed with stories about the deaths of Jacob and Joseph in Egypt. But in Genesis 47:10-12, we saw that Jacob's whole family moved to Egypt. At that time their total number was only seventy.

EXODUS 1

The Book of Exodus retells some of this earlier history, as it prepares to continue the story. Read Exodus 1:1-7.

Verse 7 suggests that the Hebrews stayed a long time in Egypt. The Bible says that they "were fruitful and prolific; they multiplied and grew exceedingly strong, so that the land was filled with them." Later, Exodus 12:40 tells us "the time that the people of Israel had lived in Egypt was four hundred thirty years."

This brief introduction of seven verses joins the story of Genesis with that of Exodus. The writer then skillfully sets the stage for the

Exodus from Egypt. The Exodus is God's great act of liberation and the Hebrews' great emancipation from slavery.

After Joseph dies and persons forget his fame, life takes a new turn for the Hebrews. The new king over Egypt sets taskmasters over them, afflicting them with heavy burdens. Exodus 1:8-22 tells how the Egyptians force the Hebrews to endure slavery and servitude. They make the Hebrews work on state construction projects and labor in the fields. Fearful that the numerous Hebrews might revolt, the Egyptians try to reduce the Hebrew population. Read Exodus 1:8-14.

Pharaoh instructs the midwives to kill all the male Hebrew babies. When they don't, the pharaoh orders his people to throw the newborn babies into the Nile River.

Three times in Chapter 1 the Book of Exodus mentions how the Israelites "multiplied." See verses 7, 12, and 20. What part of God's promise to Abraham did this Israelite population explosion fulfill? (See Genesis 15:5.)

EXODUS 2–4

During this time, a woman from the tribe of Levi gives birth to a son. Chapter 2 narrates the story of Moses' birth. Throughout the story of Moses, the writer points many times to divine providence that works in strange ways to produce unusual ends.

For example, in the birth story, Pharaoh's attempt to kill the Hebrews results in his raising a Hebrew in his own palace. After Moses' birth, his mother sets him afloat in the Nile, hoping to preserve him from slaughter. This well-known story reports how the pharaoh's own daughter rescues Moses and unknowingly secures the child's own mother to serve as a wet nurse. Pharaoh's daughter raises Moses in the court of Pharaoh, and later tradition says that Moses received the best education of his day.

As a grown man, Moses sees the humiliation of his people; and in a raging anger he kills an Egyptian who is beating a Hebrew. He buries the body in the sand and then flees the country. He goes to Midian, a district near the land of Canaan. There he takes refuge with a priest, eventually marrying one of the priest's seven daughters.

Moses was hardly aware of God's providence in his life during the first eighty years. However, the experiences of Moses during that period prepared him for leading the Israelites through the desert. The training in the court of Pharaoh gave him administrative experience. So God prepared Moses for service even when Moses was unaware that he was in training.

In Midian at a sacred mountain, God appears to Moses, commissioning him to lead the Hebrews out of Egypt. Exodus 3 and 4 report this episode. God's compassion for the people and God's aim of bringing them out of Egypt form the background for Moses' call. Verses 7 and 8 of Chapter 3 summarize these sentiments. Read Exodus 3:7-8.

God addresses Moses from a burning bush. When Moses hears of God's plan for him, Moses offers many excuses for not accepting the task. He complains that he has no special reputation as a leader. Above all, he argues that he has to know the name of the God who commissioned him. Only then can he convince his people that this God appeared to him.

God answers Moses by telling him to say to his people: "I AM has sent me to you." Here the text explains the Hebrew name for God, which is *Yahweh*. The word *Yahweh* relates to the Hebrew word meaning "to be." So Yahweh declares to Moses "I AM WHO I AM" or "I WILL BE WHO I WILL BE." Moses then tries to refuse the task by saying he is not an eloquent speaker. To meet this need, God supplies Aaron.

We often call Moses the first prophet. One common characteristic of Old Testament prophets is their initial hesitation to answer God's call. When Moses hesitates and objects that his people will not believe him, God gives him three signs to support the call. Read Exodus 4:1-9, and list the three signs.

a.

b.

c.

EXODUS 5–12

Together, Moses and Aaron return to Egypt. There they begin the task of convincing the pharaoh to let the people go. Chapters 5 to 12 report the negotiations of Moses with Pharaoh. These chapters also tell of the ten plagues God sends upon the Egyptians.

The Hebrews leave Egypt only after the first-born babies and the first-born animals of the Egyptians die. Exodus 12 tells us that future generations will continue to celebrate the Passover, to commemorate the departure from Egypt. Exodus 12:25-27 states the understanding behind the Passover ritual. Read Exodus 12:25-27.

1. Exodus 12 records the establishment of the Passover and connects it with the last of the ten plagues. Name the three foods required by the feast (Exodus 12:8).

a.

b.

c.

Moses and the burning bush

2. Read Exodus 12:13, 23. Why was the blood of the lamb in the first Passover especially important?

EXODUS 13–17

Exodus 13 to 18 describes events that happen to the Hebrews after they leave Egypt but before they arrive at Mount Sinai. In Chapters 13 and 14, they miraculously escape the Egyptians by crossing the sea on dry land.

Most of Exodus 15 is a song celebrating the escape of the Hebrews and the destruction of the Egyptians. No doubt, later Israelites sang this song frequently to mark the Passover occasion.

1. Read Exodus 14:24-25. What was the reaction of the Egyptians when their chariot wheels clogged as they pursued the Israelites?

Sculpted depiction of a wheeled ark, Capernaum synagogue

2. Read Exodus 14:31. What was the reaction of the Israelites when they saw what had happened to the Egyptians?

EXODUS 18–20

From the sea the Hebrews move toward the wilderness. The people begin to complain when the conditions become trying. This murmuring of the people is a common theme associated with the Hebrews' experience in the wilderness. To quiet their protests, God provides manna, quail, and water.

In Exodus 18 Moses and the Hebrews meet Jethro, Moses' father-in-law, in the desert. When Jethro sees how overworked Moses is, he suggests that Moses appoint judges to handle all matters, except for the most difficult cases. After following Jethro's advice, Moses lets his father-in-law depart, and Jethro returns to Midian.

At the beginning of Chapter 19 the Hebrews arrive at Mount Sinai. According to verse 1, they arrive there on the third new moon, that is, three months after leaving Egypt. Mount Sinai is the setting for the rest of the Book of Exodus, all of Leviticus, and much of the Book of Numbers. According to Numbers 10:11, the people leave Mount Sinai in the second month of the second year after leaving Egypt.

Most of the material in Exodus, Leviticus, and Numbers is legal in nature. In Exodus 19, Moses goes up the mountain and receives laws that he then proclaims to the people. Exodus 20 contains what we now call the Ten Commandments.

Read Exodus 20:1-17. Note that the first commandments describe a person's duty to God. Write out the first commandment that describes a person's duty to another human.

EXODUS 21–40

Chapters 21, 22, and 23 are a collection of laws on various topics. These topics range from the freeing of slaves, to cases involving capital punishment, to matters of civil law.

In Exodus 24 Moses goes up to the mountain again, first with seventy elders and then by himself. In Chapters 25 to 31, God gives Moses instructions about building the Tabernacle and supplying its furnishings. In these chapters we also find the regulations about the priests and their special functions and clothing.

In Exodus 32 and 33 we read the story of the golden calf. While the Hebrews wait for Moses to come down from the mountain, they make a golden calf and worship it. When Moses descends to the camp, he sees the calf and the dancing. He throws down the inscribed tablets and breaks them. The Lord punishes the people for their idolatry. The sons of Levi kill 3,000 men, and a plague falls on the others. Moses goes back up the mountain.

In Chapter 34 the Lord repeats the law previously given. This chapter, however, repeats only some of the laws in Exodus 20 to 23 and then not in the same terms. These similarities and differences in the Law suggest that Israel possessed various summaries of its laws, which have remained separate.

Exodus 35 to 40 tells how Moses assembles the people. Together they construct the Tabernacle and carry out the commandments recorded in Chapters 25 to 31.

1. God gave detailed instructions to Moses and the people for building the Tabernacle. What was the purpose of this tent? (Exodus 25:8)

2. When Moses had finished erecting the Tabernacle, how did he know that the Lord approved? (Exodus 40:34)

LEVITICUS

We now turn to Leviticus. The entire Book of Leviticus deals with laws given to Moses and Aaron for the people. These laws cover such topics as worship, clean and unclean food, and sacrifices.

Chapters 1 to 7 outline the various types of sacrifices and how to offer them. In Chapters 8 to 10, the laws concern the ordination of priests and their offering of sacrifices. Chapter 11 contains the regulations about clean and unclean food. Chapters 12 through 15 contain laws about various forms of disease and uncleanness. Much of this material discusses what is called *leprosy*. Leprosy in the Bible, however, is not what we call leprosy. Today leprosy is a very specific skin disease limited to humans. In the Bible, leprosy includes a wide range of skin diseases and is not limited to humans. Animals, clothes, and houses can have leprosy; and the laws assume that recovery is expected.

Chapter 16 relates the ritual of the scapegoat. The priests perform this ritual of sending a goat into the wilderness on the day of national repentance and atonement. Today we use the term *scapegoat* to mean a person who bears the blame for others. We base our present-day usage of the word on this ancient ritual.

Chapters 17 to 27 of Leviticus contain laws about many subjects. Many of these laws deal with matters of purity and cleanness, proper sacrifices, and festivals. While stating the demands of God, the Bible continues to emphasize love. Leviticus 19:18 says, "You shall not take vengeance or bear a grudge against any of your people, but you shall love your neighbor as yourself." Leviticus 19:34 says, "The alien who resides with you shall be to you as the citizen among you; and you shall love the alien as yourself."

1. All the sacrifices, rules, and regulations in Leviticus were intended for a purpose. Read Leviticus 17:11. What was the purpose of blood sacrifices?

2. Read Leviticus 20:7, 22-25. What was the purpose of the statutes and ordinances that God commanded the Israelites?

3. Read Leviticus 27:30-33. Why was an Israelite to practice tithing?

SUMMARY

Six major episodes in Israel's history are found in these books.

(1) God's calling of Moses, the first prophet (Exodus 3–4)
(2) The ten plagues on Pharaoh and the land of Egypt (Exodus 7–12)
(3) God's miraculous deliverance of the Israelites at the Red Sea (Exodus 14)
(4) God's giving of the Ten Commandments (Exodus 20)
(5) The instructions for the building of the Tabernacle (Exodus 25–31)
(6) God's specific laws given to the people through Moses and Aaron (the whole Book of Leviticus)

As we saw in the Genesis lesson, God is responsible for all these events in the history of the Israelites.

QUESTIONS FOR DISCUSSION

1. God promised Abraham that his descendants would be "like the dust of the earth." They would be uncountable. They numbered only seventy when they entered Egypt. Four hundred thirty years later "the land was filled with them," but they were slaves. What does this story reveal about the ways of God? How does the Exodus story affect your faith?

2. Divine providence was at work in Moses' life to produce unusual ends. Moses was forced to flee to Midian, for example. God was to use the desert experience of Moses later on to enable Moses to lead his people through that region. What does this story suggest about the role of divine providence in your life?

3. The Tabernacle represented God's presence among the Israelite people. How is God's presence realized among Christians today? When is God's presence evident in your life?

4. The Ten Commandments symbolize the covenant between God and the people of Israel. The people were obliged to keep the commandments, and God promised to be their God. They would be counted as God's own special possession among all the nations of the earth. As a Christian, how is your covenant with God different from the covenant with Israel described in Exodus 19–20?

DAILY READINGS FOR NUMBERS AND DEUTERONOMY

Day 1:   Numbers 10:1-16
Day 2:   Numbers 13:25-33; 14:1-3
Day 3:   Numbers 22:21-35
Day 4:   Deuteronomy 4:1-24
Day 5:   Deuteronomy 5:1-21; 6:1-9
Day 6:   Deuteronomy 18:9-22
Day 7:   Deuteronomy 34:1-12

NUMBERS
DEUTERONOMY

© 1981 Biblical Archaeology Society

Oasis in the Sinai desert

The books of Numbers and Deuteronomy are the fourth and fifth books of the Pentateuch or what Judaism calls the *Torah* or Law. The Hebrew name for the Book of Numbers is *bemidbar*, which means "in the wilderness." The setting for most of the book is the wilderness between Mount Sinai and the Promised Land. Our English name comes from the Greek name. In Greek the book was called Numbers because of the references to the numbering of the Israelites when they were counted in a census.

In Hebrew, Deuteronomy is called *debarim* or "Words." The English title comes from the Greek language in which Deuteronomy means "second" or "repeated law."

NUMBERS 1

Numbers opens with the Hebrews still at Mount Sinai. Deuteronomy closes with the death of Moses on Mount Nebo just before the people cross the Jordan River into the Promised Land.

The Book of Numbers has three main parts. From Numbers 1:1 to Numbers 10:10, the people are still at Mount Sinai. This Scripture forms the first main section of the book.

Chapter 1 of Numbers reports the first census of the Hebrews. God commands Moses and Aaron to count the people—that is, every male from twenty years old and upward who is able to go to war. According to Numbers 1:46, the number of such men is 603,550. If one adds the wives, the children, and the persons too old to fight, the figure rises to over two million. Many scholars believe that it would have been impossible for so many persons to survive in the desert. Some assume that the number comes from a census taken during the time of David and Solomon. The writer of Deuteronomy then recorded the same number for the desert period. Or, perhaps the writer wanted to emphasize the marvelous nature of God's works. Only the God of the Hebrews could lead two million people through the desert!

Numbers 1 tells of the census of all the able-bodied men in each tribe who were twenty years old and older. These were men capable of going to war. Read Numbers 1:47-50. Why was the tribe of Levi not included in the census?

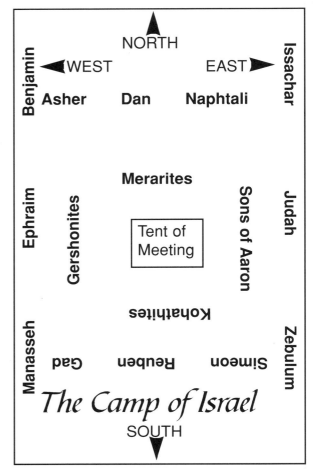

The Camp of Israel

NUMBERS 2–14

According to Numbers 2 the Hebrews encamp around the tent of meeting, facing inward. This arrangement serves to remind the Hebrews that God is in the midst of them. Each tribe receives its special place and marching position.

Chapters 3 and 4 tell about the priests and Levites, their number and duties. The Levites encamp between the ordinary Hebrews and the Tabernacle since they are more holy than the laity. According to Numbers 3:39 the number of Levites is 22,000.

Chapter 5 and 6 contain a collection of various laws. Numbers 5:5-10 states that a person is to repay the money or goods, plus twenty percent, to anyone he or she wrongs. Numbers 5:11-31 outlines the ordeal to follow when a man accuses his wife of adultery, but cannot prove the charge. Chapter 6 contains the laws of the Nazirites. The Nazirites are persons who enter a special order, giving themselves to God. They vow to drink no wine or strong drink. They also vow that they will not cut their hair or come near a dead body. In the midst of these laws, we find that great and familiar blessing of the Old Testament. Read Numbers 6:24-26.

Numbers 7 reports the sacrifices the people make during the twelve days of dedicating the altar. Chapter 8 describes the golden lampstand and the consecration of the Levites. Numbers 9:6-14 tells about the special provisions for persons who are absent or unclean when the Hebrews celebrate the Passover. These persons hold their Passover celebration a month later. Imagine celebrating Christmas on January 25! The rest of Chapter 9 describes the cloud that covers the Tabernacle and appears as fire at night. In Numbers 10:1-10 God tells Moses to make two silver trumpets to signal the people for gathering or marching out.

With Numbers 10:11 we come to the second main section of Numbers. The people break camp and leave Mount Sinai. Through Numbers 21:9 we read about the events that take place in the desert. According to Numbers 32:13 the Hebrews wander in the desert for forty years.

In Chapter 11 the people again bemoan their lack of meat. This chapter parallels several accounts already reported in Exodus 16 and 18. The parallels include God's sending of quail and the selection of seventy elders. In Numbers 12 Moses' brother and sister—Aaron and Miriam—question his authority, and Moses punishes them.

Chapters 13 and 14 tell how Moses sends men to spy out the land of Canaan. The men survey the land and its people as far as Hebron.

The spies return with stories of the land's richness and with a grape cluster so large that two men carry it on a pole between them. The spies report that the people of the land are strong and their cities are well fortified. The Hebrews are like grasshoppers against them. The people lose faith in ever taking the land. They try to replace Moses as leader and return to Egypt. Because they despise God, God condemns them to wander until the unfaithful generation dies. Among the spies, only Caleb and Joshua will enter the land.

God expected the Israelites to trust God to enable them to possess the land. When they refused to trust God, they were destined to wander in the wilderness for forty years. When Joshua was commissioned as the successor of Moses (Deuteronomy 31:23), he was told to be strong and of good courage, for the Lord would be with him. God required the people to have faith in order to be conquerors and to possess the gift of the land.

1. The camp of Israel moved northward toward Canaan. Moses sent out the twelve spies who returned with two reports. Read Numbers 13:31-32. Why did these spies return with an evil (bad) report?

2. Read Numbers 14:1-10. Caleb and Joshua brought back the minority report. Why did they encourage the people to go up to take the land?

NUMBERS 15–24

Chapter 15 contains various laws. We pick up the story line again in Chapter 16. This chapter relates the challenge of Korah and his followers to the authority of Aaron and the other priests. God vindicates Aaron in Chapter 17 by causing Aaron's rod to blossom and bear almonds.

Chapter 18 introduces laws about the tithe and support of the priesthood. Laws on the purification of uncleanness follow. Chapter 19 reports the ritual for removing impurity through the use of the sacrificial ashes of a red heifer.

Chapter 20 and Chapter 21:1-9 tell four main episodes. First, when the people have no water, Moses strikes a rock to produce water, although God commands him only to speak to the rock. Second, Moses tries to get permission from the king of Edom to pass through his territory and thus enter Canaan from the east, but the king refuses. Third, Aaron dies on Mount Hor. Fourth, because of the people's complaining, God sends snakes that bite them and cause death. Healing comes only by looking at a bronze serpent that Moses makes.

The third section begins with Numbers 21:10. Here the Hebrews come into the territory east of the Jordan after circling around Edom. They defeat Sihon, king of the Amorites, and Og, king of Bashan.

Numbers 22 to 24 contains the story of Balaam and his talking donkey. Balaam is a diviner whom Balak hires to curse the Hebrews. However, try as he might, Balaam cannot curse the Hebrews and ends up blessing them.

The story of Balaam's donkey is recorded in Numbers 22:21-35, but this is only a part of the story of Balaam. Discover other details by reading the following passages; then answer the questions.

Moses, from a wall painting in Dura-Europos synagogue, Syria

a. Where were the people of Israel encamped when this story took place? (Numbers 22:1)

b. Who was Balak the son of Zippor? (Numbers 22:4)

c. What did Balak want Balaam to do? (Numbers 22:6)

d. What was Balaam's occupation? (Numbers 22:7)

e. Why did Balak become angry with Balaam? (Numbers 24:10)

f. Why was Balaam unable to curse the Hebrews? (Numbers 24:13)

NUMBERS 25–36

According to Numbers 25 the Hebrews begin to worship the gods of the land. So God subjects them to a plague. In Chapter 26, God commands Moses and Eleazar to take a new census after the plague.

In Numbers 27:1-11 Moses judges a case that involves the inheritance right of daughters. According to the Lord's command, Moses rules that Zelophehad's daughters can inherit the property of their father if the father has no sons. The narrative of Moses' commissioning Joshua as his successor follows this inheritance story.

Numbers 28 and 29 contain laws on sabbath observance and festivals. These chapters repeat much of Exodus and Leviticus, while Chapter 30 contains regulations about vows.

We pick up the story again in Chapter 31, which reports Israel's defeat of the Midianites. The land east of the Jordan is now under Hebrew control, and in Chapter 32 the tribes of Reuben and Gad take possession of this land. They promise the aid of their tribes in the conquest of Canaan.

Chapter 33 records all the stages and stopping places of the Hebrews in their movement from Egypt to the camp east of Jordan. In Chapter 34 God reveals to Moses the boundaries of the Promised Land. In Chapter 35 God states that the Hebrews are to set cities aside for the Levites, as well as cities of refuge for the guilty, once the land is taken.

Interestingly, the daughters of Zelophehad reappear in the final chapter of Numbers. Moses rules that the daughters can inherit, but they must marry within the tribe of their father. This way, the property never transfers to another tribe.

With the close of the Book of Numbers, the Hebrews finish their long march from Egypt and begin their conquest of the Promised Land.

DEUTERONOMY

The bulk of the Book of Deuteronomy consists of speeches or sermons by Moses. The book contains his farewell and final instructions to the Hebrews before his death and their movement across the Jordan. We can imagine Moses as an elderly father who assembled his children around him to offer instructions and encouragement before his death.

The first part of Moses' speech is Deuteronomy 1:1–4:40. Here Moses reviews the people's history in the wilderness and pleads with the people to give heed to the Law and obey the statutes and ordinances. He also warns the people that if they are unfaithful, God will punish them, removing them from the land and scattering them among the nations. Deuteronomy 4:25-26 contains a good summary of such warnings. Read Deuteronomy 4:25-26.

The second part of Moses' speech is Deuteronomy 5 through 11. This speech is a passionate appeal for Israel to hear the commandments of God and to be obedient after they possess the land. It stresses the covenant made between God and Israel; and it repeats, although with some variation, the Ten Commandments found in Exodus 20.

1. Read Deuteronomy 6:4-7; then answer the following questions.

a. How should Israel love the Lord God?

b. What were the Israelites to do with the words that Moses commanded them?

2. Read Matthew 22:34-40 in the New Testament. What commandment did Jesus add to the great commandment?

DEUTERONOMY 5–34

Two themes appear in Deuteronomy 5 through 11. The first focuses on God's choosing of Israel. We see this theme in Deuteronomy 7. Read Deuteronomy 7:7-8.

The second theme is Israel's responsibility to God, which we see in Deuteronomy 10:12-13. Read this passage.

Chapters 12 through 26, the third part of Moses' speech, spell out the laws that the Israelites are to obey. Through their obedience the Israelites show their love of God. These laws emphasize that Israel is to worship one God, to worship in one holy place, to obey one set of laws (those in Deuteronomy), and to preserve their purity as a people.

In Chapters 27 and 28 Moses explains how the people are to act once they reach the Promised Land. They are to publicly exhibit the Law and participate in the ceremony of blessings and curses.

In Chapters 29 and 30 the people and Moses reaffirm the covenant while still in Moab, southeast of the Jordan. The covenant-making ceremony closes as Moses proclaims the blessings that will come if the people are obedient and the curses that will befall them if they are unfaithful.

In Chapter 31 Moses takes leave of his people, reminding them of his age. The Lord will not allow him to cross the Jordan with them. Moses commands that the Law be read at a set time every seven years. Joshua serves as his successor.

Chapters 32 and 33 are the so-called song of Moses and his blessing upon the twelve tribes. Chapter 34, the final chapter of the book, reports Moses' death. Moses dies at the age of 120. His eye is not dim, nor his natural force abated. God buries him in an unmarked place. In praise of this great man, the writer notes that "never since has there arisen a prophet in Israel like Moses, whom the LORD knew face to face."

Read Deuteronomy 34:5-12, and answer the following questions.

a. Where did Moses die?

b. How old was Moses when he died?

c. What did Moses do to designate Joshua as his successor?

SUMMARY

Five major events in the history of Israel are portrayed in Numbers and Deuteronomy.

(1) Moses and Aaron's numbering the people (Numbers 1)
(2) Moses sending spies to gather information about the land of Canaan (Numbers 13–14)
(3) Balaam's blessing the Hebrews (Numbers 22–24)
(4) Moses' commandment to love the Lord with heart and soul (Deuteronomy 6 and 10)
(5) Moses' farewell speech to the people (Deuteronomy 1–26)

God's commissioning of Joshua as the new leader over the people prepares the way for the Book of Joshua. We will continue this story in the next lesson.

QUESTIONS FOR DISCUSSION

1. At the close of Deuteronomy the Israelites were encamped in the plains of Moab opposite Jericho. They were ready to cross the Jordan and to go in and possess the land of Canaan. God had promised to give that land to the descendants of Abraham, Isaac, and Jacob (Deuteronomy 34:4). But they had to conquer the land. What does this need to conquer the land imply about God's promise to Abraham? What does this biblical example teach us about the gift of salvation in Christ for each of us? What does it teach us about overcoming ourselves? about overcoming the world?

2. We have finished our survey of the first part of the Bible, the Pentateuch. How useful are the Old Testament Scriptures to Christians? Consider the example of Jesus in Luke 4:1-13.

3. On pages 23 and 24 we paid particular attention to the story of Balaam. A surprising part of the story is that the source of Balaam's knowledge was the God of Israel (Numbers 24:13). How does this story enhance God's protective oversight of the chosen people? What applications do these ideas have to us as Christians?

4. At the close of the Book of Deuteronomy we are told that Moses does not cross over into the Promised Land. Why does God not allow Moses to cross over the Jordan? Despite the fact that Moses dies in Moab, does the story have a positive ending? Why or why not?

DAILY READINGS FOR JOSHUA, JUDGES, AND RUTH

Day 1: Joshua 1:1-11
Day 2: Joshua 6:8-21
Day 3: Joshua 23:1-13
Day 4: Joshua 24:14-31
Day 5: Judges 2:6-23
Day 6: Judges 16:18-31
Day 7: Ruth 1:1-18

Review 1 Sheet

1. What are the two major parts of the Book of Genesis, and what is contained in each part?

2. What five major characters are involved in the early history narrated in Genesis 1–11?

3. What is God's supreme test of Abraham's faith?

4. Who are the two sons of Abraham?

5. Who are the two sons of Isaac?

6. Jacob and his wives had twelve sons. Can you name them?

7. What is the story told in the Book of Exodus?

8. What does God say when Moses asks for God's name?

9. What do the Hebrews do between the time they escape the Egyptians at the Red Sea and the time they arrive at Mount Sinai?

10. What structure do the Hebrews build after receiving the Ten Commandments?

11. The laws in Leviticus cover many topics. List as many topics as you can.

12. Where do the Hebrews go after wandering in the wilderness for forty years? What river do they cross?

13. Who succeeds Moses as leader over the people?

(Answers are on page 182.)

THE HISTORICAL BOOKS

INTRODUCTION

Joshua, Judges, Ruth, First and Second Samuel, First and Second Kings, First and Second Chronicles, Ezra, Nehemiah, and Esther are called the *historical books*. They contain the history of Israel from the conquest of Canaan under Joshua to the time of Ezra. The period in history is from about 1200 to 400 B.C. Joshua, Judges, Ruth, Samuel, and Kings are set in the preexilic period. The others portray events in the postexilic period.

THE BOOKS AND THE HISTORY

The Book of Joshua takes up the story of the people of Israel after the death of Moses and before the period of the judges. The book tells of the conquest of the Promised Land and its division among the tribes of Israel. Judges describes the period between Joshua and the establishment of kingship. The period of the judges extended from about 1200 to 1040 B.C.

Samuel was the last of the judges. He was also the high priest, and in his days Saul became the first king. First Samuel provides a history of those days and an introduction to David.

David's rise to the monarchy and his accomplishments and problems are recorded in Second Samuel. Originally First and Second Samuel were a single work that was divided when the Greek translation, the Septuagint, was made in the third century B.C. This is true of First and Second Kings also. The first section of First Kings recounts the death of David and the reign of Solomon. The division of David and Solomon's kingdom into the kingdoms of Judah and Israel is recorded in First Kings, but the history of the two kingdoms continues into Second Kings. The end of the Northern Kingdom, Israel,

and the exile of the Southern Kingdom, Judah, brings the sad history to a close about 586 B.C. The Jews are in exile in Babylon.

Joshua, Judges, Samuel, and Kings are understood as a historical work of four parts that was completed during the Exile, although much of the material in them is earlier. Ruth is inserted in the historical works because the story is connected with the period of the judges.

We do not know who the writers of these books were. Jewish tradition holds that Joshua wrote his own book and the books of Judges and Ruth, and that Jeremiah wrote the books of Kings.

Chronicles, Ezra, Nehemiah, and Esther were written in the postexilic era. Chronicles is a sweeping survey of biblical history from Adam to the return from the Exile following the edict of Cyrus (538 B.C.).

More than half the information in Chronicles appears also in Genesis, Samuel, and Kings. But the books of Chronicles do not include information about the kings of Israel, the Northern Kingdom, unless a particular king has a direct connection with the history of Judah. The writer of Chronicles wanted to show that God had preserved the true covenant people in Judah. They had been ruled by the legitimate kings of the dynasty of David. The Chronicler also treats David gently. His sin with Bathsheba is not even mentioned in the history.

No one knows who the writer of First and Second Chronicles was. Jewish tradition holds that Ezra wrote Chronicles.

Ezra and Nehemiah were at one time a single book and probably a part of Chronicles. The Hebrew Bible gives verse counts for Ezra-Nehemiah as if they were one book. These works were written in the late 400's B.C. The history is of the restoration of the people from exile in Babylonia and the problems they faced in reestablishing the true worship of God in Jerusalem. Ezra contains several passages written in Aramaic, a language that was becoming increasingly important in that period.

Esther is a story set in the period of the Persian Empire, before 400 B.C. Nowhere does it contain the name of God. So pious additions were made to the book in the period between the testaments. These additions are found in the Apocrypha.

The rabbis argued the merits of including Esther in the Hebrew Bible. It won a place because of the connection of the story with the establishment of the popular Jewish feast of Purim. Also, though God is not mentioned by name, God's activity is understood to be going on behind the scenes. The Dead Sea Scroll community did not have a copy of Esther in its library, as far as we know.

IMPORTANT IDEAS IN THE HISTORICAL BOOKS

The preexilic books validate the establishment of the monarchy. The promise of God to David that one of his descendants would sit on the throne of Israel became an important idea connected with the Messiah. Another feature of these books is the word of the Lord, the revelation of God through spokesmen, the prophets. The preexilic writers were also interested in the Temple and in worship.

The postexilic writers were more interested in the Temple and its rituals. The Chronicler was fascinated with the priests and Levites, the Temple singers, and other functionaries. Many fine examples of prayers are included in the Chronicler's work.

JOSHUA
JUDGES
RUTH

Jordan River

© 1981 Biblical Archaeology Society

The books of Joshua, Judges, and Ruth portray the life of the Israelites in the period between the death of Moses and the time of Samuel.

In the Hebrew Bible, the Book of Ruth does not appear with the books of Joshua and Judges. It is found in the last section of the Old Testament, which is called the "Writings," rather than with the section called the "Former Prophets," which opens with the Book of Joshua. Persons responsible for the Greek edition of the Old Testament placed Ruth after Judges because Ruth has its setting in the same historical period. Our English translations follow the Greek order.

JOSHUA

Joshua is the first book of what is called the Former Prophets in the Hebrew Bible. Other books in this section are Judges, First and Second Samuel, and First and Second Kings. These books are not what we think of as prophecy. Rather, they present the course of Israel's history. These writings were probably called prophetic because their central themes are the fulfillment of God's promises to give the people the land, and the people's subsequent loss of the land through God's judgment upon their disobedience. Like the later prophetic books, these works center on the ideas of promise and judgment as God works in and through the history of Israel.

The Book of Joshua covers the period from the death of Moses to the death of Joshua. The book describes this period as the time when Israel is thoroughly obedient and when God's promise to give the people the land is fulfilled.

Joshua has two major parts. Joshua 1–12 tells how the Israelites conquer the land of Canaan, and Joshua 13–22 reports how the tribes divide the land. The book concludes with a speech by Joshua in Chapter 23 and a renewal of the covenant at Shechem in Chapter 24. In Joshua 1:1-9 God commissions Joshua to replace Moses and to lead the people across the Jordan.

In the second part of Chapter 1 Joshua prepares the people for the conquest. Joshua 2 tells the story of the two spies who enter Jericho. There, a prostitute named Rahab befriends and protects them. In Chapter 6, Joshua spares her life when the Hebrews capture the city. Later Jewish tradition— found outside the Bible—tells us that Rahab married Joshua after the conquest.

Chapters 3 and 4 tell us about the crossing of the Jordan River. When the priests who carry the ark of the covenant step into the river, the water halts and the people cross on dry land. As a memorial to the crossing, the people build a monument of twelve stones in the riverbed. The Hebrews reach the west bank of the Jordan. Chapter 5 tells us that while in Gilgal, they observe the Passover and eat of the grain from the Promised Land. With their eating, the manna ceases.

The crossing of the Jordan to enter Canaan parallels the crossing of the Red Sea when the Hebrews left Egypt. Joshua 4:23-24 makes this clear. Read this passage.

Just as the Hebrews observed the Passover as the last meal in Egypt—their last taste of bondage and slavery—so they observe the Passover as the first meal in Canaan—their first taste of freedom in the Promised Land.

Joshua 6 tells the story of the capture of the city of Jericho. Jericho falls after the army, following the ark, marches around the city for seven days, seven times on the seventh day.

Read the following passages in Joshua to find the answers to the questions below.

a. What was the basic attitude of mind that the Lord required of Joshua when he became the leader of the people of Israel? (Joshua 1:6, 7, 9, 18)

b. Rahab the harlot befriended the Israelite spies because she feared the God of Israel. What was the reason for her faith in and fear of the Lord? (Joshua 2:8-11)

c. How was the faith of Joshua and the priests tested when they came to the Jordan? (Joshua 3:8, 13, 16)

JOSHUA 7–24

After the battle at Jericho, Achan steals some of the booty devoted to God. Chapter 7 tells of Achan's punishment for his actions. In Joshua 8, we read how Joshua and his troops capture and destroy the city of Ai.

In Joshua 9 the citizens of Gibeon talk the Israelites into a peace treaty by pretending to be foreigners. The Israelites resume their war of conquest in Chapter 10. This chapter reports Joshua's defeat of a group of kings. Joshua 10:12-14 contains the famous episode in which Joshua commands the sun to stand still and not rise. Then his troops carry out their nighttime warfare.

The rest of Joshua 10 lists the cities the Israelites capture under Joshua's leadership. Chapter 11 reports Joshua's defeat of the city of Hazor, while Chapter 12 lists thirty-one kings of city-states in Canaan that the Israelites defeat.

The great success of the people is the keynote of the first half of Joshua. Joshua 10:40-41 provides a summary of the areas the Israelites capture in Canaan. These verses also note the thoroughness of the conquest. Read Joshua 10:40-41.

The second half of the Book of Joshua reports how the tribes divide the land after the conquest. Although in the first half of the book we saw that Joshua took the whole land, Joshua 13:1-7 contains a list of the land yet untaken.

Chapters 13 through 19 list the tribal land allotments. In Chapter 20, the Israelites choose the cities of refuge; and in Chapter 21, they allot certain cities to the Levites. In Chapter 22, Joshua allows the tribes whose territory is east of the Jordan, but who fought to take the area west of the river, to return home.

Like Moses before his death, Joshua gives a farewell address to the people and renews the covenant. His speech in Joshua 23 stresses three main points. First, he admonishes the people "to observe and do all that is written in the book of the law of Moses, turning aside from it neither to the right nor to the left." Second, he promises God's continued support if they continue to love and obey God. God will drive out the nations before them. Third, Joshua warns the people that, if they disobey, God will cause them to perish.

At Shechem, in Chapter 24, Joshua leads the community in reaffirming its faith and in renewing the covenant. Shortly after this ceremony, Joshua dies at the age of 110. The Israelites bury him in his inheritance.

1. Read Joshua 7:1-5. How did the sin of Achan affect the rest of the people of Israel?

2. List the high points in Israel's history that are summarized in Joshua 24.

a. (24:3)

b. (24:5)

c. (24:6)

d. (24:7)

e. (24:13)

JUDGES 1–2

In turning to the Book of Judges we confront a book that appears to have two introductions. The first introduction in Judges 1:1 begins like this: "After the death of Joshua, the Israelites inquired of the LORD, 'Who shall go up first for us against the Canaanites, to fight against them?' " The second introduction, Judges 2:6–3:6 continues the story of the covenant renewal ceremony at Shechem. It begins like this: "When Joshua dismissed the people, the Israelites all went to their own inheritances to take possession of the land."

We find some interesting differences when we compare the first introduction in Judges 1 and 2 to what we learned from the Book of Joshua. In the opening chapters of Judges, the Canaanites are still on the scene. They are not all slaughtered as Joshua 1 through 12 reports. In Judges, the tribes fight and capture territory individually rather than fighting as a united body of tribes.

Judges 1 has no main leader of the people. This chapter also tells us that the Israelites take possession of the hill country, but cannot drive out the inhabitants of the plain.

ISRAEL'S JUDGES

1. Othniel
2. Ehud
3. Shamgar
4. Deborah
5. Gideon
6. Abimelech
7. Tola
8. Jair
9. Jephthah
10. Ibzan
11. Elon
12. Abdon
13. Samson
14. Samuel

What are we to make of the great differences between the story of the conquest in Joshua and the account in the opening chapters of Judges? We realize that we have accounts from two different traditions. Perhaps the well-organized and completely successful conquest found in Joshua is an idealized version of how the tribes came to possess the land in Canaan.

Read Judges 2:8-19. What are the main events in the time of the judges?

a. (2:8)

b. (2:11)

c. (2:14)

d. (2:16)

e. (2:19)

JUDGES 3–16

The second introduction indicates that Israel's history following the death of Joshua will move in cycles. While a strong leader is around, the people will be faithful. But with the death of the leader, Israel will forsake God. The Lord will become angry with them, and their enemies will oppress them. When the people repent, God will hear and send another leader to save the Israelites from their enemies. Then the cycle begins again.

In Judges 3 through 16 the writer shows how Israel, time and again, moves through this cycle. A judge saves Israel who later becomes disobedient, enemies attack, Israel cries out for help, and God raises up another judge.

In Chapter 3:7-31 Othniel defeats the king of Mesopotamia, Ehud fights the Moabites and kills the king of Moab, and Shamgar defeats the Philistines.

In Judges 4 and 5 Deborah rallies the troops to battle in a war against the Canaanites under Sisera. Chapter 4 narrates her great efforts on behalf of Israel. The poetry of Chapter 5, which glorifies Deborah, was probably sung as a popular ballad in ancient Israel.

In Chapters 6, 7, and 8 Gideon saves Israel from the camel-riding Midianites after he reduces his troops from 32,000 to 300 by testing them. At the end of Chapter 8, we see that the cycle of Israel's disobedience continues after Gideon's death.

In Chapter 9 Abimelech tries to set himself up as king. But during one of his battles, a woman in a tower drops a millstone on his head and severely wounds him. Then, Abimelech's armor-bearer kills him at Abimelech's own request.

Judges 10, 11, and 12 refer to several judges, but we only receive details about Jephthah. Jephthah fights the Ammonites and wins. To fulfill his foolish vow made in battle, he sacrifices his daughter.

Samson is the hero of Judges 13 through 16. Note that in Judges 13:5 God designates Samson as a Nazirite. You will recall from the last lesson that Nazirites were a special order of persons who drank no strong drink and who did not cut their hair. We remember Samson as a long-haired, adventurous character who fights the Philistines, but whose exploits and love affairs lead to his ruin.

1. Among the fourteen judges, six are described in some detail. List the names of the six below.

a. (3:9)

b. (3:15)

c. (4:4)

d. (6:11)

e. (11:1)

f. (13:24)

2. One phrase is used repeatedly in connection with the judges (3:10; 6:34; 11:29; 13:25; 14:6). Write the phrase below and indicate what you think it means.

JUDGES 17–21

In the last five chapters, Judges breaks the pattern of telling about war heroes. These chapters include two stories. In Chapters 17 and 18 Micah builds himself a shrine and hires a professional priest, a Levite. The tribe of Dan, while migrating to another district, carries off his priest and his temple treasures.

The second story, in Chapters 19 through 21, is about the war that the rest of the tribes fight against the tribe of Benjamin. This war comes about when several men from the town of Gibeah, in the territory of Benjamin, greatly abuse a visitor's concubine. The woman dies from their harsh treatment. When the tribe of Benjamin does nothing to correct the situation, the other tribes take up arms against Benjamin and almost wipe out the tribe completely.

These last two stories in Judges 17 through 21 lay the groundwork for the rise of the monarchy that develops in the books of Samuel. The writer of Judges shows the many problems the tribes experience; for as he says in the last verse of the book: "In those days there was no king in Israel; all the people did what was right in their own eyes."

RUTH

When we move from Joshua and Judges to the Book of Ruth, we move into a different world, although the same time period.

Unlike the other two books, the Book of Ruth is not about war and fighting or the nation's fortunes. Ruth tells about a family with two women, Naomi and her Moabite daughter-in-law, Ruth.

In the Book of Ruth, Elimelech, a native of Bethlehem, goes to live in Moab. When this Israelite man dies, his sons marry Moabite women. When the sons die, Naomi, the wife and mother, decides to return to Bethlehem. Ruth refuses to stay in her homeland. She pleads with her mother-in-law to let her go with her. Her words were probably familiar to every foreign woman who converted to Judaism. Read Ruth 1:16-17.

Ruth returns to Bethlehem with Naomi. Finally, Ruth, with some intrigue on the part of her mother-in-law, marries Boaz, a distant kinsman of Elimelech. In the course of time, Ruth becomes the mother of Obed, the grandfather of King David.

Read Ruth 1:1-5. When and where does the story take place?

SUMMARY

The books of Joshua, Judges, and Ruth contain familiar stories about the people of Israel. When you think about this portion of the Bible, remember the following events in Israel's history.

(1) Joshua and the battle of Jericho (Joshua 6)
(2) Joshua's renewal of the covenant with God after the conquest of the Promised Land (Joshua 24)
(3) The cycle of faithfulness and disobedience during the period of the judges (Judges 3–16)
(4) The stories about Samson and his struggle with the Philistines (Judges 13–16)
(5) The story of Ruth and her mother-in-law, Naomi (Ruth 1–4)

By the time the Book of Ruth closes, the Israelites are established in the Promised Land. The promise of land, which God gave to Abraham, is now fulfilled.

QUESTIONS FOR DISCUSSION

1. The group of books called the "Former Prophets" in the Hebrew Bible includes Joshua and Judges. In what way can we call these two books prophetic?

2. Judges 7:1-8 describes how Gideon selected 300 warriors at the direction of God. They were selected from an original group of 32,000. Discuss the qualities of the men that separated them into the three groups. What does this story suggest about having God's person in the right place of service in the church? Where in the life of the church are your talents best used?

3. The last verse of Judges states: "In those days there was no king in Israel; all the people did what was right in their own eyes." This statement may be understood as either positive or negative. How might not having a king be preferable to having one? How might having a strong central government be an advantage in Israel? Is a strong central government an advantage or a disadvantage for us today? Give reasons for your answer.

4. Note Ruth's confession of faith in Ruth 1:16. How does the story of Ruth disprove the opinion that the Gentiles were left out by God in Old Testament times? Ruth 4:17 tells us that Ruth was the great-grandmother of King David. What is Ruth's importance in our Christian tradition? (See Matthew 1:1-18.)

DAILY READINGS FOR FIRST AND SECOND SAMUEL

Day 1: 1 Samuel 3:1-14
Day 2: 1 Samuel 7:5-17
Day 3: 1 Samuel 8:4-22
Day 4: 1 Samuel 13:5-15
Day 5: 1 Samuel 16:4-23
Day 6: 2 Samuel 7:1-17
Day 7: 2 Samuel 23:1-7

FIRST SAMUEL
SECOND SAMUEL

© 1981 Biblical Archaeology Society

Wadi in Canaan

This lesson looks at the two books of Samuel. Although these two books were once considered to be a single work in Hebrew, the Greek translators of the Old Testament divided the work into two parts. Our English tradition followed the Greek practice.

These two books tell the story of the lives and careers of three great Israelite figures: Samuel, the last judge; Saul, the first king; and David, the greatest ruler. In the first book of Samuel, the careers of these men overlap. Second Samuel deals with the reign of David.

FIRST SAMUEL 1–7

Chapters 1 through 7 of First Samuel tell about the birth, early life, and career of Samuel. Chapter 1 tells the story of Samuel's birth to Hannah. Hannah is one of Elkanah's two wives. Unlike the other wife, Hannah has no children. While attending the annual festival at Shiloh, she prays for a child and vows that if she has a son, she will give him to the Lord. God answers her prayer, and she gives birth to Samuel. Hannah weans Samuel when he is between two and three years of age. Then she presents him to Eli, the chief priest at Shiloh.

According to Chapter 2 the sons of Eli are wicked priests who are out to make a profit from religion. So religion falls on hard times in Israel. First Samuel 3:1 describes the religious conditions in the following way: "The word of the LORD was rare in those days; visions were not widespread." With Israel in this state of religious need, God calls Samuel in the night and tells him of his intention to wipe out Eli's family.

The days of Samuel are not only times of religious crisis but also of political crisis. At this time, the Philistines who settled along the southwest coast of Canaan begin threatening the Israelites. Now the Philistines start a program of expansion at the expense of the Israelites.

First Samuel 4, 5, and 6 describe a Philistine victory over Israel. The Israelites carry the ark of the covenant into battle hoping it will bring victory. However, the Philistines defeat Israel and capture the ark. They take the ark back to their territory, but the ark only brings trouble to the Philistines. The statue of their god Dagon keeps falling over, and the Lord afflicts the people with tumors. After seven months, the Philistines return the ark to Israel.

First Samuel 7 presents Samuel in a role similar to the judges. Samuel commands the troops against the Philistines, and the Israelites enjoy a victory. Samuel then sets up a stone called Ebenezer, which means "stone of help," because the Lord helped them. The end of Chapter 7 depicts Samuel as a circuit judge who moves on a yearly circuit from Ramah, to Bethel, to Gilgal, to Mizpah, and back to his hometown of Ramah.

1. God intended to wipe out Eli's family. What was the sin of Eli's sons? (Read 1 Samuel 2:15-17.)

2. What was the sin of Eli? (Read 1 Samuel 2:22-25 and 3:13-14.)

3. Read 1 Samuel 7:2-11. What factors enabled the Israelites to win the victory?

a. (7:2)

b. (7:3-4)

c. (7:5)

d. (7:6)

e. (7:9)

f. (7:10)

FIRST SAMUEL 8–15

Chapters 8 through 12 of First Samuel tell how Israel chooses the rule of a king, who provides centralized authority.

What appears to be two versions of the story of Saul can be reconciled into a single account. Saul was anointed privately by Samuel (1 Samuel 10:1), acknowledged as king by the nation (10:17-24), and established as king after his first victory in combat (11:15). But considered as two versions, the fact that the writer or compiler of First

Samuel incorporated both versions in the book seems insignificant.

One account is favorable toward Saul and kingship, and the other account is unfavorable. We find the unfavorable account in 1 Samuel 8; 10:17-27a; and 12:1-25. In this version, Samuel and God oppose kingship. Read 1 Samuel 8:4-7. These verses tell how God evaluates kingship.

The account favorable to Saul and kingship is 1 Samuel 9:1–10:16 and concludes with Chapter 11. This narrative presents Samuel as a prophet who assists Saul to be a leader at the command of God. Read 1 Samuel 9:5-17.

After Samuel anoints Saul in Chapter 10, Saul leads the Israelites in battle against the Ammonites in Chapter 11. Following this victory, the people make Saul king in Gilgal.

Chapters 13, 14, and 15 tell us a little about the reign of Saul, especially how he defeats the Philistines. In much of the Old Testament, David overshadows Saul so that we forget how important Saul was in Israelite history. Read 1 Samuel 14:47-48. These verses record some of Saul's achievements.

1. First Samuel 13 records a major mistake that Saul made. Read verses 8-12, and compare them with Leviticus 1:3-5. What was Saul's sin?

2. First Samuel 15 records Saul's second great error. Read verses 1-9, and describe that sin below.

THE UNITED MONARCHY

■ Places fortified by Solomon

— Greatest extent of the empire

Territory conquered by David

Area occupied by Saul

3. What are some of Saul's achievements? (Read 1 Samuel 14:47-48.)

FIRST SAMUEL 16–31

From First Samuel 16 through the end of First Samuel, David becomes the center of attention. First Samuel 16 and 17 tell how David first enters Saul's service. David comes to the court of Saul to play the lyre and soothe Saul's spirit.

In Chapter 18 Saul sets David over the men of war. David is such a successful soldier that Saul becomes more and more jealous of him. The close friendship between Saul's son, Jonathan, and David intensifies Saul's jealousy. This jealousy resulted in a series of confrontations between the two men. Saul's determination to kill David is portrayed in 1 Samuel 19–30. David flees from the court after Saul first tries to kill him with a spear. David builds a personal army. First Samuel 22:2 describes those who join him during his "Robin Hood" days: "Everyone who was in distress, and everyone who was in debt, and everyone who was discontented."

With his band of followers—eventually numbering 600 men—David stays on the move, running from Saul. On two occasions he has the opportunity to kill Saul, but does not because Saul is God's anointed. Read 1 Samuel 24:4-7.

David apparently secures support from the local people by running a kind of protection racket. In Chapter 25 David tries to collect from Nabal who does not know that David has been protecting him. Chapter 25 also reports the death of Samuel.

Finally, in Chapter 27 David hires out himself and his men to Achish, one of the Philistine kings fighting Saul and the Israelites.

The Philistines plan a major attack on Israel. In readying for the battle King Saul cannot get any word from God either by dreams or by prophets. In Chapter 28 Saul goes by night to a woman of Endor who practices witchcraft, a practice Saul has condemned previously. The witch calls up the spirit of Samuel, which predicts defeat for Saul and Israel.

Chapter 29 describes the Philistines' preparation for battle with Saul. The Philistines, however, do not trust David enough to take him into battle, so they send him back. In the ensuing battle in Chapter 31, the Philistines badly defeat Saul's forces. Saul, severely wounded, finally falls on his sword. He chooses to end his life rather than be captured by the enemy.

Three of his sons, including Jonathan, die with him.

1. The account of David's conflict with Goliath is a heroic story recorded in 1 Samuel 17. Read verses 37 and 46-47. What was the basis of David's courage?

2. Jonathan and David shared a close friendship. Why was this affection so unusual and so opposed by Saul? (Read 1 Samuel 20:30-31.)

SECOND SAMUEL 1–7

Second Samuel 1–5 tells how David gradually becomes king over all Israel. In Chapter 2, the men of Judah anoint David as king over Judah in the town of Hebron. The followers of Saul place Saul's son on the Israelite throne. So David is king in the south, and Saul's son, Ishbaal, is king in the north. Civil war follows.

The war between David and the house of Saul continues for some years. However, David's men eventually kill Abner, Israel's general, and King Ishbaal. After this, the tribes of Israel ask David to be king over Israel as well as Judah.

After reigning in Hebron for seven and one-half years, David's troops capture the Jebusite city of Jerusalem. David makes Jerusalem his capital. Second Samuel 6 reports how David's chosen men bring the ark to Jerusalem. With the ark's return, Jerusalem becomes the religious capital as well as the political capital.

David wants to build a temple in Jerusalem for Yahweh, Israel's God. In 2 Samuel 7, the prophet Nathan reports that David's building a house is not God's will.

Instead God will build David a house—a family to rule over Israel forever. God promises David that he and his family will sit on the throne forever.

1. David wanted to build a temple in Jerusalem for God. Why did the Lord refuse that offer? (Read 2 Samuel 7:4-6.)

2. Read 2 Samuel 7:1-16, and answer the following questions.

a. How will the Lord make David a house?

b. Whom did the Lord appoint to build a house?

SECOND SAMUEL 8–24

Chapter 8 summarizes David's military conquest and lists his cabinet officers. David not only defeats the traditional enemies of Israel, but he extends Israel's rule over neighboring states to create an empire.

Beginning with Chapter 9, Second Samuel focuses on David's court and family. In Chapter 9 he restores all the land of Saul to Mephibosheth, the crippled son of Jonathan.

The war with the Ammonites and Arameans, described in Chapter 10, forms the background of the David-Bathsheba story, which Chapters 11 and 12 relate. David steals Bathsheba, commits adultery with her, and has her husband Uriah put to death. Nathan reprimands David and promises him that evil will rise up against him from his own house. Read 2 Samuel 12:9-11.

Nathan's promise comes true. In Chapter 13, Amnon, the son of David, rapes his half-sister, Tamar. Tamar's brother, Absalom, kills Amnon and then flees. And in Chapter 14, after Absalom returns from exile, he leads a revolt against his father, David. Chapters 15 through 20 tell this story of Absalom's revolt. David flees from his son. But Joab, David's commander-in-chief, kills Absalom, whom he finds hanging from a tree after Absalom's hair becomes entangled in a tree limb. David mourns Absalom's death.

The final four chapters of Second Samuel are diverse. Chapters 22 and 23 contain poems attributed to David. Second Samuel 22:2-51 also appear in Psalm 18:2-50. This poem describes how God chooses David and protects him in times of great trouble.

1. Second Samuel 12:1-6 is a parable told by Nathan to David. Read these verses, and explain the point of the parable.

2. Read 2 Samuel 22:1-4. David praised the Lord by recounting God's attributes. List eight of them below.

a. (22:2)

b. (22:2)

c. (22:2)

d. (22:3)

e. (22:3)

f. (22:3)

g. (22:3)

h. (22:3)

SUMMARY

The books of First and Second Samuel tell us about some of the most important figures in Israel's history. The following episodes are the highlights of these books.

(1) Samuel's career as the last judge in Israel (1 Samuel 7)
(2) The reign of Saul as the first king over the Israelites (1 Samuel 13–15)
(3) The anointing of David as Saul's successor (2 Samuel 1–5)
(4) The story of David and Bathsheba (2 Samuel 11–12)
(5) David's psalm of praise to God for delivering Israel from her enemies (2 Samuel 22)

With the close of Second Samuel, we move into the era of the kings.

QUESTIONS FOR DISCUSSION

1. In 1 Samuel 8 the elders of Israel assemble at Ramah and ask Samuel to appoint a king who would govern over them. Samuel is not pleased with their request. Read 1 Samuel 8:10-18, in which Samuel warns the people about the effect a king will have upon their lives. The people are not convinced by Samuel's arguments. Do Samuel's predictions seem realistic to you? How would you have responded to these warnings? Would you have changed your mind about the request for a king? Why or why not?

2. Ancient Israel told two versions of how Saul became king. The biblical writer, however, incorporated both versions in the account without explanation or apology. Does this method help us understand the Bible as the Word of God? Or does this peculiarity cause doubts about the inspiration of the Bible? Why might it cause doubts? How can the two accounts be understood positively? What are some similar situations in our time where more than one version of an event is circulated?

3. Read David's lament over the death of Saul in 2 Samuel 1:19-27. Think back about the history of the relationship between Saul and David. Are you surprised at David's ability to forgive Saul after the animosity that existed between them? Why do you think David forgave Saul? What part does forgiveness play in your life?

4. We are all familiar with the story of David and Bathsheba. In order to "cover up" his illicit relationship with Bathsheba, David has her husband, Uriah the Hittite, killed in a battle. Think about the covering up of one crime with another. How is that pattern reflected in American political history?

DAILY READINGS FOR FIRST AND SECOND KINGS

Day 1:	1 Kings 2:1-12
Day 2:	1 Kings 10:23–11:18
Day 3:	1 Kings 19:1-18
Day 4:	2 Kings 5:1-14
Day 5:	2 Kings 17:1-18
Day 6:	2 Kings 22:1-13
Day 7:	2 Kings 25:1-12

FIRST KINGS
SECOND KINGS

Stone ramp leading to an altar on Mount Ebal at Shechem

The books of First and Second Kings tell the history of the chosen people from the time of Solomon until after the destruction of Jerusalem, the end of Judah, and the beginning of the Exile. The books cover a period of over five centuries.

The first section of the books of Kings is 1 Kings 1 through 11. These chapters cover the reign of Solomon, which lasted forty years.

FIRST KINGS 1–2

First Kings opens with the aged David on his deathbed. Adonijah, David's oldest son, assumes he will become king. But Bathsheba, the mother of Solomon, has other ideas. First Kings 1:7-8 tells us who supports whom. Read 1 Kings 1:7-8.

The army commander and the priest of the old tribal religion support Adonijah. Zadok the priest from Jerusalem, Nathan the prophet, and David's men support Solomon.

Bathsheba connives with Nathan, the court prophet, to convince David of his earlier promise to Bathsheba that Solomon would be his successor. David accepts the arguments of Bathsheba and gives orders for the coronation of Solomon.

In Chapter 2 Solomon kills his major opponents. This chapter closes with words as final as the sound of the executioner's ax: "So the kingdom was established in the hand of Solomon."

First Kings 1–2 describe the power play for the throne of David before he died. Skim these chapters, and find the answers to the following questions.

a. What phrase in 1:4 indicates that David was becoming senile?

b. Why did Adonijah think that he had a right to become king? (1:6)

c. What did Bathsheba mean by her statement in 1:21?

d. Name the three major supporters of Solomon to succeed David as king. (1:32)

FIRST KINGS 3–7

First Kings 3 through 11 describes the reign of Solomon. The Bible's presentation of Solomon emphasizes a number of aspects about his rule.

First Kings 3 and 4 focus on Solomon's wisdom and administrative expertise. God grants Solomon wisdom in response to Solomon's request. The story about Solomon's advice to divide a child between two women who both claim to be its mother illustrates his wisdom.

In Chapter 4 we read about Solomon's administration and the extravagance of his court. This chapter includes a list of his cabinet members in verses 1 through 6, a list of the provinces in his reorganization of the state in verses 7 through 19, and a list of the needs for his court for a single day in verses 22 through 28. Solomon and his staff consume 10 oxen, 20 cattle, and 100 sheep every day! The end of Chapter 4 lists Solomon's accomplishments in the area of wisdom. Read 1 Kings 4:24-34.

Chapters 5 through 9 focus on Solomon as the city and temple builder. With the support of Hiram, king of Tyre, Solomon builds a palace and administrative buildings in Jerusalem. The most famous of Solomon's construction projects is the Jerusalem Temple. Chapters 6 and 7 discuss the building of the Temple and its furnishings. The project takes seven years.

1. Read 1 Kings 3:4-13 for the answers to the following questions.

a. For what did Solomon ask in his dream?

b. What is the evidence that Solomon's request pleased God?

2. Solomon's Temple was a thing of beauty, but what did it symbolize? (Read 1 Kings 6:13; 8:29.)

FIRST KINGS 8–11

Chapter 8 describes the great celebration Solomon holds to dedicate the Temple. Solomon does not limit his construction projects to the palace and Temple complex. First Kings 9 reports on his construction of the walls of Jerusalem, his rebuilding of numerous cities throughout the land, and the projects he carries out to provide for his new chariot forces. At the close of Chapter

9 Solomon builds a merchant fleet on the Red Sea for trade with foreign countries.

First Kings 10 focuses on Solomon as the great international trader and merchant. Chapter 10 notes the results of that trade. The queen of Sheba visits Solomon, gold and silver flow into Jerusalem, Solomon develops a great military machine and supplies the surrounding nations with horses and chariots.

Not all of Solomon's reign is successful. First Kings 11 tells us something of his problems and troubles. Many of the women in Solomon's life are foreigners and worshipers of pagan gods. They bring foreign worship into Jerusalem.

Solomon's last days were troubled by problems. Skim 1 Kings 11:14-33 for the answers to the following questions.

a. Who was the first adversary that God raised up against Solomon? (11:14)

b. Who was the second adversary that God raised up against him? (11:23)

c. Who was the third adversary that God raised up against the king? (11:26)

FIRST KINGS 12–22

Solomon's empire begins to disintegrate. The Edomites and Arameans revolt. Jeroboam, the head of Solomon's forced labor, leads a rebellion against Solomon. Finally, a prophet named Ahijah rises up to oppose Solomon. Ahijah predicts that Solomon's kingdom will crumble and that ten of the Israelite tribes will withdraw from the Israelite union.

Following Solomon's death the kingdom that Saul founded, that David established, and that Solomon ruled separates into independent states. The two kingdoms are Judah in the south and Israel in the north. First Kings 12 tells the story of the division of the United Kingdom. The rest of First Kings and 2 Kings 1–17 narrate the history of the Northern and Southern Kingdoms.

According to 1 Kings 12 the ten northern tribes secede when Solomon's son, Rehoboam, refuses to lighten the heavy tax burden or to change the labor policies of Solomon. Jeroboam, who led the earlier revolt against Solomon, becomes the first king in the north.

The writer of the history of the Divided Kingdom does not give a full account of events that take place under the various kings. The writer gives a summary of the reigns, and then he often refers to other sources of information. The writer mentions one such source in 1 Kings 14:19 where he states, "Now the rest of the acts of Jeroboam, how he warred and how he reigned, are written in the Book of the Annals of the Kings of Israel." Unfortunately, the royal chronicles that writer mentions no longer exist.

The writer of First and Second Kings follows a pattern in telling us about the reigns of the various kings. He completes one king's rule, and then he traces the reign of the king or kings who ruled in the other kingdom at the same time. The writer tells us when each king begins his reign and a few facts about each reign. The writer then refers to further material on each king and makes a statement about the king's death and successor.

For the Judean, or southern kings, the writer also tells us the names of their mothers since the queen mother seems to function as first lady. And he also compares each Judean king's rule with that of David.

The writer condemns the Israelite, or northern kings, for separating from Judah and for continuing to worship at shrines built by Jeroboam. He never compliments any of the northern kings. This attitude probably comes from the fact that the information was edited from a southern perspective.

In some places the writer expands the accounts of various kings. This expansion usually occurs when the events concern prophets, Temple activities, or major wars.

First Kings 17 through 2 Kings 9 contains narratives about the prophets Elijah and Elisha. They are independent prophets who have bands of followers, and who try to preserve true religion and ethics threatened with extinction. These stories about Elijah and Elisha demonstrate the need for such prophets if the true worship of Yahweh is to survive in the north.

This need for survival is especially important during the reign of King Ahab and his Phoenician wife, Jezebel. During their reign, Elijah carries out a contest with the prophets of Baal on Mount Carmel. In Chapter 18, we read the story of this contest.

In Chapter 21 King Ahab seizes the vineyard of Naboth in order to turn it into a royal vegetable garden. Elijah opposes this illegal act.

© 1991 Biblical Archaeology Society

Horned incense altar

1. The sins of Jeroboam, the son of Nebat, are remembered again and again in the Bible. Read 1 Kings 12:25-33; then list his sins below.

a. (12:28-30)

b. (12:31)

c. (12:31)

d. (12:32-33)

e. (12:32-33)

2. The confrontation between Elijah, the prophet of the Lord, and the prophets of Baal is recorded in 1 Kings 18. Read verses 20-24 to find the answers to the questions below.

a. What was the test on Mount Carmel supposed to prove?

b. What evidence indicates that the worship of Baal was more popular than the worship of the Lord?

c. How were the people watching to know whether Baal or the Lord was God?

SECOND KINGS

The writer of the books of Kings wants to show that events took place in Israel and Judah according to the predictions of the prophets. Second Kings 9, in the account of the death of Queen Jezebel, gives an example of this attitude. Read 2 Kings 9:36-37.

Second Kings 17 reports the final days of the Northern Kingdom. To understand how the states of Israel and Judah fall, we need to know a little about their geographic location.

In ancient times, the land of Canaan formed a bridge joining the continents of Africa and Asia. In Africa, to the south of Canaan, was the rich and populous state of Egypt. To the north were the powerful countries of Assyria and Babylonia. When those countries were weak, Israel and Judah became fairly strong. But when Egypt, Assyria, and Babylonia were strong, each could dominate the surrounding regions including Canaan. When both Egypt and Assyria or Babylonia were strong, Israel and Judah served as buffer states and a battleground between the two.

In the eighth century B.C., Assyria expanded its territory in every direction. This expansion finally brought Assyria into contact with Israel. In Israel the shadow of the Assyrians caused panic. Many Israelite kings were killed in revolts and rebellions. Israel tried to make peace with Assyria, but later tried to fight Assyria with Egypt's help. Eventually, in 722 B.C. the capital city of Samaria fell and many members of the ten northern tribes were taken into exile. Many of these exiles were never heard of again, thus forming the basis for the legend of the ten lost tribes of Israel.

Second Kings 18 through 25 tells the story of the surviving state of Judah until Babylonia destroys it in 586 B.C. The writer praises and discusses in detail two Judean kings. These kings are Hezekiah, whose career the writer notes in Chapters 18 through 20, and Josiah, whose reign the writer discusses in Chapters 22 through 24. Both kings try to reform Judean religion and limit worship to the one Temple in Jerusalem. Josiah carries out this reform on the basis of a law book found in the Temple. This book was probably a form of the Book of Deuteronomy.

Throughout most of her last 150 years, Judah was ruled alternately by Assyria and Egypt. She was caught up in international struggles. Finally the new kingdom of Babylonia under King Nebuchadnezzar captured and destroyed Jerusalem.

Second Kings 24 and 25 tell about this destruction. The Babylonians burn the city and Temple and deport thousands of Judeans to Babylon. They take the Judean king into captivity. Here the Book of Second Kings ends. But the writer leaves the reader with a glimmer of hope in the story of the Judean king's release from prison.

1. Second Kings reports the destruction and exile of Israel, the Northern Kingdom, and Judah, the Southern Kingdom. Skim 2 Kings 17:1-8 for the answers to the questions below.

a. What nation destroyed Samaria, and who was its king?

b. Why did the Assyrians decide to invade and besiege Samaria?

c. What did the Assyrians do with the Israelites?

d. Why did the Lord allow these events to happen to Israel?

2. Now read 2 Kings 25:8-11, and answer these questions.

a. What king destroyed Jerusalem, and over what nation did he rule?

b. What did Nebuchadnezzar do with the captives?

3. Read 2 Kings 23:26-27. Why did the Lord allow these events to happen to Judah?

SUMMARY

Six major events in Israel's history, which are discussed in First and Second Kings, are listed here.

(1) The death of King David and Solomon's coronation (1 Kings 1)
(2) The accomplishments of Solomon and the disintegration of his empire (1 Kings 2–11)
(3) The division of the kingdom (1 Kings 12)
(4) The stories of Elijah and Elisha (1 Kings 17–2 Kings 9)
(5) The destruction of Samaria, the capital of Israel (2 Kings 17)
(6) Nebuchadnezzar's defeat of Judah and the beginning of the Babylonian Exile (2 Kings 24–25)

We can see that the books of Kings conclude at a turning point in the Old Testament history.

QUESTIONS FOR DISCUSSION

1. Discuss the last days of David as they unfold in 1 Kings 1–2. What statements suggest that he was becoming senile? What

passages reflect that a spark of his old fire still remained? What can we anticipate from these events about the future of the Israelites?

2. In doing the workbook questions for this lesson, you saw that God punished both King Solomon and King Ahab for worshiping other gods. In addition, the reforms of King Josiah were largely an attempt to eliminate such idol worship. In our modern culture, what is the equivalent of worshiping idols? Can we expect punishment for worshiping other gods? Why or why not?

3. The marriage of King Ahab of Israel to the Phoenician Jezebel, who worshiped idols, illustrates the influence of a dominant person in a marriage. Consider the influences of Jezebel on Ahab. (Read 1 Kings 16:29-34; 19:1-2; and 21:1-29.) What does this example suggest about marrying outside the faith? How should the realities of such a marriage be handled by one partner who is a committed believer?

4. Josiah instituted reforms after he discovered the "book of the law." Second Kings 23 lists the reforms. Soon after Josiah's death, Nebuchadnezzar marched into Jerusalem, and a decade later he destroyed the city. Thirty-five years after Josiah's reforms, the people of Judah were in exile in Babylon. Why do you think Josiah's reforms had no lasting effect?

DAILY READINGS FOR FIRST AND SECOND CHRONICLES

Day 1:   1 Chronicles 11:1-10
Day 2:   1 Chronicles 14:1-17
Day 3:   1 Chronicles 22:1-13
Day 4:   1 Chronicles 29:20-30
Day 5:   2 Chronicles 1:1-13
Day 6:   2 Chronicles 6:1-11
Day 7:   2 Chronicles 36:17-23

FIRST CHRONICLES
SECOND CHRONICLES

Model of Herod's Temple, Jerusalem

This lesson looks at the books of First and Second Chronicles. These books duplicate much of the information found in Genesis through First Kings. Originally the books of Chronicles were one book. Greek scholars divided them into two works much later. Like the Book of Ruth, the books of Chronicles appear in the third part of the Hebrew Old Testament. The Hebrews call the third part the Writings. The Writings represent books written rather late in the history of the chosen people.

If the books of Chronicles duplicate what we find in Genesis through Second Kings, why did someone write them? Ancient scholars also thought about this question. Their answer is partially seen in the name they gave the books. The Greek and Latin Bibles call them "the books of the things left out." They contain information left out of the earlier books.

First and Second Chronicles were the work of Jews living in the period after the Exile—a period when the nation, although politically dependent, enjoyed some measure of self-rule by favor of the overlords to the East. The priesthood guided the nation, and the Law was its charter. The Temple and its ritual in Jerusalem were the center of national life. In addition to this framework of law and ritual, great interest existed in personal devotion, in wisdom doctrines, in the memory of past glories and failures, and in the promises of the prophets.

FIRST CHRONICLES 1–10

The first nine chapters of First Chronicles are primarily lists of ancestors. These chapters, which begin with Adam, summarize the books of Genesis through Judges, but only by listing names. They present history in a genealogical nutshell. These chapters show a special interest in the ancestors and descendants of David, including some that lived after the Exile.

Chapter 1 tells us about the people who lived from Adam until the time of Jacob, whom the writer calls Israel. Beginning with 1 Chronicles 2:3, we have the descendants of the tribe of Judah. Turning over to Chapter 3 we see the names of persons from the house of David. In Chapter 4 we have an account of the southern tribes. In Chapter 5 we find a record of the tribes who live across the Jordan. Chapter 6 gives the lineage of the high priests. Chapter 7 tells us about the northern tribes, while Chapter 8 describes the tribe of Benjamin. Chapter 9 discusses families of Jerusalem and their tasks. Chapter 10 describes the death of Saul.

1. Early in First Chronicles we are given evidence that the book was written after the Babylonian Exile and return. Read 1 Chronicles 9:1-2. Summarize the evidence below.

2. Read 1 Chronicles 10:13-14. What was the main reason that Saul died?

3. List the three specific proofs that Saul had been unfaithful to the Lord.

a.

b.

c.

FIRST CHRONICLES 11–20

Chapters 11 through 29 introduce the history of David who is the main figure in the rest of First Chronicles. First Chronicles 11:1-9 narrates David's accession to the throne in Hebron. Chapters 11 through 14 describe David as a strong king. Warriors surround him and ensure his kingdom. These chapters tell us about David's palace at Jerusalem, about his children, and about his victories over the Philistines. Read 1 Chronicles 14:16-17.

Chapter 15 tells about the preparations for the moving of the ark from a place called Kiriath-jearim to Jerusalem, and then Chapter 16 describes the service the Levites perform in front of the ark.

First and Second Chronicles give us a very idealized picture of David. These books do not record many of David's weaknesses found in the books of Samuel. First Chronicles omits any account of the hostility between Saul and David, as well as David's sin with Bathsheba. The book does not mention David's domestic disputes or the dissension within his household. Chapter 17 gives prominence to the prophecy of

Nathan in which the prophet tells David that one of David's sons will build the Temple.

Chapters 18, 19, and 20 describe some of David's military victories. David and his army defeat the Philistines, the Moabites, the Arameans, the Edomites, and the Ammonites.

1. Turn to 1 Chronicles 18, and read verses 5-11. Then answer these two questions.

a. Who is responsible for all of David's victories? (18:6)

b. How does David acknowledge that God is the one responsible for his victories? (18:10-11)

2. How did God help David establish a strong kingdom among the other nations? (14:17)

FIRST CHRONICLES 21–29

Chapters 21 through 29 discuss the organization of worship in the Temple. Chapter 21 tells about David's numbering of the Israelites and the plague that God sends on Israel because of God's displeasure with the census. In the remainder of Chapter 21, we read about David's purchase of the land where his son will build the Temple.

In Chapter 22, David makes the preparations necessary to build the Temple. He charges his son Solomon with the responsibility for its construction. Chapters 23 through 26 tell about the organization of the Levites, the priests, the musicians, and the gatekeepers. Chapter 27 gives the division of the people into armies and lists the leader of each army. In Chapter 28, we read that David leaves to his son Solomon the task of putting all these plans into effect. In its final verses, 1 Chronicles 29 tells about the end of David's reign and the succession of Solomon. Read 1 Chronicles 29:26-30.

SECOND CHRONICLES 1–6

When we turn to the Book of Second Chronicles, we find in the first nine chapters an account of Solomon and his reign. A few paragraphs ago we referred to the prophecy of Nathan, which is found at the beginning of 1 Chronicles 17. In 1 Chronicles 17:12 Nathan tells David that David's son will build a house for God. So the Book of Second Chronicles begins with an account of Solomon's building of the Temple. In 2 Chronicles 6 we read Solomon's prayer of dedication.

Solomon's prayer at the dedication of the Temple begins in 2 Chronicles 6:14 and ends in verse 42. In this prayer, Solomon asks God for forgiveness in seven different situations. Read the verses below, and list the seven situations.

a. (6:22)

b. (6:24)

c. (6:26)

d. (6:28)

e. (6:32)

f. (6:34)

g. (6:36)

SECOND CHRONICLES 7–36

As we continue our survey of Second Chronicles, we see that Chapters 7, 8, and 9 give us additional information about the reign of King Solomon. The last two verses of 2 Chronicles 9 tell us about Solomon's death.

Just as in the case of David, the writer of Chronicles presents Solomon in all his glory. In Chronicles, we find none of Solomon's problems and none of the negative evaluations of him that we saw in Second Kings.

At the close of 2 Chronicles 10, the kingdom of Solomon becomes the two separate states of Israel and Judah. Read 2 Chronicles 10:17-19.

The writer does not tell us very much about the reasons for this division of the kingdom. From this point on, the Book of Second Chronicles deals only with the history of the tribes in the South. The writer believes that the king of the southern tribes is the legitimate successor to David and that the ten tribes of the North are rebels against this legitimate lineage. So the remaining twenty-seven chapters of Second Chronicles deal only with the kingdom of Judah. Much of the history in these chapters duplicates the events in 1 Kings 12 through 2 Kings 25.

SUMMARY OF CHRONICLES

Let us summarize now what we have discovered about the books of Chronicles. First, we see why they are called "the books of things left out," that is, things left out of the books that come before Chronicles—from Genesis through Second Kings. The books of Chronicles are also a "retelling" of the earlier historical books. The characters are more religious, more pious, and more idealized.

Second, we see that David is the real hero of the books of Chronicles. His heroism passes on to his son Solomon and to the other kings of Judah who are a part of his house and lineage.

Third, we see that the writer's concern is not so much with history, but with helping the people at a later time gain a sense of national pride as they struggle to preserve themselves, their identity, and their religion.

Fourth, the books stress that the important thing in the people's past is not so much their history, as their religion and their response to the will of God. The writer also wishes to demonstrate the supremacy of the Jews and their religion over all other people and cults. He accomplishes this by showing how God dwells in the Temple at Jerusalem.

Although the tiny kingdom of Judah seems insignificant in the eyes of the great peoples of the world, to the writer of First and Second Chronicles Judah is a kingdom with a noble past and a glowing future. Further, these books show that those who worship God exclusively and obey God's laws are rewarded, and those who do not find punishment.

Books in the ancient world usually end on a happy note somewhat like our fairy tales, where everyone lives happily ever after. The books of Chronicles are no exception. They jump across the period of the Exile to tell the reader about the Persian king, Cyrus, who issues a decree that allows the Jews to return home from exile. We will examine this part of Jewish history in the next lesson.

1. According to the writer of Second Chronicles, why was Judah invaded and defeated by another nation? (Read 2 Chronicles 36:16-17.)

2. According to the writer of Chronicles, what is the reason that Judah could prevail over its enemies? (Read 2 Chronicles 12:6-7; 13:18; 14:11-12.)

3. Second Chronicles 15:1-2 mentions prophets, the messengers of God. What message did Azariah bring to Asa, king of Judah?

4. Second Chronicles 16:7-9 mentions Hanani the seer. What point did he stress in his message to the king of Judah?

SUMMARY

Four main events in Israel's history, which are found in First and Second Chronicles, are listed here.

(1) The death of Saul and David's succession to the throne (1 Chronicles 10–11)
(2) The military victories under David's rule (1 Chronicles 18–20)
(3) The building and dedication of the Temple in Jerusalem (2 Chronicles 1–6)
(4) The division of David's kingdom into the separate states of Israel and Judah (2 Chronicles 10)

The end of Second Chronicles prepares the way for the return from the Exile, which we will study in the next lesson.

QUESTIONS FOR DISCUSSION

1. Ecclesiastes 3:1 states: "For everything there is a season, and a time for every matter under heaven." A few verses later the point is made that there is "a time to keep silence, and a time to speak." The writer of Chronicles chose to keep silent about King David's fateful sin—his adultery with Bathsheba. Why do you think the writer of Samuel told the story in full while this writer was silent about it? Think of examples from your experience where the repetition of a story may be appropriate at one time but not at another. Share your examples with the group. How might this situation in the Bible provide instruction for us today?

2. In the workbook questions on page 49, you learned that God slew Saul because of Saul's disobedience. (See 1 Chronicles 10:13-14.) Now read 1 Chronicles 10:1-7, which tells how Saul takes his own life. How can we reconcile these two parts of 1 Chronicles 10?

3. Compare 2 Chronicles 32:32-33 with 33:1-6 and 33:18-20. How can you explain that Hezekiah, the father, was such a godly person while Manasseh, the son, was such an ungodly king? Are you aware of similar examples today? What are some possible explanations of such unexpected and opposite characteristics in fathers and sons, or mothers and daughters? How can we respond to children or parents who disappoint us?

DAILY READINGS FOR EZRA, NEHEMIAH, AND ESTHER

Day 1: Ezra 1:1-11
Day 2: Ezra 6:1-12
Day 3: Ezra 7:1-10
Day 4: Nehemiah 1:1-11
Day 5: Nehemiah 8:1-8
Day 6: Esther 2:1-11
Day 7: Esther 9:23-32

EZRA
NEHEMIAH
ESTHER

Aerial view of the Temple Mount in Jerusalem

© 1986 Biblical Archaeology Society

The books of Ezra and Nehemiah pick up the history of the Jewish people at the point where Second Chronicles leaves off. We cannot tell whether Ezra and Nehemiah were once a single work with First and Second Chronicles. But the connection between the narratives in the two books is obvious to the reader. Chronicles ends with the decree by Cyrus of Persia about rebuilding the Temple in Jerusalem. The opening of the Book of Ezra gives the reader a full copy of Cyrus's decree.

To understand some of the issues and events in Ezra and Nehemiah, let's look at the historical background. The state of Judah fell to the Babylonians in 586 B.C., a little over 500 years after the time of

David. Many Judeans were carried into exile in Babylonia. The Jews in exile were granted a limited amount of freedom so they could preserve many of their religious practices. Many looked forward to returning to their homeland.

About 550 B.C. the Persians under Cyrus began to rise to prominence and take over territory from the Babylonians. In 538 B.C. Babylon was captured by Cyrus, and the Babylonian Empire came to an end. Cyrus was a very considerate ruler who encouraged many of the ethnic groups, whom the Babylonians had deported, to return home. He also encouraged a revival of their religion and granted them a certain amount of independence as long as they paid their

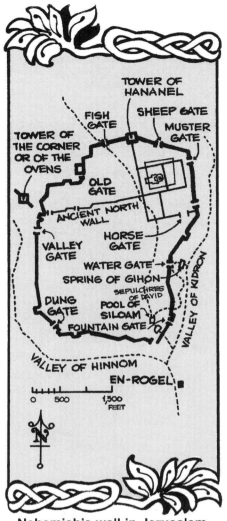

Nehemiah's wall in Jerusalem

EZRA 1–3

Ezra 1 through 6 tells the story of the return of the Jews from Babylon and their work in rebuilding the Temple. The famous edict of Cyrus introduces the story of return. Read Ezra 1:2-4.

This edict contains several elements. First, Cyrus assumes a limited personal responsibility to see that the Temple in Jerusalem is rebuilt. Second, Cyrus permits interested Jews to return to Judah to work on the Temple. Third, Cyrus calls upon others who could not return, or did not want to return, to aid those returning.

Sheshbazzar, a prince of Judea, leads the return from exile. He takes with him the sacred vessels that Nebuchadnezzar had carried out of the Temple. Cyrus restored these to the Jews.

Ezra 2, which is repeated as part of Nehemiah 7, is a list of the returning families. According to the writer, 42,360 persons return, along with 7,337 servants and 200 singers. The text even reports the number of horses, mules, camels, and donkeys that accompany those returning.

Chapter 3 reports that reconstruction work begins under the direction of the high priest Jeshua and the Davidic descendant Zerubbabel. Work progresses slowly.

The edict of Cyrus is an important statement that closes the Book of Second Chronicles and opens the Book of Ezra. Read Ezra 1:1-4 for the answers to these questions.

a. Why did Cyrus want to have the Temple in Jerusalem rebuilt?

b. What prophet had predicted the return of the people in exile to Jerusalem?

taxes to the Persian treasury. So Cyrus's treatment of the Jews was not unique, but it was characteristic of the way the Persians treated the peoples under their rule.

With this historical summary in mind, let us now return to the books of Ezra and Nehemiah. We can divide the two books into four sections. The first section reports the return from exile and the rebuilding of the Temple. The second section treats the return of Ezra and his initial work of reforming Jewish life in Jerusalem. The third portion tells of Nehemiah's return to reconstruct the city walls of Jerusalem. The fourth part reports the work of Ezra and Nehemiah in reforming and restructuring Jewish life in the city of Jerusalem.

c. Who was to decide which individuals would return to Jerusalem to rebuild the Temple?

d. What responsibilities did those who remained in Babylon have to help rebuild the Jerusalem Temple?

EZRA 4–7

Chapters 4 and 5 discuss the opposition to the rebuilding of the Temple. The people of the land—persons of uncertain identity—volunteer to help in reconstructing the Temple. Jeshua and Zerubbabel refuse to allow this, so the people of the land try to stop all work. The Samaritans in the north also oppose the rebuilding of the Temple. Finally a decree by King Artaxerxes officially halts the work.

Chapter 6 reports that Darius, the Persian who becomes king in 522 B.C., commands his servants to search the archives. They find a copy of Cyrus's edict permitting the Jews to rebuild the Temple. Darius allows the Jews to resume working, and they complete and dedicate the Temple in 515 B.C.

A central emphasis in these first six chapters of Ezra is the role that foreign rulers play in the rebuilding of the Temple. The rebuilding demonstrates the respect Persian rulers gave to foreigners and their religions.

The second division of Ezra and Nehemiah is Chapters 7 through 10 of Ezra. These chapters report Ezra's return to Jerusalem. Ezra is a priest and a scribe skilled in the law of Moses.

According to Chapter 7 Ezra returns with the permission of the Persian king Artaxerxes. The king grants Ezra the authority to regulate Jewish life according to the Law.

Chapter 8 lists those who return with Ezra and tells the story of their trip back to the homeland. In Chapter 9, Ezra learns that the Jews in Judea are marrying non-Jews, thus mixing the holy race. In Chapter 10, Ezra gathers all the men in the open square and tells them to separate from their foreign wives. But because of heavy rain the men ask Ezra to allow officials to stand for the whole assembly. So Ezra appoints a committee to draw up a list of those who married foreign women. After two months, this committee submits a list of names of those who married non-Jews. The Book of Ezra ends with this list.

Read the portions of Ezra 7 listed below, and answer the questions.

a. Read Ezra 7:6. What are Ezra's qualifications?

b. Read Ezra 7:10. What is Ezra's mission?

NEHEMIAH 1–4

The Book of Nehemiah opens with a description of Nehemiah's desire to return and rebuild the walls of Jerusalem. Read Nehemiah 1:1-3.

Nehemiah is cupbearer to the Persian king Artaxerxes. The cupbearer is not only a taster of the king's wine but also serves as guardian of the royal apartment. Nehemiah returns to Jerusalem with the king's permission. Nehemiah 1 through 6 reports how Nehemiah returns to the city, surveys the ruins, organizes work groups, and rebuilds the city walls in fifty-two days. The Jews continue to work despite threats by the Samaritans, the Ammonites, the Arabs, and others who do not want the wall rebuilt.

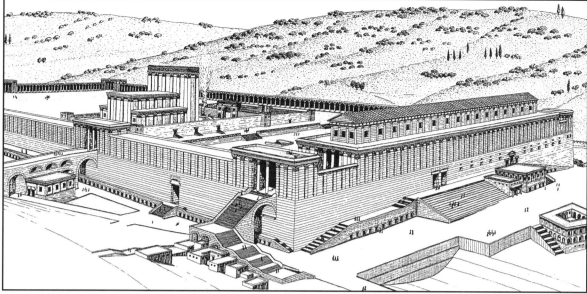

Artist's drawing of the Second Temple

Ecclesiasticus (also known as Sirach), a wisdom book that was written after Ezra but before the time of Jesus, says this of Nehemiah: "The memory of Nehemiah also is lasting; he raised our fallen walls, and set up gates and bars, and rebuilt our ruined houses" (49:13). Skim Nehemiah 1:1–2:8 to discover why and how he was able to rebuild Jerusalem. Then find the answers to these questions:

a. How did Nehemiah become aware of conditions in Jerusalem?

b. What did Nehemiah do when he heard about the sorry state of Jerusalem?

c. After the king agreed to allow Nehemiah to go to Jerusalem, what two things did Nehemiah request of the king? (Nehemiah 2:7-8)

NEHEMIAH 5–13

Chapters 5 and 6 report Nehemiah's attempts to ease the economic burdens on the population. He forbids the taking of interest on loans and reduces the taxes on the people.

The final section of Nehemiah is Chapters 8 to 13. In these chapters Ezra reads the law aloud to the people in the square in front of the Water Gate. Then they enter a covenant to obey the law. Read Nehemiah 10:28-31.

In Chapters 11 and 12 we read that the population of Jerusalem increases by ten percent of the population then living outside the city. The people cast lots, and one of every ten families moves into the city. Following this move, the Jews dedicate the walls of Jerusalem. Chapter 13 reports some of Nehemiah's other reforming works. He excludes non-Jews from the Temple, he enforces sabbath observances, and he requires a pledge from the men that they will not marry foreign women.

Ezra and Nehemiah are partially autobiographical. Both tell parts of their stories in the first person. Notice, for example, the last two verses of the Book of Nehemiah. Read Nehemiah 13:30-31.

These verses suggest that the writer of Ezra and Nehemiah actually possessed memoirs of these men and incorporated them into his work.

ESTHER

Esther, the third book in today's lesson, has little to do with the content of Ezra and Nehemiah. We consider Esther with these two books because it follows them in the Protestant Bible. And like Ezra and Nehemiah, the story in Esther is set during the time when the Persians ruled the ancient world.

The Book of Esther is a historical romance that takes place during the reign of King Ahasuerus, probably the king we know as Xerxes who ruled from 486 to 465 B.C.

In the story Ahasuerus dismisses his queen for insubordination. In Chapter 2 the officers of Ahasuerus bring all the beautiful virgins in the area to the court. The one who most pleases the king will become queen. Esther, the cousin of Mordecai the Jew, is one of the virgins the officers bring to the court. Esther finds favor in the king's eyes, and he chooses her as his queen. However, Esther does not tell the king she is Jewish. Read Esther 2:9-10.

The plot thickens in Chapter 3 when Haman, the prime minister, wants everyone to bow down to him. Mordecai refuses. Haman gets the king's permission to destroy the Jews. The king circulates a decree throughout the empire that all Jews will be killed on the thirteenth day of the month Adar. In Chapter 5 Haman's wife encourages Haman to build a gallows about seventy-five feet high to hang Mordecai. Of course, Haman's plots fail, because the king discovers that Mordecai once saved his life. Chapter 8 tells us that at Queen Esther's request the king changes the edict to allow the Jews to put their enemies to death. The king's servants hang Haman on the gallows he built for Mordecai.

Many persons wonder why Esther, with its sense of vengeance and lack of any reference to God, is in the Bible. The ancient Greek translators recognized some of the objections to the book and added numerous sections to make Esther pious and to relate God to the course of events. Our English versions place these additions to Esther in the Apocrypha, under the title "Additions to the Book of Esther."

Jewish tradition has the Book of Esther preserved and canonized because it explains why Jews celebrate the festival of Purim on the fourteenth day of the month of Adar. The festival commemorates the Jews' survival and existence in a hostile world. Read Esther 9:20-22.

The plot of Haman against the Jews is recorded in Esther 3:7-15. Read that section to find the answers to these questions.

a. What two reasons did Haman use to convince the king to permit the Jews to be destroyed?

b. The decree that Haman had sent out called for the people to kill the Jews on a certain day. What else were they to do on that day?

SUMMARY

We conclude this study of Ezra, Nehemiah, and Esther by listing four main events in Israel's history that are found in Ezra, Nehemiah, and Esther.

(1) The edict of Cyrus, which releases the exiles from Babylon (Ezra 1)
(2) The rebuilding of the Temple in Jerusalem (Ezra 3–4)
(3) Nehemiah's restoration of the wall around Jerusalem (Nehemiah 1–6)
(4) Esther's saving her people from death (Esther 7)

With the books of Ezra, Nehemiah, and Esther we come to the end of the historical books in the Old Testament. Next we will begin our study of the Wisdom Literature.

QUESTIONS FOR DISCUSSION

1. In Chapter 1 of Ezra, we find the edict of Cyrus. This edict allowed the people of Judah to return from the Exile and rebuild the Temple in Jerusalem. In the introduction in Ezra 1:1, the writer states that the Lord "stirred up the spirit of King Cyrus of Persia." What is your thinking about God's use of a pagan king as an instrument to fulfill the divine purpose?

2. Both Ezra (9–10) and Nehemiah (13:23-30) required the end of mixed marriages. (Note also 2 Corinthians 6:14. The New Testament does not oppose interracial marriages *between believers*. It does warn against marrying unbelievers.) Discuss why they emphasized this in their reforms. Read these passages for clues. Is this principle still valid for God's people today? Why or why not? Think of examples in your own experience to support your answer.

3. When Nehemiah wanted to rebuild the wall, he faced two types of obstacles. Read Nehemiah 4–5. Identify the obstacles and how Nehemiah responded to them. Think of examples where some worthy work has been proposed in your church or community. Have similar obstacles arisen in opposition? How does the response of Nehemiah to his situation provide a model for us in such matters? (The outside obstacle was that the enemies of the Jews ridiculed them, then plotted and fought against them. Nehemiah's quick response was prayer (4:4–5). He followed the prayer with practical action (4:16, 21). The obstacle within was the rich taking advantage of the poor. Nehemiah called on the rich to fear God.)

4. The word *God* does not appear in Esther. Draw attention to the famous passage in Esther (4:13-16) in which Mordecai challenges her to do what she can for the cause of the threatened Jews. Have the class members note the reference to relief arising from "another quarter." Is this a reference to the unseen presence of God in the story? Probably so. Ask the class members to think of examples from history or their experience where God seemed to be in command behind the scenes. What indication do we have that the sovereignty of God is at work behind the scenes? Where in your church or community does God appear to be at work behind the scenes? How is our secular society today an echo of the society in Persia in Esther's day?

DAILY READINGS FOR JOB

Day 1:   Job 1:1-12
Day 2:   Job 1:13-22
Day 3:   Job 2:1-13
Day 4:   Job 3:1-10
Day 5:   Job 9:1-12
Day 6:   Job 38:1-11
Day 7:   Job 42:1-17

Review 2 Sheet

1. What six books are the Former Prophets in the Hebrew Bible?

2. What major task does God commission Joshua to do?

3. What does Joshua do in a ceremony at Shechem after the conquest is completed?

4. What cycle is portrayed over and over again in the Book of Judges?

5. Why does the Book of Ruth have special meaning for those who have converted to Judaism?

6. What three Israelite figures are portrayed in the books of First and Second Samuel?

7. Who are the main enemies of Israel throughout the books of First and Second Samuel?

8. Who succeeds David on the throne of Israel?

9. Into what two kingdoms does Solomon's monarchy divide?

10. What major power defeats the Northern Kingdom (Israel) in 722 B.C.?

11. What major power defeats the Southern Kingdom (Judah) in 587 B.C.?

12. What two Old Testament books parallel the history told in First and Second Kings?

13. What major task faced the Jews who returned to Jerusalem from the Babylonian Exile?

14. What two Old Testament historical books tell about the return of the exiles to Jerusalem?

15. What Israelite festival is connected with the Book of Esther?

(Answers are on page 182.)

WISDOM LITERATURE

INTRODUCTION

The wisdom literature of the Bible is usually identified as the books of Job, Proverbs, and Ecclesiastes. Wisdom is connected with wise men or sages, just as law is connected with the priest and the word with the prophet.

In Jewish tradition, Solomon is *the* wise man of the ages, for we are told in 1 Kings 4:31-33 that he was wiser than all others. Besides his wisdom about nature, he spoke 3,000 proverbs and composed 1,005 songs. To Solomon, therefore, tradition attributes the writing of most of the Proverbs, all of Ecclesiastes, and Song of Solomon.

WISDOM IN THE BIBLICAL WORLD

Thanks to archaeological research in the past 150 years, we know today that wisdom literature similar to that in the Bible existed long before Solomon in the biblical world. From ancient Babylonia, Syria, and Egypt have come examples of ancient wisdom. The Egyptian wisdom is the most important because of the close connections that the people of the Nile Valley had with ancient Canaan and Israel over long periods of time.

Biblical wisdom shares basic characteristics with the wisdom of the ancient Near East. First, wisdom is focused on the individual rather than the nation. The law taught by the priest is concerned primarily with statutes and commandments that keep the nation holy before God. The prophets emphasize the moral requirements of God and the shortcomings of the people that threaten national judgment. But the sages provide instruction for the individual.

The wisdom of Babylonia and Egypt consists of the two types that we meet in the Bible—practical and philosophical. Practical wisdom helps the individual develop a sane, workable attitude toward life. Wisdom includes technical skills, such as weaving and goldsmithing; administrative skills, such as governing and leading in war; and artistic skills, such as composing poetry and songs or playing musical instruments. The sayings are short and easy to remember. They help the individual get along with others. The intent of practical wisdom is to guide a person through the difficulties of life to success.

Biblical wisdom was practical, but also religious. It was not concerned with religious ritual, but it was always understood that "the fear of the LORD is the beginning of knowledge [wisdom]" (Proverbs 1:7). Wisdom was recognized as coming from God, but it was frequently portrayed as a woman (see Proverbs 1:20-33; 3:13-20; and 8:1-31). This personification of wisdom helps us understand the personification of the Word (Logos) in John 1:1-18.

Job and Ecclesiastes are two examples of the philosophical type of wisdom in the Bible. They wrestle with such issues as why the innocent suffer and how to find a rational explanation for the purpose of life in the face of humankind's inevitable death.

WISDOM LITERATURE AND THE BIBLE

Job, Proverbs, and Ecclesiastes are found in the third section of the Hebrew Bible. This section seems to be held together by the idea of wisdom, just as the Pentateuch is by law and the prophetic section is by the idea of the prophetic word. Thus Psalms can be seen as the result of wisdom, along with the other collections of poems, Lamentations, and Song of Solomon. Daniel is included in this third section, rather than among the prophets, because Daniel is clearly a sage.

Biblical wisdom literature, though written at least 2500 to 3000 years ago, is a vital source of moral instruction today.

JOB

Mimi Forsyth

This lesson looks at the story of Job, whose capacity for articulate complaint excels his reputation for patience. As we flip through the Book of Job in the New Revised Standard Version, a major difference in the style of the book becomes immediately apparent. The first two chapters, 32:1-5, and the final eleven verses are in story or narrative form. The rest of the book, Chapter 3 through the first six verses of Chapter 42, is poetry.

The narrative portions at the beginning and the end of the book make up the prologue and the epilogue. The poetry forms the main body of the book. First of all let us quickly survey the book's content. Verses 1 through 5 begin the prologue by telling us of Job's piety. Read Job 1:1-5.

A conversation follows between God and Satan. Satan questions the motivation of Job's piety. He argues that Job is pious only because God protects and rewards him. To prove that this is not the case, God allows Satan to bring misfortune upon Job and his family. This misfortune occurs without Job's knowing the source of his troubles. Three concerned friends then arrive to offer condolence to the suffering Job. Job and his friends speak about the reason for his suffering. In these speeches, Job claims that he is innocent of wrong-doing and wishes that God would state the charges against him and explain the reason for his suffering. Finally, Job personally confronts God who points out that only God has the power to do mighty works and reminds Job that there is much in life that Job cannot understand.

The epilogue in Job 42:7-17 resolves Job's problems. God restores his possessions and his sons and daughters. Job's intercession on behalf of his friends who have displeased God appears to motivate these rewards.

Many scholars believe that the story of Job originally circulated in an oral form. Egyptian and Mesopotamian cultures had stories similar to that of Job. All these stories deal with the problem of a righteous person who suffers without apparent reason. The prologue and epilogue probably once existed as a complete short story without the speeches. Later storytellers enhanced the story by adding the conversations between Job and his friends and God's speeches in poetry form. In expanding the narrative, the poets were attempting to explore the problem of suffering in greater depth.

The original narrative form of Job pictures him as a man of patience and long-suffering. The later poetic speeches present an impatient Job who bitterly complains of his condition.

JOB 1–2

The prologue in Chapters 1 and 2 introduces Job, a family man who is righteous, wealthy, and highly respected. He lives in the land of Uz. Verses 4 and 5 tell about his sons and daughters who celebrate together on special days. Job expresses his parental concern through sacrifices for the possible sins of his sons. The picture is one of a very happy family.

We meet Satan for the first time in Job 1:6. He presents himself before God. Here Satan appears as a servant of God. Satan devises a plan to test Job. By testing Job, Satan hopes to show that Job is faithful only because of what he gets from God.

Job 1:13-19 tell of the dramatic destruction of Job's servants, livestock, and children. In verses 20 to 22 we read about Job's reaction in the face of trouble. Job

remains sinless and does not accuse God of acting in an unacceptable manner. In verse 21 he confesses, "Naked I came from my mother's womb, and naked shall I return there; the LORD gave, and the LORD has taken away; blessed be the name of the LORD."

In Chapter 2 Satan comes to make another deal with God. God vouches for Job's integrity, but Satan is sure he can break down Job. This time God grants Satan power to afflict Job further, stating only that Satan must spare Job's life.

Satan immediately afflicts Job with "loathsome sores" from head to foot. Job's affliction makes him unclean. He leaves his house for an ash heap where he sits scraping himself with a potsherd. Job's wife tries to talk him into ending it all. "Do you still persist in your integrity? Curse God, and die," she says. Job reproves his wife for her foolish ways and expresses his acceptance of both good and evil from the hand of God.

1. In the prologue, God and Satan meet twice to discuss Job. Read Job 1:6-12 and 2:1-6, then answer these questions.

a. In the first meeting, how did Satan desire to test Job's loyalty to God?

b. When Job passed the first test, what did Satan suggest as an additional test?

c. What limit did God place on the first test of Job?

d. What limit did God place on the second test of Job?

2. The Bible reports on how Job performed in the second test. Read Job 2:9-10, then explain what you think the statement, "Job did not sin with his lips," means.

JOB 3–8

At the end of Chapter 2 the narrator reports the visit of Job's three friends who come to console and comfort him. Job's deplorable condition shocks Eliphaz, Bildad, and Zophar; and at first they do not recognize him. After wailing, tearing their robes, and sprinkling dust on their heads, they sit with Job in silence—day and night—for a week.

With this setting the writer of the poetic section of Job presents the speeches of Job and his friends. Job begins with a complaint and a denunciation of life. In turn the friends and Job answer one another. A friend speaks, Job responds; another friend speaks, Job responds, and so on. In three sets of speeches, Job and his friends take turns stating their cases and their understanding of the situation. The first two sets of speeches are well preserved in Chapters 4 through 21. The third round of speeches in Chapters 22 through 27 is in fragmentary form. No one knows why this third cycle was not preserved intact. Now that we know the writer's pattern, let us go back and examine some of the arguments of the various speeches.

In Chapter 3 Job curses the day of his birth. He reasons that to never see life might be better than suffering the miseries of his tormented state. Read Job 3:2-5.

The speeches of Job and his friends are actually individual monologues. The speakers frequently do not address one another or take seriously what the other has said. The writer obviously has a reason for this technique. This approach allows the writer to speculate on practically every conceivable approach to the problem of evil and suffering without declaring any one of these as the right understanding.

Job's friends propose any number of possible interpretations of Job's trouble: he is guilty of some sin he needs to confess, God is chastening him for his ultimate good, Job is guilty of arrogance before God, and Job is suffering the misery that befalls all persons to lesser and greater degrees.

Read the verses listed below, and write in your own words the reasons that Job's friends suggest for his suffering.

a. (4:8)

b. (8:4)

c. (8:13)

d. (15:31)

JOB 9–31

None of the traditional answers to the problem of human misery satisfy Job. He argues that no cause-and-effect relationship exists in his experience. Nothing in his life warrants the misery Job encounters.

Job does not content himself to respond only to his friends. He takes on God. Job directs many of his speeches to the divine rather than to his friends. For Job, God is more the enemy than the friends.

Job complains that God will not leave him alone. Even when he lies upon his bed, God scares him with dreams and terrifies him with visions. Job cannot get God to respond to his complaint. Read Job 9:32-33.

Job pleads with God to clearly state the case against him. In spite of his misery Job refuses to admit guilt or at least any guilt sufficient to produce his torment. In Job 19:23-29 Job wants to record his words in a book or chisel them into stone. He believes that ultimately his Redeemer will vindicate him. Job hopes to find God and argue his case directly and hear God's response.

In Chapter 31 Job ends his arguments with a confession where he lists numerous sins of which he claims innocence. He places himself under a curse if he is guilty.

1. Despite his desperate physical condition, Job yet looked to God for vindication. Read Job 19:23-27. Describe in your own words Job's hope.

2. In Chapter 31 Job denies that he has committed a number of sins. Identify these sins.

a. (31:5)

b. (31:9)

c. (31:13)

d. (31:16)

e. (31:24-25)

f. (31:29)

g. (31:33)

JOB 32–42

In Chapters 32 through 37 a young man named Elihu puts in his first appearance. He offers his understanding of Job's condition. Elihu really offers no new perspective on the issue, but summarizes many of the arguments already put forth.

Finally God responds to Job twice—first in Chapters 38 and 39, and again in Chapters 40 and 41. God does not refute Job's arguments directly. Instead God points out the futility of human wisdom and affirms a divine, if mysterious, purpose in creation. Against the marvelous world of creation and the power of the Creator, humankind is weak and without answers. Read Job 40:6-9.

Job responds to God twice but can no longer defend himself. He confesses that over against the mysteries of creation, he is of little account and will argue his case no more. Job receives no explanation for his sufferings. God transcends his sufferings. God directs Job and the reader away from the issues of suffering and justice and toward God. The impatient and persistent Job willingly confesses that to see and hear God is in itself sufficient. Read Job's confession in Job 42:1-6.

Re-read Job's confession in Job 42:1-6 to find the answers to these questions.

a. What does Job say to God in verse 2? Write it in your own words.

b. What is Job saying to God in verse 3?

c. What does Job do at the end of his confession?

SUMMARY

With the Book of Job we enter a new phase of our book-by-book study of the Bible. Until this lesson we have studied historical books. With Job we begin a group of books that are poetic in nature.

Five important parts of this book are listed below.

(1) Satan's testing of Job (Job 1–2)
(2) The visit from Job's friends and the dialogue that takes place among the four men (Job 2)

(3) Job's conclusion that he is innocent (Job 31)
(4) The speeches of God to Job (Job 38–41)
(5) The confession of Job and the restoration of his fortunes (Job 42)

QUESTIONS FOR DISCUSSION

1. We noted in question 2 on page 56 that Job had not sinned *with his lips*. Discuss why this idea was stressed in the prologue. How are speech and deeds related? How might Christians today be guilty of sinning with the lips? When have you committed this kind of sin?

2. Try to put yourself in Job's place. Then think about the advice that Job's friends give him. Do you think Job's friends are a positive or negative influence on him? Do they help him or make matters worse? How can we use this biblical example to become better friends to other people?

3. The question of why the innocent must suffer is found not only in the Book of Job, but elsewhere in the Bible and in literature. Humankind has always looked in vain for a sure answer to this question. It is all right to disagree with the answer Job gives. According to this book Job, the innocent man is suffering because God has willed it. Job spends forty chapters trying to discover why God has willed his suffering. What answer does the Book of Job give to this question? Why do you agree or disagree with its answer?

DAILY READINGS FOR PSALMS

Day 1:   Psalm 1
Day 2:   Psalm 8
Day 3:   Psalm 23
Day 4:   Psalm 46
Day 5:   Psalm 67
Day 6:   Psalm 100
Day 7:   Psalm 150

PSALMS

Jean-Claude Lejeune

The Book of Psalms, which we study in this lesson, is probably the best known of all the Old Testament books. Many people in our churches know at least one psalm by heart.

Throughout history, people have respected and appreciated the Book of Psalms. Martin Luther called it a Bible in miniature. John Calvin described the book as a mirror that reflects the anatomy of all the parts of the soul. We especially see the disquieting emotions such as grief, sorrow, fear, care, and anxiety as well as hope, joy, gratitude, and praise.

The word *psalms,* which became the title of the book, comes from the Greek language. In classical Greek, *psalmos* originally referred to the playing of a stringed instrument. Gradually it came to mean the music produced by such playing. Still later, *psalmos* included the song that accompanied the playing of a stringed instrument.

Our present Book of Psalms, based on the Hebrew text, contains 150 psalms. We divide the 150 psalms into five books. The four doxologies that appear at the end of four psalms make us aware of this five-book division.

Psalm 72:20 says, "The prayers of David, the son of Jesse, are ended." The doxology in Psalm 89:52 states, "Blessed be the Lord forever! Amen and Amen." A slightly more elaborate doxology appears at the end of Psalm 106:48.

The last psalm in the book, number 150, does not contain a final doxology; the

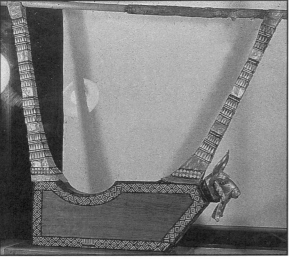

Four-foot-high lyre, from Ur

entire psalm is a doxology in itself. Read Psalm 150.

The doxologies divide the larger book into five smaller books. Book One is Psalms 1 to 41, Book Two is Psalms 42 to 72, Book Three is Psalms 73 to 89, Book Four is Psalms 90 to 106, and Book Five is Psalms 107 to 150.

These doxologies suggest that the book was edited to produce what the ancient rabbis called the five books of David that parallel the five books of Moses. This fivefold division of the book was probably made at a time when the psalms were read in worship services along with the books of the Law. Book One, or Psalms 1 to 41, would be read with the Book of Genesis; Book Two with the Book of Exodus, and so on.

All but thirty-four of the psalms have headings or introductions. Many of these introductions to individual psalms associate the psalms with David. Seventy-two psalms refer to David in the headings. Besides the references to David, these headings supply other information. We can no longer clearly understand many of these introductory statements to the psalms. If you compare a number of modern translations and notice the differences, this fact becomes immediately apparent.

Look at the heading of Psalm 59. The words *To the leader* suggest that this psalm was probably sung by a choir. *Do Not*

Destroy may refer to the tune to which the psalm was sung. The word *Miktam* seems to refer to the kind of psalm. The Israelites employed this word in a way similar to our use of such terms as *ballad* or *western* when we describe types of songs. We do not know the meaning of *Miktam,* and therefore scholars leave the word untranslated. *Of David* generally means that David wrote the psalm. The rest of the heading associates the psalm with an episode in David's life.

We can see then that the Israelites associated David with many psalms. Later tradition tended to assume that David wrote all the psalms, but the headings do not support this assumption. The many references to David do, however, show that the psalms were closely associated with the royal family in Jerusalem.

When most people read through the Book of Psalms, they notice two things. Different psalms repeat the same phrases and ideas. So the psalms usually appear repetitious. Also, the subject and tone of the book often changes drastically from one psalm to the next. A boastful and almost irreverent psalm follows a pious psalm. These changes give the book a sense of great diversity. In light of its great similarity and equally great diversity, how can we speak of the book as a whole?

Persons commonly speak of the Book of Psalms as the hymnbook of the Jewish Temple. In some respects, this description is true. Many of the psalms may have originally been sung as hymns in Temple services. Others describe the Book of Psalms as the prayer book of ancient Israel. This description is also partially true since many psalms are prayers addressed to God.

No single description is appropriate for all the psalms. Some of the psalms are addressed to God either in praise and thanksgiving or in words of petition and request. Other psalms speak not *to* God but *about* God and assume a human audience. Some psalms contain the words of God addressed to persons. Some psalms read

Canaanite incense stand with musicians

ing. Sometimes services were for individuals, at other times for the whole community, and at other times for the king. The worshiping community used the psalms again and again, just as modern congregations use prayer books and hymnals.

The priests offered ceremonies in the Temple for private individuals when persons were sick or facing death, when they felt threatened by enemies, or when they were wrongly accused of some crime. On these occasions, the priest offered psalms to God along with sacrifices as he asked for God's help. Psalm 5 is a prayer for a person who has many enemies. Psalm 6 is an example of a psalm used during time of sickness. Psalm 7 is a psalm for someone falsely accused of some misdeed. Some individuals prayed laments during times of trouble and distress. And persons used some psalms, such as Psalm 51, when they had committed some sin and were asking for forgiveness. Read Psalm 51:1-2, 15-17.

The priests held services of thanksgiving after God saved a person from trouble or distress or forgave that person's sin. Psalms used in thanksgiving rituals looked back on the trouble from which God granted delivery. Psalm 32 is a psalm of thanksgiving for forgiven sin. Other psalms offered thanksgiving for healing from disease or for rescue from one's enemies.

The community had its troubles and times of thanksgiving also. Psalms such as 74 and 79 are prayers by the people after the destruction or defilement of the Temple. These psalms and others like them express the hope that the enemy will be destroyed and that the Temple and the chosen people will be restored. Some of these psalms, such as Psalm 137, are prayers for vengeance on Israel's enemies.

Many psalms are majestic hymns that proclaim God's greatness in creating the world, in bringing the Hebrews out of Egypt, in saving and protecting the people from their enemies, in choosing Jerusalem as God's sacred city, and in making the family of David the chosen dynasty. The

like sermons. The Book of Psalms, therefore, is really a collection of poems.

The psalms were an important part of worship in the Jerusalem Temple. The choirs, priests, and worshipers recited and sang the psalms as part of worship services. Other worship activities included sacred processions, sacrifices, weeping, feasting, and dancing. The variety in the psalms reflects the variety in worship services. Sometimes worship services were joyful and thankful; at other times, sad and lament-

worshipers probably sang these hymns at the great spring and fall religious festivals. These festivals were the Feasts of Passover and Tabernacles. Read Psalm 100.

Just as the psalms gave expression in worship to the diverse needs, emotions, and conditions of the ancient Israelite people, so they still allow us to identify with these same feelings and hopes. They are an eloquent expression of universal sentiments. Thus the psalms have an abiding relevance.

The first kind of psalm we will look at is the *hymn of praise*. Read Psalm 19 aloud. Then answer the following questions.

a. What is describing God's glory in speech without words? (verses 1-4)

b. What is the main theme of verses 7-11?

c. What is the psalmist praying in verses 12-14?

INDIVIDUAL LAMENTS

A second kind of psalm in the Psalter is an *individual's lament to God*. Read Psalm 51 aloud. Then answer these questions.

a. What is the psalmist confessing in verses 1-4?

b. What is the psalmist asking God to do? (verse 7)

c. What is the acceptable sacrifice before God? (verse 17)

INDIVIDUAL PSALMS OF THANKSGIVING

The third kind of psalm, *the individual psalm of thanksgiving*, corresponds to the individual lament. In the individual psalm of thanksgiving the psalmist offers thanks to God for something God has done. Read Psalm 32 aloud. Then answer the questions below.

a. According to the psalmist, who is the blessed one? (verses 1-2)

b. Why had the psalmist suffered? (verses 3-4)

c. How could the psalmist find happiness and joy? (verse 5)

PRAISE OF ZION PSALMS

A fourth kind of psalm we find in the Psalter is the *praise of Zion* psalm. This type of psalm glorifies the holy city of Zion, or Jerusalem. Read Psalm 2 aloud. Then answer the following questions.

a. Who set themselves against the Lord and God's anointed? (verses 1-3)

b. Where does God sit? (verse 4)

c. Where did God set the king? (verse 6)

COMMUNAL PSALMS OF THANKSGIVING

A fifth kind of psalm found in the Psalter is the *communal psalm of thanksgiving*. In this psalm the congregation offers thanks to God for something God has done. Read Psalm 67 aloud. To whom is this psalm addressed? (verses 3-7)

COMMUNAL LAMENTS

Just as a community addresses thanksgiving to God, it may also lament to God about its collective troubles. Read aloud Psalm 137, *a communal lament*. Then answer these questions.

a. Where did the people sit down and weep?

b. What is the reason for the people's lament?

SUMMARY

Six kinds of psalms are found in the Psalter, with these listed as examples.

(1) Hymns of praise (Psalm 19)
(2) Individual laments (Psalm 51)
(3) Individual psalms of thanksgiving (Psalm 32)
(4) Zion psalms (Psalm 2)
(5) Communal psalms of thanksgiving (Psalm 67)
(6) Communal laments (Psalm 137)

The beauty of this poetry is best appreciated when the psalms are read aloud.

QUESTIONS FOR DISCUSSION

1. Take a few minutes to think about the times in your life when you have experienced joy, sorrow, anxiety, anger, grief, or any other deep emotion. Which psalms did you find meaningful at these times?

2. The Book of Psalms is a collection of quite varied poems. This was the hymnbook of Judaism and the early church, so the poems were sung. Discuss the value of singing as a worship experience rather than just reading.

DAILY READINGS FOR PROVERBS, ECCLESIASTES, AND SONG OF SOLOMON

Day 1:   Proverbs 8:22-31
Day 2:   Proverbs 10:1-12
Day 3:   Proverbs 31:10-31
Day 4:   Ecclesiastes 1:1-11
Day 5:   Ecclesiastes 3:1-9
Day 6:   Ecclesiastes 12:1-14
Day 7:   Song of Solomon 8:1-7

PROVERBS
ECCLESIASTES
SONG OF SOLOMON

Palestinian farmer in field of ripe grain

This lesson deals with three books: Proverbs, Ecclesiastes, and Song of Solomon. These three books fall together primarily for two reasons. First, tradition ascribes all three books to Solomon; and second, all three books relate to ancient Israelite wisdom.

The Old Testament presents Solomon as the wisest of men in ancient times. Read 1 Kings 4:32-34, which indicates something of Solomon's wide learning and wisdom.

This passage presents Solomon as not only the composer of proverbs and songs but also the writer of encyclopedic works about plants, beasts, birds, reptiles, and fish.

Each of these books begins with a state-ment that attributes it to Solomon. Proverbs begins "The proverbs of Solomon, son of David, king of Israel." Ecclesiastes opens with "The words of the Teacher, the son of David, king in Jerusalem." The third book begins "The Song of Songs, which is Solomon's."

Scholars today do not assume that Solomon wrote any of these books. The language and ideas in the books suggest a time much later in Israel's history than the reign of Solomon. The Book of Proverbs itself attributes much of the material con-tained within it to persons other than Solomon. Perhaps Solomon's reputation as the wisest of men and the patron saint of

© 1981 Biblical Archaeology Society

wisdom in Israel led later editors and writers to credit material to him. Two books—The Wisdom of Solomon and The Psalms of Solomon—are ascribed to him but are in the Apocrypha, not in the Protestant Bible. Let us now look at the three books in this lesson.

PROVERBS

The Book of Proverbs takes its name from its content. The book contains proverbs or wise sayings that offer advice and make suggestions about the art of living. The Hebrew word that translates as *proverb* has a wider range of meaning than our term *proverb*. In Hebrew, a proverb, or *mashal*, designates material ranging from short pithy sayings to long discourses or complex allegories.

The Book of Proverbs is actually made up of seven smaller collections. Each collection has its own introduction. Most of these collections relate to Solomon in some way, although they also refer to such unknown writers as Agur and Lemuel.

Some of the wisdom found in the Book of Proverbs is more like what we call philosophy. We find examples of this type of wisdom in Proverbs 1 to 9. Perhaps the Israelites used these chapters in school where students were considered to be the son of the teacher, who was called "the father."

These longer poems personify wisdom and folly as two women who invite the student to embrace them and live with them.

Read the introduction to the Book of Proverbs in 1:2-7. Then answer the following questions.

a. What was the purpose for which the book was written? Write the purpose in your own words.

b. According to verse 7, how can we begin to acquire knowledge? What must we do first?

Most of the Book of Proverbs is made up of two-line sayings or proverbs. The collection that begins with Proverbs 10:1 and extends to Proverbs 22:16 contains 375 individual proverbs. Many of these proverbs are similar in intent to our sayings such as "Haste makes waste," or "A stitch in time saves nine." They attempt to sum up an insight into life in a catchy and easily memorized fashion.

The proverbs take various forms. Some are merely descriptions of persons and actions. Read Proverbs 10:26 as one example.

Sometimes the proverb states the truth in such a way that the truth appears to be the opposite of what it is. An example is Proverbs 13:24. Turn to this proverb and read it.

And turning to Proverbs 17:1, we find that one particular type of life is preferable to another kind. Read Proverbs 17:1.

These simple proverbs were probably a part of the folk culture of ancient Israel. They were used wherever people were learning how to live life in the best way. Above all, parents and grandparents used these proverbs in teaching their children what was expected of them in life and what were the best ways to confront life with all its problems and difficulties.

We can sum up the philosophy of life found in the Book of Proverbs in several statements. First of all, the book and its practical wisdom assume that a person can discover a general order to life and existence through wisdom and thought. Second, once one discovers the order of existence, then a person can live in harmony with that order in the realm of creation. Third, one tends to get out of life what one puts into it. As we would say, you reap what you sow. Fourth, one ought to live a life based on self-interest that serves and loves others, because in the long run, such love and service benefit everyone concerned.

1. Proverbs emphasizes the power of words and speech, for good and for ill. Read the following passages, and write down what you learned from them about words and speeches.

a. (10:19)

b. (12:18)

c. (15:1)

d. (16:28)

e. (18:13)

f. (20:19)

g. (27:2)

2. Proverbs also emphasizes family relationships. Read the following passages, and write down what you learned from them.

a. (13:24)

b. (15:20)

c. (20:20)

d. (29:15)

ECCLESIASTES 1:1–3:15

When we turn to the Book of Ecclesiastes, we encounter a book almost totally opposite from the Book of Proverbs. Some translations of the Bible also call this book "The Teacher," which is a translation of the Greek term *Ecclesiastes*. The writer of this book teaches a philosophy of life that he sums up in his motto: "Vanity of vanities! All is vanity." Or, as we may loosely translate it: "Nonsense, Nonsense! Everything is nonsense."

If we look at the early chapters of Ecclesiastes, we can see some of the emphases of the writer. The first ten verses promote the idea that there is nothing new under the sun—life is simply the same old thing over and over again.

In Ecclesiastes 1:12-18 the writer argues that wisdom does not give a person the key to life, since knowledge raises more questions. In Ecclesiastes 2:1-11 the writer argues that life's happiness is not found in the search for pleasure. The rest of Chapter 2 expounds the idea that death robs persons

Types of weights used in everyday life in Bible times

of both wisdom and the fruit of toil. In Ecclesiastes 3:1-15 the writer tells us that although a predetermined pattern for life exists, we can neither understand nor change it.

According to the writer of Ecclesiastes, what things are really empty in our lives? List the examples of empty things found in the following verses.

a. (1:16-18)

b. (2:1)

c. (2:18-20)

d. (5:10)

ECCLESIASTES 3:16–12:14

The rest of Chapter 3 and all of Chapter 4 demonstrate that life has no justice and that persons cannot count on a life after death where matters will make sense. The remaining eight chapters of the book develop in various ways the central ideas found in the first four chapters.

In many ways Ecclesiastes seems to dispute and disprove the philosophy of life found in the Book of Proverbs. Proverbs is very optimistic about life and very positive about human potential to do the best in life. Ecclesiastes is the skeptical opposite.

Yet while Ecclesiastes appears to be very negative, it is not totally so. Ecclesiastes recommends that a person enjoy life as much as possible and engage in some work that is enjoyable. Above all do not expect too much of life nor live wickedly and foolishly. Read Ecclesiastes 3:12-13. These verses give us the basic philosophy of the book.

SONG OF SOLOMON

The third book in this lesson is Song of Solomon. This book is a collection of love poems describing courtship, love, and human intimacy. The poems depict the male and female lovers in very sensuous and erotic imagery. The popularity of these songs through their association with Solomon and their use in wedding festivities established them firmly in the lives of the Israelites. Christian tradition has interpreted Song of Solomon as an allegory of the covenant love between God and God's people. These songs became part of sacred Scripture because their writer was said to be King Solomon.

Read Song of Solomon 8:6-7, in which the writer discusses the nature of love. List three evidences of the power of love that are found in these verses.

a. (8:6)

b. (8:7)

c: (8:7)

SUMMARY

Four kinds of Wisdom Literature are found in the books of Proverbs, Ecclesiastes, and Song of Solomon.

1. Long poems that praise the pursuit of wisdom (Proverbs 1–9)
2. Short poems that give insight into life (Proverbs 10–26)
3. A treatise on the theme "All is vanity" (Ecclesiastes 1–12)
4. A collection of love poetry (Song of Solomon 1–8)

QUESTIONS FOR DISCUSSION

1. The Book of Proverbs gives advice for daily living. These proverbs were probably produced in the everyday life of the people of ancient Israel. Read aloud at random from Chapters 10–26 in Proverbs. What issues did you encounter in Proverbs that are relevant for your life today? Share with the group any nonbiblical proverbs that you know or use as a guide to right action or thought.

2. According to a Jewish tradition, Solomon wrote Song of Solomon when he was young, Proverbs when he was middle-aged, and Ecclesiastes when he was old. What characteristics of these books may have contributed to the development of that tradition?

3. Song of Solomon was included in the Old Testament canon because tradition assumed that it was written by Solomon. But critical scholarship has discounted the possibility that Solomon wrote this love poetry. Protestant tradition has tended to de-emphasize this book because of its largely secular quality. This sensual poetry about the love between a man and a woman is not expressly religious. What other reasons can you think of for its inclusion in the Old Testament?

DAILY READINGS FOR ISAIAH

Day 1: Isaiah 5:1-7
Day 2: Isaiah 6:1-13
Day 3: Isaiah 7:1-17
Day 4: Isaiah 40:1-11
Day 5: Isaiah 45:1-13
Day 6: Isaiah 52:13–53:12
Day 7: Isaiah 61:1-11

Review 3 Sheet

1. What three Old Testament books are Wisdom Literature?

2. How do Chapters 1, 2, and 42 of Job differ from the rest of the book?

3. What is the main question raised in the Book of Job?

4. What does Job confess at the end of the book?

5. Name six kinds of psalms that are found in the Hebrew Psalter.

6. What two kinds of Wisdom Literature are found in the Book of Proverbs?

7. What is the general philosophy of the writer of Ecclesiastes?

8. What kind of literature is contained in Song of Solomon?

(Answers are on page 182.)

THE PROPHETIC LITERATURE

INTRODUCTION

Our Old Testament contains a number of books that we classify as prophetic literature. Isaiah, Jeremiah, and Ezekiel are called the *Major Prophets* because the books that bear their names are longer than the books of Daniel, Hosea, Joel, Amos, Obadiah, Jonah, Micah, Nahum, Habakkuk, Zephaniah, Haggai, Zechariah, and Malachi (called the *Minor Prophets*, primarily because their length is shorter than the Major Prophets).

Daniel is not included among the prophets in the second section of the Hebrew Bible. That book is placed in the third section of the canon, the Holy Writings (*Hagiographa*). Daniel is considered a sage in Jewish tradition, which helps to explain the book's place in the third section, composed primarily of books of wisdom.

PROPHETS IN ISRAEL

In the Bible, non-Israelite prophets are acknowledged (Numbers 22:2), but the prophetic tradition in Israel was extraordinary in the numbers and fervor of the prophets. Before the establishment of the monarchy, tradition recalls Abraham, Aaron, Miriam, Deborah, and Moses as prophets. Six important figures appeared from the eleventh to the ninth centuries: Samuel, Nathan, Ahijah, Elijah, Micaiah, and Elisha. To all of them the term *prophet* was applied. These are the "non-literary" prophets. They were endowed with prophetic and sometimes miraculous powers. Sometimes groups of persons were associated with a major prophet, such as Elisha.

The great age of prophecy was during the Divided Kingdom period and into the Exile. About 750 B.C., the earliest "literary prophet," Amos, appeared. In the book that bears his name we have a collection of his oracles, visions, and some biographical information. Similar materials are found in the other writing prophets. We often speak of the *preexilic prophets*—Amos, Hosea, Isaiah, Micah, Zephaniah, Nahum, and Jeremiah, and perhaps Habakkuk and Obadiah. The dating of some of the prophets is uncertain. Jonah is more a story about a prophet than a collection of prophetic oracles. The story is set in the preexilic period.

The Old Testament prophets warned Israel and Judah of a national disaster that would come upon them from the Lord because of religious corruption and social injustice. They spoke out against kings, priests, and people as spokespersons for the Lord. The key phrase that introduces their oracles again and again is, "Thus says the LORD."

Before Israel, the Northern Kingdom, was destroyed by the Assyrians in 722 B.C., Amos and Hosea had prophesied there. The remainder of the literary prophets spoke to the kingdom of Judah. The oracles of the preexilic prophets were carried to Babylon by devout disciples. There they played an important role in the religious reforms of the people before the return.

All of Ezekiel and the last half of Isaiah encouraged the Jews in exile. Obadiah and possibly Daniel are also set in this period. They gave hope of restoration. After the return to Jerusalem and until the time of Ezra (about 430 B.C.), Zechariah, Haggai, Joel, and Malachi prophesied. They are called the *postexilic prophets*. According to Jewish tradition, the prophetic spirit left Israel in the time of Ezra.

THE PROPHETIC MESSAGE

Prophets were spokespersons for God. They were "forthtellers" more than "fore-tellers." Their predictions usually concern the *day of the Lord,* an approaching day of destruction, due to the sin and rebellion of the people. But later generations could often see how the words of the prophets spoke to their times and to the future. This characteristic of prophecy is in line with the recognition that the word of God is living and active.

The influence of the prophets grew after the destruction of Jerusalem when the doom they had foretold came about. The prophets inspired the religious concept of ethical monotheism. This is the concept of God as the only ruler of the universe.

The biblical prophets emphasized the relationship between God and Israel through the covenant. They were well ahead of their time in social, moral, and humanitarian issues. They taught that religious ritual without a genuine concern for the welfare of the weaker members of society was unacceptable before God. This idea prepared for the survival of the Jewish religion when the Temple was destroyed.

While they described the suffering that would come as the result of transgression, the prophets also planted the idea that a remnant would return. This idea gave rise to the messianic hopes of postexilic times. Even in the postexilic era, the prophets continued to look forward to a bright future for God's people. Thus Malachi, the last of the Old Testament prophets, closes with the promise: "Lo, I will send you the prophet Elijah before the great and terrible day of the LORD comes" (4:5). John the Baptist was the fulfillment of that prophecy (Matthew 11:11-15).

ISAIAH

Isaiah, wall painting in Dura-Europos synagogue, Syria

With the Book of Isaiah we come to the first of the prophetic books in the Old Testament. Isaiah, however, is not the earliest prophet.

The Old Testament speaks about prophets in the early days of Israelite history. Prophets assisted in the early wars of the Hebrews as they struggled to take the land from the Canaanites. The Bible describes Samuel as a prophet who associated with a band of prophets, as Elijah and Elisha did in later times. Several prophets were associated with the royal court during the time of David. Frequently the historical books mention prophets. Here the prophets appear as both supporters and critics of the king and state policies. In 2 Samuel 7:4-9 we see the prophet Nathan at work as an advis-er to King David. Read 2 Samuel 7:4-9.

The historical literature in the Old Testament gives us important information about prophets and prophecy. Prophets were an important element in Israelite culture from the earliest days. They sometimes functioned as lone individuals and sometimes in groups. They could be either male or female. These prophets were often closely associated with the royal court and with military undertakings, although some prophets opposed the military activities of the kings. None of the early prophets left us any books of their sermons and preaching. Amos is the first prophet from whom we have a book. Amos, however, dates from about 750 B.C., two centuries after the time of David.

If prophets were a basic element in Israelite life, what can we say about their functions and characteristics? The prophets whose books were preserved saw themselves as divinely appointed spokespersons of their times. For this reason, many of the prophets give us accounts of how they received their calls and commissions.

The prophets were also critics of the religion and culture of their day. All aspects of the life of their times were viewed in the light of God's judgment upon human ambitions and achievements. The prophets tried to awaken persons to the reality of sin and evil in their midst, especially when the people were unaware of the presence of such evil in their lives. And the prophets proclaimed what lay ahead in the future if the lives of the people continued on the same course. The prophets therefore "foretold" the future. They could speak of this future as a time of judgment or as a time of salvation. The prophets functioned as social critics and as foretellers and proclaimers of the future.

In light of this brief discussion of the history and nature of prophecy, let us return to the Book of Isaiah. Read Isaiah 1:1-3.

Isaiah 1:1-3 gives us some pertinent information about this prophet. Read these verses, and answer the following questions about the person and work of Isaiah.

a. Who was Isaiah's father?

b. What were the subjects of Isaiah's visions?

c. During which kings' reigns did Isaiah prophesy?

d. For whom did Isaiah speak his prophecy?

ISAIAH 1:4–6:13

Keep in mind that the Book of Isaiah is perhaps the most complex and involved of all the prophetic books. Today, most scholars agree that the present Book of Isaiah contains materials from several prophets and editors who lived during a period of over two hundred years. Thus we can actually speak of three Isaiahs—First, Second, and Third. However, we know nothing historical about any of these Isaiahs except for the first. Chapters 1 through 39 make up the Book of First Isaiah, Chapters 40 through 55 are Second Isaiah, and Chapters 56 through 66 are Third Isaiah.

This division of the book into three smaller collections represents the attempt of scholars to explain some of the problems and issues that arise from the material itself. These problems are historical, literary, and theological. Let us look at the historical arguments for dividing the book.

The historical backgrounds for the three collections appear to be quite different. In Chapters 1 to 39 Assyria is the major world power. Jerusalem and Judah are hard-pressed to defend themselves, their city, and the Temple against the invading enemy. Isaiah warns the people about their possible capture by the Assyrians. In Chapters 40 to 55 Babylonia is the world ruler, but Cyrus and the Persians are about to take over. The Jews are in exile and the Temple and city of Jerusalem are in ruins. In Chapters 56 to 66 the Exile is over, the Jewish community is restored, and the people are trying to settle down to a new life in the land of promise. Thus the Book of Isaiah spans several centuries.

Chapters 1 through 12 in Isaiah contain oracles and speeches about Judah and Jerusalem. Much of Isaiah's prophecy condemns Judean and Jerusalemite society for

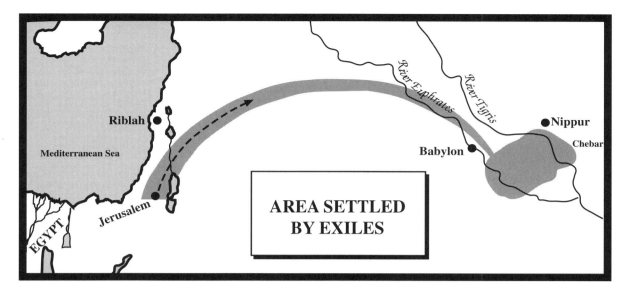

AREA SETTLED
BY EXILES

its lack of righteousness and social justice. In Isaiah 1:21-23 the prophet assesses the city's evil. Read these verses.

The prophet also argues that what God demands more than worship is genuine ethical obedience. In verses 10 through 15 God, speaking through the prophet, condemns all forms of worship, including prayer. Verses 16 and 17 stress what God does require. Read Isaiah 1:10-17.

In Isaiah 1 through 12 we also find some information about the prophet himself. For example, Isaiah 6 tells us about the prophet's vision in the Temple. This vision results in his call and commissioning as a prophet. According to Isaiah 6:9-13 the Lord gives Isaiah a message of judgment to proclaim to a people that is already condemned. Read Isaiah 6:9-13. As best as we can tell, Isaiah received this message about 740 B.C.

The call of Isaiah in Chapter 6 is a well-known passage in the Old Testament. Read Isaiah 6:1-8, and answer the following questions about the prophet's call.

a. What did Isaiah see?

b. Why did Isaiah feel lost?

c. How was Isaiah cleansed?

d. How did God challenge Isaiah to become a prophet?

ISAIAH 7–12

Also in these first twelve chapters of Isaiah we see the prophet's emphasis on the need for a trusting faith in God. By such faith Isaiah means that the people and their rulers will rest confidently in the promises of God and not try to impose human solutions on the problems of the day. He warns King Ahaz in Isaiah 7:9 that if Ahaz does not believe, he will not be established.

When the nations of the ancient world—including Judah—are trying to throw off the yoke of their Assyrian conquerors, Isaiah advocates a policy of peace. In all the furious activity to gain the nation's freedom, Isaiah speaks out for a policy of faith and trust, rather than for military solutions. Read Isaiah 8:11-15.

The prophet Isaiah looks forward to the time when all the promises of God to Jerusalem will be realized. Chapter 2 envisions the time when Jerusalem, or Zion as he calls it, is a world center where true religion and law are taught. As a result, war-weary people "beat their swords into plowshares, and their spears into pruning hooks." Chapter 11 relates the rule of the ideal member of the house of David, a rule that results in the ideal kingdom, where even the world of nature lives in tranquility and peace.

In the Book of Isaiah, there are several prophecies on the coming of a messiah. Read Isaiah 7:14 and 9:6-7, and answer the following questions.

a. What was the sign of the Lord? (7:14)

b. What was the child to be named? (7:14)

c. How was the Messiah to come? (9:6)

d. What was to be his name? (9:6)

e. How long was he to reign on the throne of David? (9:7)

ISAIAH 13–66

Chapters 13 to 23 are speeches against such foreign nations as Babylonia, Moab, Ethiopia, and Egypt. Chapters 24 to 27 consider the end times and the acts of God in judgment and salvation. We sometimes call these chapters the Isaiah Apocalypse. Chapters 28 to 33 are words the prophet speaks with regard to the Assyrian invasions of Judah. Chapters 34 and 35 tell of the end of the nations that oppose Judah, and these chapters discuss Jerusalem's final salvation. Chapters 36 to 39 tell about the seige of Jerusalem by the Assyrians during the reign of King Hezekiah.

We find the next main section of Isaiah in Chapters 40 through 55. We usually call this part of the book Second, or Deutero-Isaiah. Two main themes characterize Chapters 40 to 55. First of all, Second Isaiah proclaims that the end of the Exile is near. A new day is dawning for the oppressed Jews who are living dispersed among the nations. Second, these chapters depict God as personally leading the people home in a triumphant march, while transforming the world of nature. In Isaiah 43:18-19 God speaks of the future. Read these verses.

Chapters 56 to 66, or Third Isaiah, look at not only great theological issues, but also such matters as keeping and observing the sabbath, the place of converts in Judaism, and the proper sacrifices and their nature. These chapters look forward to the people's obedience to God and to God's transformation of the world. Read the words about the future in Isaiah 65:17-18.

Read Isaiah 55:6-11 and answer the questions below.

a. What does the writer of the book exhort persons to do?

b. Why should persons obey the exhortation?

c. How do the thoughts and ways of God compare to our ways and thoughts?

d. Describe in your own words the character of God's word as it is pictured in verse 11.

SUMMARY

Remember the following three points that constitute the message of Isaiah.

(1) Judgment on Judah for her disobedience to God, in First Isaiah (Isaiah 1–39)
(2) God's deliverance of his people from exile in Babylon, in Second Isaiah (Isaiah 40–55)
(3) God's future transformation of the world into a place for rejoicing, in Third Isaiah (Isaiah 56–66)

QUESTIONS FOR DISCUSSION

1. Scholars hold the opinion that our present book is actually made up of the work of three prophets. Many persons still hold the traditional view that one Isaiah, Isaiah of Jerusalem, wrote the complete book. If there were three distinct writers, how might these works have been brought together? Why would the memory of this joining be lost? If the scholarly opinion about the book is correct, how does it affect our understanding of the book as the Word of God?

2. The call of Isaiah was a powerful spiritual experience. Not every prophet left a record of his call, but the prophetic calls we know about are different from one another. You might want to compare the call of Moses (Exodus 3–4) with the call of Isaiah. Paul's call (conversion) on the road to Damascus is a New Testament example (see Acts 9). Discuss the call of God in Christ in the New Testament and in our time. Discuss the range of spiritual experience that different people undergo when they sense God calling them. How have you felt God calling you?

3. The Book of Isaiah is the source of many statements about the Messiah. Jews before Jesus' time referred to the book as they thought about his coming. Was Jesus the Messiah? Read Isaiah 61:1-2, then turn to Luke 4:16-21. Read it and discuss how Jesus answered the question of whether he was the Messiah.

4. Read the Servant Song in Isaiah 52:13–53:12. What does the prophet say about this servant that reminds you of Jesus Christ?

DAILY READINGS FOR JEREMIAH AND LAMENTATIONS

Day 1:	Jeremiah 1:1-12
Day 2:	Jeremiah 7:1-15
Day 3:	Jeremiah 20:7-18
Day 4:	Jeremiah 31:23-37
Day 5:	Jeremiah 32:6-25
Day 6:	Jeremiah 52:12-27
Day 7:	Lamentations 5:1-22

JEREMIAH
LAMENTATIONS

Assyrian soldiers with battering ram attacking Lachish (2 Kings 18:13-14)

© 1993 Biblical Archaeology Society

The career of the prophet Jeremiah spanned the most turbulent years in the history of Jerusalem and Judah. Called to be a prophet in 626 B.C., his last activity of which we have knowledge occurred in the late 580's. For almost forty years he carried the burdens of Judah's life. But he could not turn the tide that eventually led to the destruction of the state, the holy city of Jerusalem, the sacred Temple, and the chosen dynasty of the Davidic family.

In order to understand the career of this prophet as well as the book that bears his name, let's sketch briefly the main historical events of Jeremiah's day.

The time of Jeremiah's call coincided with the beginning of the demise of the hated Assyrian Empire. For over one hundred years the Assyrians had ruled most of the Near East, including Judah. They had governed with an iron hand and a heart of stone. War scenes dominated Assyrian art—towns being captured, exiles being led away, prisoners being impaled on sharp stakes. The Assyrians kept meticulous count of the number of cities they destroyed and the persons they killed. Their art shows scribes tabulating decapitated heads or piles of right hands. Thus, when Assyria began to lose her grip on subject states, moves toward freedom erupted everywhere.

In Jeremiah's time King Josiah asserted Judah's independence. He carried out radical religious and political reforms and moved to re-establish some of the glory and territory of the old state of David and Solomon. From about 625 to 610 B.C. Josiah was successful. Egypt and Babylonia engaged in a power struggle to fill the vacuum left by Assyria's demise. The Egyptians killed Josiah in 609 B.C. at the battle of Megiddo.

With Josiah's death the light of Judean independence flickered and went out. In turn Judah was subject first to Egypt and then to Babylonia. As a Babylonian subject, Judah again longed for independence. Relying on Egyptian promises of aid, Judah and other states rebelled.

The Babylonian king Nebuchadnezzar captured Jerusalem twice. The first time was March 15, 597 B.C.—an exact date we know from Babylonian records. At that time the Babylonians spared Jerusalem, and they deported only the royal family and the upper classes. The second revolt and capture of Jerusalem in 586 B.C. turned Judah into a bloodbath and the city into a bonfire. Again leading citizens were exiled.

After the destruction of Jerusalem, a band of rebels murdered Gedaliah, the governor appointed by Nebuchadnezzar. Despite Jeremiah's counsel to remain in the land, the rebels fled to Egypt, taking Jeremiah and his secretary with them.

With this background we now turn to the Book of Jeremiah. We can divide the book into four major sections. Chapters 1 to 25 are primarily prophecies and proclamations against Israel, Judah, and Jerusalem. Chapters 26 to 45 are biographical narratives about Jeremiah, which contain several prophecies. Chapters 46 to 51 are Jeremiah's speeches denouncing foreign nations. The final chapter, Chapter 52, is a historical narrative about the fall of Jerusalem and the deportation of Judean citizens.

We find most of Jeremiah's prophetic preaching in Chapters 1 to 25. Chapters 1 to 6 appear to contain preaching from the time of King Josiah.

Jeremiah 1:4-10 records the call of Jeremiah. It is a conversation between the prophet and the Lord. Read these verses for the answers to the following questions.

a. Four words in verse 5 record actions of God. List them below.

b. Why did Jeremiah object to God's call?

c. How did the Lord respond to Jeremiah's objection?

d. How will Jeremiah both destroy and build?

JEREMIAH 2–6

Chapter 1 gives the account of Jeremiah's call. Apparently he becomes a prophet at an early age. He complains that

Babylonian king (left) and vassal

he is only a youth despite God's assurance that he was destined to be a prophet before he was born. Jeremiah finally accepts his commission, realizing that his task is both to tear down and to build up. He knows his career will mean isolation and loneliness.

In Chapters 2 through 6 Jeremiah's preaching has two primary emphases. First, he condemns Judah for her worship of many gods and for her devotion to idolatrous religious practices. Jeremiah describes the people as an unfaithful bride who becomes an international prostitute, cavorting with Egypt and Assyria in infidelity and worshiping pagan gods on every high hill and under every green tree. Read Jeremiah 3:6-7.

Second, in these early prophecies Jeremiah proclaims that an enemy from the north is on the move to bring destruction to Judah and Jerusalem. Although he does not identify this foe from the north, he probably was speaking of the Chaldeans. Apparently Jeremiah made these prophecies early in the reign of Josiah—before the king's attempts to reform the nation's religion were under way.

1. Jeremiah 5:15-19 describes the foe from the north. Read the passage, and list below five characteristics of that nation.

a. (5:15)

b. (5:15)

c. (5:15)

d. (5:15)

e. (5:16)

2. What five threats against Jeremiah's people are mentioned in 5:17?

a.

b.

c.

d.

e.

JEREMIAH 7–20

After the death of Josiah at Megiddo, Josiah's son Jehoahaz II succeeds him. However, the Egyptians remove him from the throne and replace Jehoahaz with another of Josiah's sons whom they call Jehoiakim. Chapters 7 through 20 of the book are best seen against the time of King Jehoiakim who reigns from 609 to 597 B.C.

Jeremiah considers Jehoiakim to be totally incompetent, extravagant, and pompous. He is quite a contrast to his father, Josiah. Jehoiakim spends much of his reign building a palace in a Jerusalem suburb. Jeremiah chastises Jehoiakim for this indulgence. Read Jeremiah 22:13-14.

In addition to the condemnation of the king, Chapters 7 to 20 contain many emphases not found in Chapters 1 to 6. In Chapter 7 the prophet condemns the people for believing that God will not destroy the city of Jerusalem simply because the Temple is there. According to Chapter 26 the priests and prophets of the Temple charge Jeremiah with treason for this sermon. But those who judge the case release him because Micah, an earlier prophet, had preached similarly without being executed.

In Chapters 7 to 20 Jeremiah symbolically acts out the coming destruction of Jerusalem. The most noteworthy of these symbols is in Chapter 19. Jeremiah buys a pottery jar and smashes it in public. As he breaks the flask, Jeremiah proclaims these words: "Thus says the LORD of hosts: So will I break this people and this city, as one breaks a potter's vessel, so that it shall never be mended." For such preaching, Pashhur, the priest, beats Jeremiah and puts him in the stocks.

In Chapters 7 to 20 Jeremiah often complains to God. He laments over his life and calling. Many of his words remind us of Job's complaints. The following two passages give the tone of Jeremiah's complaints. Read Jeremiah 20:7. Here Jeremiah complains that God deceived him. Also read Jeremiah 20:14-15, where Jeremiah laments the day of his birth.

One of Jeremiah's symbolic acts is recorded in Jeremiah 13:1-11. Read the passage, and answer these questions.

a. What did the linen loincloth symbolize?

b. With what two evils did the Lord charge the people?

JERAMIAH 21–31

Much in Chapters 21 to 25 comes from the time of Zedekiah, the last king of Judah. During his reign, Jeremiah advises the king not to rebel against Babylonia; and after rebellion breaks out, Jeremiah counsels surrender to the foreigners as the will of God.

Chapters 26 to 45 describe numerous episodes in the life of the prophet Jeremiah. These chapters were partially written by Baruch who functioned as Jeremiah's secretary. Like the prophet Isaiah—who went around Jerusalem unclothed for three and one-half years—Jeremiah pickets and demonstrates to get his word across. According to Chapters 27 and 28 he wears an ox yoke to demonstrate that the Judeans will be placed under the Babylonian yoke.

In Chapter 29 Jeremiah writes letters to

those taken into exile. He advises them to settle down and not to expect a return home during their lifetime. On numerous occasions persons imprison Jeremiah or keep him under house arrest.

After Jerusalem fell the Babylonians gave Jeremiah special treatment. This action probably convinced many of his contemporaries that he was a traitor all along. Although the Babylonians gave him freedom to settle where he wished, Jeremiah chose to remain with those left in the land of Canaan.

The Book of Jeremiah is not totally pessimistic. Many passages speak about the good future to come, a new day after the coming judgment of God. The prophet's preaching shows that he not only expects a new day to dawn but he also believes the new day will see a new humanity that is faithful to God and the Law. The new age will be characterized by a new covenant and a new way of life. Read Jeremiah 31:33-34.

The letter of Jeremiah to the exiles is found in Chapter 29. Verses 10-14 contain a message of hope. Read Jeremiah 29:10-14 and answer these questions.

a. What did the Lord plan to do for the exiles?

b. After the return to Jerusalem, how will the people respond to the Lord?

c. How will the Lord respond when found by the people?

LAMENTATIONS

This hope of the new covenant seems to be set aside as we move into the Book of Lamentations. The Greek version of the Old Testament associates the Book of Lamentations with Jeremiah. The Hebrew Bible does not. This association probably resulted from the fact that 2 Chronicles 35:25 mentions the fact that Jeremiah uttered a lament for Josiah.

The five poems in the Book of Lamentations express the sense of loss and despair that characterized the people after the destruction of Jerusalem. They bemoan the fate of the city while recognizing that God destroyed it as an act of judgment in accordance with his word. Read Lamentations 1:1-2.

The first four poems in Lamentations are alphabetical. The first line or first verse begins with the first letter of the Hebrew alphabet, the second verse begins with the second letter, and so on through the twenty-two letters of the Hebrew alphabet. The Book of Lamentations was later used in worship services on the anniversary of Jerusalem's destruction.

Read Lamentations 3:19-26, and answer these questions.

a. In the midst of affliction, why does the poet have hope?

b. To what kind of person is the Lord good?

c. What should a person in distress do?

d. What is the subject of the Book of Lamentations?

SUMMARY

Like the prophet Isaiah, Jeremiah made a significant contribution to Israelite prophecy. The most important parts of this prophetic book are listed here.

(1) God's call of Jeremiah (Jeremiah 1)
(2) Jeremiah's prophecies about the foe from the north (Jeremiah 2–16)
(3) Jeremiah's predictions about the destruction of Jerusalem (Jeremiah 17–20)
(4) The prophet's hope for the new covenant (Jeremiah 31)

The Book of Lamentations is important for its portrayal of the people's grief over the loss of Jerusalem.

QUESTIONS FOR DISCUSSION

1. Jeremiah was strengthened in his life by the promise of God's sustaining power. Read Jeremiah 1:18-19. However, Jeremiah knew suffering. He was beaten and put in the stocks (20:2-3), imprisoned (37:15), and cast into a slimy cistern (38:6). Through forty years God saved Jeremiah from destruction even though he was under attack. God protected him not for the sake of Jeremiah but so that he could fulfill God's purpose in life, to preach God's word. What is the relationship between God's promise to Jeremiah and the suffering he experienced? What instruction for our Christian experience comes from Jeremiah?

2. Jerusalem had been besieged but not captured in over three hundred years. The Judeans considered Israel in error for breaking away from the rule of the Davidic dynasty. Perhaps they thought that the end of the kingdom of Israel a century earlier was because of God's anger with Israel, but that God protected Judah and Jerusalem at that time. So the Judeans had a superstitious belief that God would not allow Jerusalem to be destroyed because the Temple was there. The prophet refers to this belief in his great Temple sermon. Read Jeremiah 7:1-15. Why might the people have held this belief? Why was it in error? What are some examples of unfounded superstitions today? Share these examples with the group. How can we learn to let go of such superstitions?

3. On several occasions, Jeremiah uses symbolic actions—such as smashing a clay pot in public (Chapter 19) and wearing an ox yoke (Chapters 27–28)—to get his message across. In both political and religious life today, persons perform symbolic actions. What examples can you think of? What is the value of such symbolic actions?

4. Lamentations 1:7-12 gives a brief glimpse at the misery of a destroyed Jerusalem. To what do the images of nakedness and skirts refer? What is the grievous sin? Read Lamentations 3:19-33. What are the images of hope?

DAILY READINGS FOR EZEKIEL

Day 1:	Ezekiel 1:1-14
Day 2:	Ezekiel 2:1-10
Day 3:	Ezekiel 4:1-17
Day 4:	Ezekiel 19:1-14
Day 5:	Ezekiel 37:1-14
Day 6:	Ezekiel 40:1-16
Day 7:	Ezekiel 47:1-12

EZEKIEL

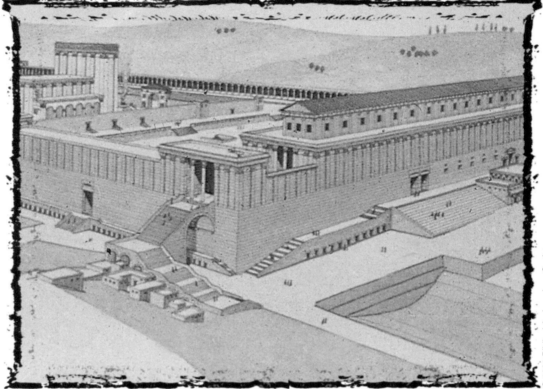

© 1991 Biblical Archaeology Society

Artist's drawing of Herod's Temple, Jerusalem

The prophet Ezekiel was a contemporary of the prophet Jeremiah. His ministry spanned the time period in which Jerusalem fell and the Temple was destroyed

Ezekiel was one of the persons taken into Babylonian exile in 597 B.C., when Nebuchadnezzar first captured Jerusalem. According to Ezekiel 3:15 and 8:1 Ezekiel had his own house in exile. He lived in the city of Tel-abib on the river Chebar.

According to Ezekiel 1:2 he receives a call to be a prophet in the fifth year of the Exile—probably 593 B.C. The last oracle in the book that has a specific date is in Chapter 29. Ezekiel 29:17 refers to the twenty-seventh year of exile, which was 571 B.C.

Ezekiel's career as a prophet lasted for at least two decades. It could have been longer since much of Ezekiel is not dated and could have come from a later period.

Before looking at the specific content of the Book of Ezekiel, two general comments about Ezekiel will help us better understand the book as a whole. First of all Ezekiel came from a priestly background. Thus, unlike most of the other prophets, Ezekiel was strongly interested in priestly matters, in worship, in dietary laws, in ceremonial forms, in matters of clean and unclean, and in meticulous fulfillment of the Law.

Second, Ezekiel's activity was far more unusual and imaginative than that of any other prophet. For example, Ezekiel lived in exile, hundreds of miles from Jerusalem, and carried out his ministry there.

Nonetheless, he did much of his preaching as if he were actually in Jerusalem addressing its citizens rather than speaking to the exiles. He claimed that the Spirit carried him from Babylon to Jerusalem.

The Book of Ezekiel falls into four distinct parts. Chapters 1 to 24 are prophecies of judgment and warning to Judah and Jerusalem about the coming destruction. These prophecies primarily date to the time before the fall of Jerusalem.

Chapters 25 to 32 are speeches against or condemnation of foreign nations, especially Egypt and the Phoenician city of Tyre, as well as other neighbors of Judah. These prophecies come from various times in Ezekiel's career.

Chapters 33 to 39 are prophecies about the judgment and future restoration of the people. These date from after the fall of Jerusalem.

Chapters 40 to 48 describe the ideal and restored land of Israel, the sacred city, and the holy Temple, which the prophet sees in a vision. Now let us examine the book more closely.

The first three chapters of the book describe the prophet's call and commission. Ezekiel sees a vision of God that comes with a stormy wind out of the north accompanied by a great cloud and lightning. From the wind and cloud come four creatures with composite features, partly human and partly animal, each possessing four wings and four faces. The faces are those of a human being, a lion, an ox, and an eagle. Accompanying the creatures are four wheels with rims and spokes—with eyes filling the rims. Wheels are inside the wheels, and as the creatures move, so do the wheels.

Over the creatures and wheels Ezekiel sees a platform with the likeness of a throne, on which one sits with the likeness of a human form. The one on the throne then commissions him. Ezekiel 2:3-7 describes Ezekiel's commission. Read verses 3 and 4.

The prophet then sees a hand holding a scroll that has writing on it, front and back.

God commands the prophet to eat the scroll. He does so, and it tastes as sweet as honey. The rest of Chapter 3 describes how the prophet sits overwhelmed for many days before he begins his activity.

The vision of Ezekiel is a revelation of the glory of the Lord. Read Ezekiel 1:26-28 for a description of that glory. Then answer these questions.

a. How did Ezekiel describe the throne of the Lord God?

b. Ezekiel described the appearance of the Lord. Write that description below.

c. To what did Ezekiel liken the brightness round about God?

EZEKIEL 4–11

Chapters 4 and 5 describe acts the prophet carries out to symbolize the coming fall of Jerusalem and the destruction of the chosen people. He draws a portrayal of Jerusalem on a brick and then attacks it with war toys. He lies on his side for many days, symbolizing the length of time the

Coin with facade of Jerusalem Temple on one side

people will be punished. He eats a sparse diet that symbolizes God's breaking of the staff of bread. Ezekiel cuts off the hair of his head and face and uses it to symbolize the people of Jerusalem, some of whom will die by the sword, others will burn, and the remainder will scatter to the winds.

Ezekiel tells his people that God's glory is leaving the people and the Temple. He describes the reasons for God's leaving in Chapters 7 through 11. Chapter 8 especially describes the pagan forms of worship that the prophet sees in his vision of the Jerusalem Temple.

1. The destruction of Jerusalem is depicted in Ezekiel 5. Read Ezekiel 5:7-12 for the answers to the following questions.

a. Why was God determined to execute judgment in the midst of Jerusalem? (5:7)

b. How extreme were conditions in Jerusalem to be when God executed judgment? (5:10)

c. What part of the people might survive the war, and what would become of them? (5:12

2. Now read Ezekiel 6:8-10. What is God's purpose in the destruction of Jerusalem and the scattering of the survivors?

EZEKIEL 12–32

In Chapter 12 Ezekiel carries out further symbolic acts. And in Chapter 13 he preaches against the prophets. Chapter 16 presents Ezekiel's vision of Jerusalem's history. God describes her as a harlot.

In Chapter 18 Ezekiel argues that each person is responsible for his or her own sins and that God judges each person according to her or his condition at the time of the judgment. The prophet here opposes the view of some of his contemporaries who argue that their troubles are due to the sins of their fathers. The people try to excuse themselves by quoting the proverb: "The parents have eaten sour grapes, and the children's teeth are set on edge." Ezekiel speaks of this principle of divine judgment in Ezekiel 18:20. Read this verse.

In Chapter 20 Ezekiel gives his version of the people's history. He pictures that history as one of continual sin and faithlessness that began even before the people left Egypt. The rest of Ezekiel's sermons of judgment in Chapters 20 to 25 are similar in content to those mentioned previously. Chapters 25 to 32 contain speeches against foreign nations.

Skim through Ezekiel 25–32, which contains oracles against foreign peoples. Which peoples does Ezekiel condemn in these prophecies?

a. (25:2)

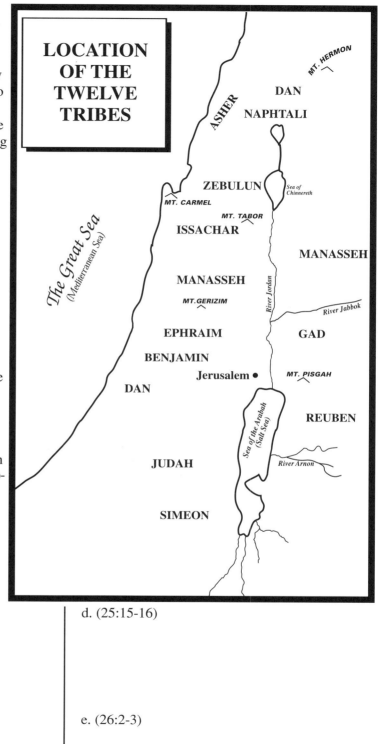

LOCATION OF THE TWELVE TRIBES

MT. HERMON

ASHER

DAN

NAPHTALI

MT. CARMEL

ZEBULUN

Sea of Chinnereth

MT. TABOR

ISSACHAR

MANASSEH

The Great Sea
(Mediterranean Sea)

MANASSEH

MT. GERIZIM

River Jordan

River Jabbok

EPHRAIM

GAD

BENJAMIN

Jerusalem ●

MT. PISGAH

DAN

Sea of the Arabah
(Salt Sea)

REUBEN

River Arnon

JUDAH

SIMEON

b. (25:8-9)

c. (25:12-13)

d. (25:15-16)

e. (26:2-3)

f. (28:20-21)

g. (29:2)

EZEKIEL 33–39

We find Ezekiel's hopeful prophecies of the good time beyond the judgment in Chapters 33 to 39. Chapter 37 is a typical proclamation of Ezekiel. In this chapter, he views the people in exile as a valley filled with unburied bones. He discusses with God whether the bones can live. God commands Ezekiel to prophesy to the dry bones. Read Ezekiel 37:7-10, where he describes the events that follow.

Ezekiel then envisions the restoration of both Israel and Judah under the rule of David.

Chapters 38 and 39 are rather unique. In them, Ezekiel talks about Gog from the land of Magog who attacks the chosen people, wages war against them, and finally loses. We do not know who Ezekiel is describing in these chapters, but persons throughout history have associated Gog with a particular enemy of their time.

Chapter 34 is an oracle about the shepherds (leaders) of Israel. They have failed in their responsibilities. A messianic promise follows. God will appoint a new shepherd. Read 34:23-31, and respond to these questions.

a. With whom is the messianic shepherd identified? (verse 23)

b. In the messianic days, how will the Lord relate to the sheep (people)? (verse 25)

c. God will meet two needs of the people in those days. What are those needs? (verse 29)

d. What will be the mutual relationship between the Lord God and the people of Israel at that time? (verses 30-31)

EZEKIEL 40–48

Chapters 40 to 48 contain a sketch of the restored community in the land of promise. Ezekiel first of all describes the structure of the restored Temple, giving measurements of its courts, gates, and chambers as well as descriptions of the Temple building and its decorations. In Ezekiel 43:2 the prophet says he sees the glory of God returning to the restored Temple. Chapters 43 through 46 describe the various activities in the Temple. Ezekiel even comments in 46:21-24 on the kitchens in the new Temple. He tells us that this is "where those who serve at the temple shall boil the sacrifices of the people."

In Chapter 47 Ezekiel describes a great stream—perhaps the river of life—which he sees flowing from beneath the Temple. The stream is full of fish, and its sweet waters flow into the Dead Sea, making it fresh. Along the stream grow trees that bear fresh fruit each month and whose leaves are for healing. Finally, he sees the land of Canaan divided into twelve equal districts—a district for each of the twelve tribes. This allotment of territory and the location of the tribes form the content of Chapter 48.

SUMMARY

Ezekiel paints a marvelous portrait of expectation about the renewed people, with a new Temple in a renewed land where life is idyllic, almost like that in the garden of Eden. When you think about the contents of Ezekiel's prophecy, remember the following elements.
(1) Ezekiel's predictions of the coming destruction of Jerusalem (Ezekiel 1–24)
(2) Ezekiel's condemnation of foreign nations (Ezekiel 25–32)
(3) Ezekiel's vision of the valley of dry bones (Ezekiel 37)
(4) Ezekiel's vision of a battle between Gog and Israel (Ezekiel 38–39)
(5) Ezekiel's vision of the restored community in Jerusalem (Ezekiel 40–48)

QUESTIONS FOR DISCUSSION

1. A key phrase in the Book of Ezekiel is *the glory of the Lord/God*. You will recall seeing it on page 93 of the workbook questions (Ezekiel 1:28). The glory of the Lord departed from the Temple in Jerusalem and came to Chaldea (Babylon), we are told in 11:22-24. Later, in his vision of a new city and Temple, Ezekiel sees the glory of the Lord return to Jerusalem and the Temple (43:1-5). Discuss what this movement of the glory of the Lord might have symbolized. If you had been in exile in Babylon and Ezekiel described these visions to you, do you think you would have been uplifted or depressed as a result? Where is the glory of God today?

2. Ezekiel was called to be a watchman for the house of Israel (3:16-21). God told him that, "if . . . you give them no warning, . . . their blood I will require at your hand." How does this warning apply to every Christian today? Compare the responsibility that God gave Ezekiel with the one now given to Christians. How are the two warnings similar? How are they different?

3. A prevalent idea in the Old Testament was that the penalty for the sins of one generation could fall on following generations. Deuteronomy 5:9 mentions God's "punishing children for the iniquity of parents, to the third and fourth generation." But in 18:1-32, Ezekiel calls the people to personal accountability. They cannot blame their misfortunes on their ancestors. What aspects of our modern life could cause future generations of Americans to condemn us?

4. Ezekiel's vision of the valley of dry bones teaches that God is the key to life, that the presence of God's spirit makes the difference between death and life. Where do you see examples of the Spirit bringing life today?

DAILY READINGS FOR DANIEL

Day 1: Daniel 1:1-7
Day 2: Daniel 2:31-45
Day 3: Daniel 5:13-28
Day 4: Daniel 7:1-14
Day 5: Daniel 7:15-28
Day 6: Daniel 9:1-10
Day 7: Daniel 12:1-13

DANIEL

Three-foot-high bull on Ishtar Gate, Babylon

© 1993 Biblical Archaeology Society

The subject of this lesson is the Book of Daniel. In Christian Bibles, Daniel follows the Book of Ezekiel and is therefore considered one of the books of the prophets. In the Hebrew Bible, Daniel follows the Book of Esther and precedes the Book of Ezra. That is, its place is among the Writings rather than among the Prophets.

The ancient Greek version of the Book of Daniel is much longer than the Hebrew version. It contains three episodes of 174 verses not found in the Hebrew text. These additions to the book are the Song of the Three Young Men, Susanna, and Bel and the Dragon. These additions are found in Catholic Bibles or in Protestant versions of the Apocrypha.

The origin, nature, and content of the Book of Daniel have been some of the most controversial issues in the history of biblical scholarship. Even in the early church, Christian scholars debated the question of the original content of the book, as well as whether the book was written in the sixth or second century B.C.

The introduction to Daniel in 1:1-2 suggests the historical background of the book. Read these verses, and answer the questions below.

a. Who came to Jerusalem and besieged the city?

Daniel 3:24-25

b. Who gave the king of Judah into his hand?

c. What is the location of Shinar?

DANIEL

Daniel belongs to a class of literature that we call *apocalyptic*. The other biblical example of this type of literature is the New Testament Book of Revelation. The word *apocalyptic* comes from a Greek word meaning *an unveiling* or *revelation.* In apocalyptic literature, a person receives revelation—through angels or other media-tors—of coming events in history or of heavenly conditions in the other world. The last six chapters of Daniel, Chapters 7 to 12, are especially apocalyptic. Because apocalyptic literature tends to speak in veiled images and in puzzling ways about rulers and events, it is difficult for a later audience to understand fully the original meanings.

We can divide the Book of Daniel into two equal halves. Chapters 1 to 6 contain stories about Daniel and his friends who live among the exiles. In these chapters Daniel and his companions are presented as very loyal Jews who remain faithful to their religious beliefs and practices in spite of all threats. The writer depicts Daniel as an interpreter of dreams and various other omens. In Chapters 7 to 12 Daniel is no longer the interpreter. Daniel himself has visions that he cannot interpret and ques-tions that he cannot answer. The angel explains these to him.

The Book of Daniel appears to have been written during the time of the Babylonian Exile. However, the book was probably composed during the second cen-tury B.C. Daniel was written to encourage the faithful during a time of religious per-secution. But some of the material—partic-ularly the stories in Chapters 1 to 6—could be much older than the second century.

Today most scholars place the Book of Daniel against the background of the perse-cution of Jewish religion during the reign of the Syrian king Antiochus IV. Antiochus, with his capital at Antioch, ruled over Palestine from 175 to 164 B.C. About 168

B.C. Antiochus issued his famous edict outlawing the worship of any God except Zeus. He erected an altar to Zeus in the Jerusalem Temple. Loyal Jews fled the country, went into hiding, or took up arms against Antiochus. The Book of Daniel was probably written to reveal to the community how long its suffering would last or how long before God would intervene to set matters right.

DANIEL 1:3–2:49

Let us now take a closer look at the contents of the book. In Chapter 1 we meet Daniel and his friends. They are taken into exile in the third year of King Jehoiakim of Judah—or 606 B.C. Daniel requests that they be allowed to eat only vegetables and drink water while they are in training for service at the royal court. The request is granted. After their period of training the youths are found to be superior in every way to the trainees who ate from the king's table. This story demonstrates that faithfulness to God and the dietary laws can bring reward and that God watches over the faithful.

In Chapter 2 the Babylonian king Nebuchadnezzar has a dream. He wants his advisers—the magicians, enchanters, sorcerers, and Chaldeans—to reveal not only the meaning of the dream but also the dream itself. After all the others fail to meet the king's demands, Daniel makes known the dream and its interpretation.

Read Daniel 2:27-28.

Daniel tells the king that he saw a great statue with a head of gold, breasts and arms of silver, belly and thighs of bronze, with its legs of iron and its feet partly of iron and partly of clay. In the vision a stone uncut by human hands smashes the statue. The stone then grows into a mountain and fills the whole earth.

Daniel tells Nebuchadnezzar that the parts of the statue represent various kingdoms. These kingdoms will rule from the time of Nebuchadnezzar until the time when God will destroy all earthly kingdoms and set up God's own kingdom that will never be destroyed. Nebuchadnezzar is the head of gold. Daniel does not identify the earthly kingdoms represented by the other metals. He only gives a general description of them. For revealing and interpreting the dream Nebuchadnezzar makes Daniel ruler of the province of Babylon and gives him other honors as well.

Daniel 2:36-45 gives Daniel's interpretation of Nebuchadnezzar's dream. Read these verses, and answer the following questions.

a. To whom does the head of gold refer? (2:38)

b. What will the fourth kingdom of iron do? (2:40)

Ron Martin

MENE MENE TEKEL PARSIN

Daniel 6

c. What will the stone—the kingdom that will never be destroyed—do? (2:44)

DANIEL 3

In Chapter 3, Daniel's companions—Shadrach, Meshach, and Abednego—refuse to bow down and worship an image set up by the king. For their refusal Nebuchadnezzar's men throw them into a fiery furnace. When Nebuchadnezzar calls them forth from the flames, they are unharmed. In light of this miraculous event, the king elevates them in the royal administration.

The experience of the three friends in the fiery furnace shows the willingness to die for one's belief. This willingness to be a martyr for the faith is illustrated by the men's words in verses 17 and 18. Read Daniel 3:17-18.

Read Daniel 3:19-30, and answer these questions.

a. Whom did the king throw into the fire? (3:23)

b. How many figures did the king see in the fire? (3:25)

c. According to the king, who was the fourth man in the fire? (3:25)

d. What did the king do to these three men after they came out of the fire? (3:30)

DANIEL 4–7

In Chapter 4 Nebuchadnezzar dreams again—this time of a great tree that grows to the heavens, but is cut down. The stump is left in the field. Daniel says the dream refers to the coming madness of the king. He will live in the fields with the beasts—as a beast—until he admits that the Most

High rules the world. The chapter then reports that this interpretation comes true.

Chapter 5 tells the story of King Belshazzar's feast, which is interrupted by the fingers of a hand, writing on the wall. Daniel interprets the inscription—MENE, MENE, TEKEL, PARSIN—to mean that God has numbered the days of the Babylonian Empire. He has weighed the empire and found it wanting. The kingdom will be given to the Medes and Persians. Chapter 5 records that the king was slain that very night, and Darius the Mede took over his kingdom. Read Daniel 5:26-28.

Chapter 6 reports a plot against Daniel. The king's assistants persuade him to issue an edict prohibiting prayer to any god except the king. Because Daniel remains loyal to the offering of prayer three times a day, the king orders him cast into a den of lions. When no harm befalls him the king again rewards Daniel. King Darius then decrees that all his subjects should tremble before the God of Daniel. Read this decree from Daniel 6:26-27.

Thus we see that all of the stories in Chapters 1 to 6 offer encouragement to those who would remain loyal to their faith even when threatened with oppression and persecution. In Chapters 7 to 12 Daniel dreams or has visions. He interprets these to mean the end of the persecution of the Jews and the establishment of God's kingdom on earth.

In Chapter 7 Daniel sees four beasts rise from the sea and plunder the earth. God deposes the four beasts—a lion, a bear, a leopard, and an indescribably horrible fourth beast. God then gives universal dominion to one "like a human being" (or "son of man," see footnote in the New Revised Standard Version)—that is, to a human-looking figure, probably an angel. For Daniel the dream refers to the kingdoms that will exist before God's intervention through one "like a son of man/human being."

In the latter part of Chapter 7 Daniel interprets his vision of the four beasts. Answer the following questions about Daniel's interpretation of this vision.

a. What is different about the fourth kingdom? (7:23)

b. What is the meaning of the ten horns? (7:24)

c. How much time will be given into the hand of the eleventh king? (7:25)

d. What will be given to the people of the holy ones of the Most High? (7:27)

DANIEL 8–12

In Chapter 8 Daniel again dreams of a battle, this time between a ram and a male goat. After the goat wins, a little horn grows from one of the four horns on his head. This horn grows large. It defiles the Temple and makes sacrifice cease. This dream refers to the Persian and Greek Empires. Many scholars believe that

Antiochus IV was the arrogant little horn.

In Chapter 9 the angel Gabriel interprets Jeremiah's statement that Jerusalem would be desolate for only seventy years. The seventy years are not just seventy years, but seventy weeks of years or 490 years. The remainder of the chapter describes what will happen during these seventy weeks of years. Read Daniel 9:24-27.

According to the writer's calculation, the last half week of the seventy weeks, which amounts to three and one-half years, will be the time when sacrifice ceases. Dating from 168 when Antiochus took over the Temple, the writer sees the end of the 490 years as falling in 164 B.C.—or in his own day.

Chapters 10 and 11 give a history of the Near East and Jerusalem from Persian times until the writer's own day. The exactness of this history suggests that most of it had already occurred before the writer predicted it. The end of Chapter 11 predicts that the persecutor of the Jews will die encamped between Jerusalem and the Mediterranean Sea. According to Chapter 12, resurrection follows the death of the persecutor. The just are rewarded, and the evil are punished. Read Daniel 12:1-4.

According to Daniel 12:2 to what shall the people awake after the resurrection?

SUMMARY

The Book of Daniel is both strange and familiar to most of us. Five familiar episodes found here are those listed below.

(1) Daniel and his friends enter the court of King Nebuchadnezzar (Daniel 1)
(2) Nebuchadnezzar has a dream, and Daniel interprets it (Daniel 2)

(3) God delivers Shadrach, Meshach, and Abednego from the fiery furnace (Daniel 3)
(4) The hand writes on the wall during the feast of Belshazzar (Daniel 5)
(5) God delivers Daniel from the lions' den (Daniel 6)

QUESTIONS FOR DISCUSSION

1. Apocalyptic literature, such as Daniel and Revelation, is based in part on visions. This kind of literature deals with the struggle in the world between the opposing forces of good and evil. What evidences do you see in our world today of the conflict between the forces of good and evil? How do writers and/or media productions represent this conflict? How is the conflict evident in your everyday life?

2. Apocalyptic writings are tracts for hard times. Daniel becomes an example for later generations of a wise servant of both God and his political sovereign. Which of Daniel's qualities are worthy of copying? How can these qualities sustain Christians in a time of turmoil and persecution?

3. Recall the stories of the three young men in the fiery furnace and of Daniel in the lions' den. These stories encouraged the original audience of this book—Jews undergoing persecution. In what ways do Christians suffer persecution today? How can we encourage those who suffer?

DAILY READINGS FOR HOSEA, JOEL, AND AMOS

Day 1:	Hosea 1:1-11
Day 2:	Hosea 3:1-5
Day 3:	Hosea 14:1-9
Day 4:	Joel 1:1-12
Day 5:	Amos 4:1-13
Day 6:	Amos 5:14-27
Day 7:	Amos 7:1-17

HOSEA
JOEL
AMOS

Servants bringing their tribute to the Assyrian king

With this lesson we come to the first three books in a prophetic collection that Christians call the Minor Prophets. In the Jewish canon the twelve books in this group make up what is called the Book of the Twelve. In ancient times literary works were written on scrolls. Often a work was not long enough to fill up an average scroll. Therefore, several short works were written on the same scroll. All twelve of the shorter prophetic books were written on one scroll. Thus the Hebrews call this collection the Book of the Twelve. We base our Christian designation—the Minor Prophets—on the fact that these prophets' surviving works are much shorter than the works of the Major Prophets Isaiah, Jeremiah, and Ezekiel.

We are not certain how the order for the twelve Minor Prophets was established. Today scholars assume that Amos was the first prophet from whom we have a book. However, in the Book of the Twelve Hosea comes first. From references within the book, we know his career spanned the final troubled days of the Northern Kingdom of Israel.

HOSEA

During Hosea's career Israel's life was characterized by anarchy and constant political moves. During these years—from about 745 to 720 B.C.—the Assyrians overran most of the Near East. The Assyrians used a policy of exile and deportation to weaken their conquered lands.

After the last strong northern king died in about 746 B.C., one ruler followed another on the Israelite throne. One ruled for six months and was assassinated. His successor ruled for one month and was assassinated. His successor ruled for seven years, but his son was assassinated after two years. So, the murder of one ruler after another characterized this period. We need to view Hosea's prophetic career against the canvas of this larger political background.

We can easily divide the Book of Hosea into two main parts. The first part is Chapters 1 to 3, which are biographical and autobiographical. The second part, Chapters 4 to 14, contains the preachings and prophecies of Hosea.

Let us examine the first three chapters. In Chapter 1 God commands the prophet to marry a prostitute and to have children of prostitution. Read Hosea 1:2.

Hosea marries Gomer. She conceives and bears a son whom Hosea names *Jezreel* after the place where the reigning Israelite dynasty had taken over in a bloody massacre. The child's name is a prediction that God will punish the reigning house for the blood of Jezreel. Gomer next bears a daughter. The prophet names her *Not pitied*, saying that God will not pity Israel any longer. A second son is born—whom Hosea names *Not my people* to symbolize that Israel is no longer God's people.

As in most prophetic books the introduction to Hosea in 1:1 gives us some information about the prophet and his time. Read Hosea 1:1-3, and answer these questions.

a. During the reigns of which kings did Hosea prophesy?

b. By what figure does the book describe the problem of the land at that time?

HOSEA 2–14

In Chapter 2 Hosea compares Gomer to Israel and uses his marriage to illustrate the relationship between Israel and her God. Hosea sees God as the husband and Israel as the prostituting wife. As God's wife Israel has gone after other gods and worshiped Baal.

In Chapter 2 we encounter a basic emphasis in the Book of Hosea, namely, his preaching against the people's acceptance and practice of the Baal religion of the Canaanites. Baal worshipers closely associated the powers of nature and the seasons of the year with the gods. The Canaanites worshiped many deities, of which Baal and his consort were the most important. The worshipers related the fertility of the field, the flock, and the family to these deities.

Baal died in the spring with the coming of the dry, hot summer. After his death vegetation dried up and died. In the fall, with the coming of the rainy season, Baal returned to life. Life returned to the world of vegetation. The people thus regarded Baal as the giver of life and fertility. In Hosea, God speaks out strongly against this belief that it is Baal who gives the increase. Read Hosea 2:8.

Since the gods were sexual beings, and their sexual relations were part of the cycle of nature, the worshipers of Baal imitated the god in sexual rituals in their worship. Cultic prostitution and sexual activities were part of their religion. Gomer probably continued as a sacred prostitute in a temple even after marrying Hosea.

The prophet's opposition to this sexual

aspect that entered Israelite life through the Baal cult is an important emphasis in the book. The prophet tries to show the people that it is their God Yahweh, not the Canaanite god Baal, who is the source of life and fertility. For Hosea use of sexual rituals in worship was unnecessary and actually degraded worship.

In Chapter 3 we return to narrative about the prophet. This time the information is autobiographical rather than biographical as in Chapter 1. Here the prophet reports that he purchases a woman for fifteen shekels of silver, a homer of barley, and a measure of wine. Many scholars have questioned whether this woman was Gomer and under what conditions the purchase was made. Although we cannot prove any view, most persons understand this chapter as Hosea's purchase of Gomer from the temple. Although she is his wife, she was previously temple property.

After securing all rights to Gomer, Hosea isolates her so that she does not even function as his companion in marriage. He does this, as he says in Hosea 3:4, to symbolize the time when Israel (God's wife) will have to live without king or prince or religious establishment and practices. Read Hosea 3:3-4. Here Hosea is pointing to the time of Israel's coming destruction.

Chapters 4 to 14 of the book are a collection of Hosea's prophecies of judgment. They are not organized chronologically or according to subject matter, but represent an anthology of his preaching. Because of the order in which these prophecies appear, the book ends on a happy note with a prediction of a good time coming.

The following are themes and ideas in these chapters. First, Hosea condemns the people because they have forsaken their knowledge of God. This fault results in their living without faithfulness and kindness. Hosea blames the religious leaders— that is, the priests and prophets—for this fault. Read Hosea 4:1-3.

Second, Hosea condemns the religious practices where men associate with harlots and cult prostitutes. Third, he condemns the political events, royal assassinations, and kingship in general. Fourth, he pronounces the coming judgment of God— when God will devastate the people and the land. Hosea describes this as a "return to Egypt," that is, to the time when the people of Israel did not exist.

The book ends on a very positive note, which speaks of the restoration of the people after the time of judgment. After the people confess that they no longer trust in worldly powers or military might, God responds with the promise that God will heal them and make their land productive. God will truly be Israel's husband and give her the fertility that Baal promised. Read Hosea 14:4-7.

Chapter 11 of Hosea describes the love of God for the rebellious nation. *Ephraim* is used here as a symbol for the whole kingdom. Read Hosea 11:1-9, and answer these questions.

a. When did God love Israel, and how was God's love shown? (11:1)

b. How is God's love described in verse 3?

c. How is the inner feeling of God toward the rebellious nation described in verse 8?

Joel 1:4

Charles Shaw

d. Why does God not execute fierce anger? (11:9)

JOEL

Next we turn to the Book of Joel. We cannot date this little book of three chapters with any certainty. Notice that the first verse of the book does not try to place the prophet in any historical context. Joel 1:1 simply says, "The word of the LORD that came to Joel, the son of Pethuel."

In the first chapter Joel presents a picture of the coming destruction, which takes the form of a locust plague. Joel mentions all types of locusts and describes all the destruction they do. In Chapter 2 Joel describes the judgment day of God or the day of the Lord. God calls upon the people to repent, to fast, to pray, and to return.

In Joel 2:19 the tone changes and God proclaims a blessing that sharply contrasts with the judgment of the locust plague. God tells the people that they will receive God's spirit. Read Joel 2:28-29.

The early church believed this passage was fulfilled on the Day of Pentecost.

In the final verses of Chapter 2 and in

the opening verses of Chapter 3, the prophet again proclaims the coming time of trouble. However, Chapter 3 ends with words about salvation after and beyond the judgment and turmoil.

Read Joel 2:28-32, and answer the following questions.

a. On what will God's spirit be poured out? (2:28)

b. What kind of signs will be given in the heavens and on the earth? (2:31)

c. How is the coming day of the Lord described? (2:31)

d. Who will be delivered on that day? (2:32)

AMOS 1–2

Finally, let us turn to the Book of Amos. This book opens—in Chapters 1 and 2—with speeches denouncing most of the neighboring states of Israel. These states include Damascus, Gaza, Tyre, Edom, Ammon, Moab, and Judah.

The Lord, through Amos, condemns these foreign nations for their war atrocities and slave trade. This condemnation assumes a widely recognized standard of international behavior, which these countries had broken and for which they were judged.

No doubt Amos's preaching against these foreign nations got him an audience. However, he moves from condemning for-

Amos's vision of a plumb line (7:7)

eign nations to condemning Israel in the remainder of the book (Amos 2:6–9:15). Here we can only summarize the main themes of his preaching of judgment. He condemns the people for their lack of social justice. They abuse the poor, misuse those standing for righteousness, sell second-rate products, pervert justice, and are falsely religious.

Amos preached at a time when Israel and Judah had reached the summit of their prosperity. The leaders of the people were devoted to pleasure. Read Amos 2:6-8, and summarize in short sentences the transgressions of Israel.

a. (2:6)

b. (2:7)

c. (2:7)

d. (2:8)

e. (2:8)

AMOS 3–9

Amos describes the upper classes as living in luxury—drinking wine from silver bowls, sleeping in ivory beds, and anointing themselves with fine oil. They eat from the fat of the land and with no concern for the poor. They have no desire to see justice done in the land.

For their sins the prophet pronounces the coming judgment when God will destroy the cities and scatter the people. Chapters 7, 8, and 9 relate Amos's visions of the coming judgment. Amos describes his intercession on behalf of the people, but God finally has had enough and says that judgment must come.

The Book of Amos—like Hosea and Joel—ends with the promise of a good future. God will restore the land and cities. The land will become so fertile and productive that one crop cannot be harvested before planting time for the next.

The closing chapters of Amos contain five visions of the prophet. Read the verses listed here, and describe in a brief phrase the content of each vision.

a. (7:1-2)

b. (7:4)

c. (7:7)

d. (8:1)

e. (9:1)

SUMMARY

With the books of Hosea, Joel, and Amos we begin our study of the twelve Minor Prophets. Remember the following highlights of these three prophetic books.

(1) Hosea's marriage to Gomer, which points to God's relationship to Israel (Hosea 1–3)
(2) Hosea's condemnation of Israel's religious and political practices (Hosea 4–14)
(3) Joel's prediction of the locust plague symbolizing the destruction of the people (Joel 1)
(4) Amos's speeches against the foreign nations (Amos 1–2)
(5) Amos's concern for social justice (Amos 3–9)

QUESTIONS FOR DISCUSSION

1. Hosea's marriage to Gomer is a prophetic symbol of God's relationship to Israel. God is the husband and Israel is the adulterous wife. What qualities help assure a good marriage? What qualities threaten a marriage relationship? Discuss the ways in which a religious commitment is like a marriage vow.

2. Hosea was the first prophet to use marriage imagery to depict Israel's relationship to God. Hosea was a northerner, speaking to the Kingdom of Israel before it fell to the Assyrians.

Hosea's words must have been carried south to Judah when Israel was taken into exile. There they survived, and apparently Jeremiah read them. Read Jeremiah 3:1-10. Discuss the probable connection between these words of Jeremiah and the prophecy of Hosea. Hosea was active about 740 B.C. Jeremiah's ministry was near 600 B.C. How do these prophecies affect our understanding of prophetic inspiration?

3. The vision of Joel 2:28-32 foresees a day of great spiritual power. Discuss the images. What do they represent? What might this mean now? Review also Acts 2:1-23. How are Joel's words used and interpreted in that Pentecost experience?

4. Amos 5:21-27 shows that the people's sin lay in their belief that God would look favorably on the nation—in spite of sin—if the people continued their religious rituals. However, Amos was more concerned with right living than with formal worship. How do we relate these two aspects of religious expression—right living and worship—in the church today? How can worship contribute to right living? right living to worship? What does 5:23-24 mean in today's world?

DAILY READINGS FOR OBADIAH, JONAH, MICAH, NAHUM, AND HABAKKUK

Day 1: Obadiah 1-21
Day 2: Jonah 2:1-10
Day 3: Jonah 4:1-11
Day 4: Micah 5:1-15
Day 5: Micah 6:1-8
Day 6: Nahum 1:1-15
Day 7: Habakkuk 1:1-11

OBADIAH
JONAH
MICAH
NAHUM
HABAKKUK

Assyrian soldiers

This lesson examines the books of Obadiah, Jonah, Micah, Nahum, and Habakkuk, which are part of the Minor Prophets.

OBADIAH

The first of these five books is Obadiah. It is the shortest book in the Old Testament, having only one chapter. We know nothing about the prophet Obadiah. The opening verse tells us that the book is a vision of Obadiah, but it gives no historical context and no biographical information. The name *Obadiah* means "servant of Yahweh." This name was fairly common in ancient Israel. Thirteen Obadiahs appear in the Old Testament.

The Book of Obadiah is primarily a denunciation of the state of Edom. It describes the calamities that the prophet sees befalling the Edomites, who are related to the Israelites. The Edomites traced their lineage back to Esau, the twin brother of

Jacob. Thus the Edomites and the Israelites claim the same ancestors.

Much of the Old Testament expresses a great hostility toward the Edomites. Psalm 137 speaks of the Edomites and declares as blessed anyone who takes their little ones and dashes them against the rock.

Why did such harsh feelings exist between Edom and Israel? The answer probably lies in the fact that the Edomites fought together with the Babylonians when the Babylonians took and destroyed Jerusalem in 586 B.C. Edom, rather than aiding Jerusalem, proved to be an enemy. Obadiah proclaims that the coming devastation of Edom is its reward for its role in Jerusalem's fall. Verses 10 to 14 clearly describe Edom's action in the day of Jerusalem's trouble: she would not aid Jerusalem, she rejoiced when Judah fell, she helped loot the city after its fall, and she killed Judean fugitives trying to flee from the Babylonian army. Read Obadiah 8-10.

Read Obadiah 1-4, and answer the following questions.

a. What has deceived the Edomites?

b. Where do the Edomites live?

c. What will God do to them?

JONAH

Turn now to the Book of Jonah, which contains a familiar story. The Book of Jonah differs from all the other prophetic books because it is really a narrative about a prophet and contains almost nothing of his preaching. Jonah's one proclamation in Jonah 3:4 contains, in Hebrew, only five words.

In Chapter 1 God calls Jonah to preach to Nineveh, the ancient capital of the Assyrians. But Jonah tries to flee. He boards a ship. A great storm arises, and the mariners finally throw Jonah overboard. A great fish then swallows Jonah.

Chapter 2 is Jonah's prayer that he offers to God while in the belly of the fish. It is actually a thanksgiving psalm similar to many of the poems in the Book of Psalms. After being vomited out of the fish, Jonah, in Chapter 3, hastens to Nineveh and proclaims the destruction of the city. To his surprise the people and even the animals repent and wear sackcloth, and God spares them. In Chapter 4 Jonah sulks because God spared the city. He sits above the city, awaiting the destruction he hopes will still come. While Jonah waits, God supplies a plant to shade him from the sun. After a time God has a worm destroy the plant. Jonah becomes angry over the loss of his plant. When Jonah has pity for the plant, God questions Jonah. Read Jonah 4:9-11.

The Book of Jonah is fascinating and appealing. But what is its message? Certainly it is not merely a fish story. One can argue that it sets out to show that a prophet cannot escape his call. The book also stresses that God will save whomever God will—even non-Israelites—if they genuinely repent. One may view the book as a protest against any narrow Jewish nationalism that stressed one people's election over all others. It is interesting to notice that the strongly anti-Edomite Book of Obadiah and the pro-Assyrian Book of Jonah follow each other. This placement seems to indicate that persons must hold the sentiments of nationalism and those of universalism in tension.

Chapter 2 of Jonah is his prayer to God. Read Jonah 2:4-9, and answer these questions.

a. Jonah fled from God's calling and was cast into the sea. How did he feel about God then?

b. When his soul fainted within him, what did Jonah do?

c. Why did Jonah give thanks to God?

MICAH

When we move to the Book of Micah, we again encounter a prophetic book similar to Isaiah, Jeremiah, Amos, and Hosea. The opening verse tells us something about the prophet and his historical context. From the introduction, we know that Micah was a contemporary of Isaiah who prophesied during the days of the Assyrian Empire.

Micah is from a small village called Moresheth. In many ways his preaching parallels that of his urban contemporary, Isaiah. Micah says a great deal about the perversion of justice by the leaders of Judah. Read Micah 3:9-11.

In one of the most perceptive passages of the Old Testament, Micah tries to define what religion is all about. He asks whether God will be pleased with sacrifice—even the sacrifice of one's own child. Read Micah 6:8 for Micah's own answer to his question.

Micah is the first prophet to preach about Jerusalem's destruction. In Micah 3:12 he predicts that Jerusalem will be plowed like a field and become a heap of ruins, and that the Temple mount will become a wooded height.

Christians usually recall one particular passage from Micah. This passage is his prophecy of the coming ruler from the house of David and the town of Bethlehem. Read this prediction in Micah 5:2.

Micah 6:7-8 gives us a simple definition of true religion. Answer the questions after reading these verses.

a. What does God require?

1.

2.

3.

b. With what other things have people thought to please God, but in vain?

1.

2.

3.

4.

NAHUM

The fourth book in this lesson is the Book of Nahum. All three chapters in this book proclaim and celebrate the fall of Nineveh. The city of Nineveh, capital of the Assyrian Empire, fell to invaders in 612 B.C. The Book of Nahum originated shortly before or just after the fall of the city. It was probably preserved in the canon because it graphically depicts the end of one of Judah's great enemies.

Although the celebration of the fall of Nineveh may strike us as odd, we might remember the joyful celebration that occurred in the Western world with the capture of Berlin and the end of World War II. With the fall of Nineveh an oppressive power that had ruled and plundered the Near East for over a century finally came to an end. Assyria's destruction meant others' salvation.

Sense the joy of the news of Nineveh's fall as you read Nahum 1:15.

At the same time, the prophet presents the fall of the city in dramatic detail. Read Nahum 3:1-3.

The subject of the Book of Nahum is the destruction of Nineveh. However, Nahum starts with a description of God who will bring about the fall of the city. Read the following passages, and summarize the main idea about the Lord contained in each.

a. (1:2-3)

b. (1:4-5)

c. (1:6)

d. (1:7)

e. (1:8-10)

HABAKKUK

The final book for today's consideration is the Book of Habakkuk. This prophetic book of three chapters is interesting in that it contains dialogues between the prophet and God. In Habakkuk 1:1-4 the prophet complains to God, who answers him in verses 5 to 11. The prophet then responds to God in Habakkuk 1:12–2:1. God then answers the prophet in Habakkuk 2:2-5.

Habakkuk complains that he cannot understand the events of his day and why things are as they are. The prophet wonders why the Chaldeans, or Babylonians, go on plundering, and God does not intervene. In Habakkuk 1:17 he asks, "Is he then to keep on emptying his net, / and destroying nations without mercy?" God answers the prophet by stating that the end awaits its time.

In 2:6-20 Habakkuk proclaims a number of woes upon various types of sinful behavior—especially the acquisition of extravagant wealth and property and deceitfully acquired gain. The book concludes with a poem or psalm, which is primarily a hymn of praise. Read Habakkuk 3:17-19.

The introduction in Habakkuk 3:1 and

the final line of the last verse suggest that this psalm once existed as an independent writing. Perhaps the prophet offered the psalm in worship, and it was later incorporated into his book.

Read Habakkuk 2:1. Write in your own words what the prophet did before he received the answer to his complaint.

SUMMARY

The books we studied in this lesson are some of the lesser-known books in the Bible. Try to remember at least one fact about each of these books.

(1) Obadiah denounces the country of Edom.
(2) Jonah, after being imprisoned within a great fish, proclaims the destruction of Nineveh.
(3) The prophet Micah, a contemporary of Isaiah, proclaims the defeat of Jerusalem by the Assyrians.
(4) Nahum celebrates the fall of Nineveh in 612 B.C.
(5) Habakkuk warns of the impending fall of Jerusalem to the Babylonians.

QUESTIONS FOR DISCUSSION

1. There are three alternatives for the message of Jonah: a prophet cannot escape his commission; God could save non-Israelites, even Assyrians, if they repent; and Jews must not think of themselves as chosen by God over all others. What do you think is the message of Jonah? If you do not agree with any of these possibilities, what other or others can you suggest?

2. We noted Jonah's prayer in the workbook questions on page 112. Look again at Jonah 2:4 and 2:8. Discuss what these verses reveal about Jonah's idea of where God was. Do we tend to identify a specific place with the presence of God? Why is or is not such identification appropriate?

3. We studied the memorable passage in Micah 6:6-8. Look at these verses again, noting the seventh verse: "Shall I give my firstborn for my transgression, / the fruit of my body for the sin of my soul?" This is a reference to human sacrifice in the Canaanite religion. See 2 Kings 3:26-27; 21:6; and Leviticus 18:21. That a man would permit the slaughter of his first-born son in an effort to make payment for the sin of his soul is an indication of his sense of the importance of sin. In ancient Israel, sin was a major problem to be redeemed through blood sacrifice. Discuss how this verse provides an insight into the thinking of ancient people about the problem of sin. How do we look upon the problem of sin today?

4. Habakkuk 2:4 states: "Look at the proud! / Their spirit is not right in them, / but *the righteous live by their faith*" (italics added). The last half of the verse is quoted several times in the New Testament. What does the phrase mean to you? Discuss the way the quotation is used in the following passages: Romans 1:16-17; Galatians 3:10-14; and Hebrews 10:32-39.

DAILY READINGS FOR ZEPHANIAH, HAGGAI, ZECHARIAH, AND MALACHI

Day 1:	Zephaniah 1:1-9
Day 2:	Zephaniah 3:14-20
Day 3:	Haggai 1:1-11
Day 4:	Zechariah 1:7-17
Day 5:	Zechariah 9:1-10
Day 6:	Malachi 1:1-14
Day 7:	Malachi 4:1-6

ZEPHANIAH HAGGAI ZECHARIAH MALACHI

Mimi Forsyth

ZEPHANIAH

With this lesson we come to the last four writings in the Book of the Twelve. The first of these books is Zephaniah. In the opening verse of the book, we learn two things about Zephaniah. First of all the verse traces his family line back four generations. No other prophet receives such a pedigree. Why is Zephaniah an exception? Perhaps the identity of one of his ancestors is important. He is said to be a descendant of Hezekiah—maybe the king of that name who ruled about a century before Zephaniah. Thus Zephaniah would be a relative of the reigning king of Judah at the time of his prophetic activity.

A second thing we learn about Zephaniah in this opening verse is that the word of the Lord that he proclaims comes to him during the reign of King Josiah. Josiah ruled from 640 to 609 B.C. We also know that Jeremiah was active during this same period. So Jeremiah and Zephaniah were contemporaries, although neither mentions the other.

We can divide the Book of Zephaniah into three parts. These three parts do not correspond to the present chapter divisions. In Zephaniah 1:2–2:3 Zephaniah prophesies against Judah. In Zephaniah 2:1–3:8 he prophesies against foreign nations. In the remainder of Chapter 3 Zephaniah tells of the good time coming in the future.

As we have seen, many of the prophetic books have a similar outline—judgment against the chosen people, followed by judgment against foreign nations, followed by predictions of a promising future.

In Zephaniah's preaching against Judah the central theme is the coming day of the Lord, the coming day of judgment. On this day God will punish the officials, the king's sons, those who worship other gods, those who deny that God can bring judgment, and those guilty of amassing wealth and trusting in possessions. Read Zephaniah 1:14-16. These verses describe the day of the Lord.

At the end of his sermon to Judah on the coming judgment, Zephaniah issues a call for repentance and conversion. Read Zephaniah 2:1-3.

In the second part of the book the prophet proclaims judgment upon the nations of the region: the Philistines and the seacoast, Moab and Ammon, Ethiopia and Assyria. In Zephaniah 3:8 we read about God's indignation and anger toward these nations. God's jealous wrath will consume the earth.

The final part of Zephaniah describes the new conditions that will exist for the "humble and lowly" who survive the purifying judgment of the day of the Lord. Arrogant sinners will be gone, the remnant will live in obedience, God will be king, and the exiles will return home.

The Book of Zephaniah, which starts with a prophecy of judgment, ends with predictions of a promising future. Read the last verse, 3:20, and write down what God will eventually do for the people.

a.

b.

c.

HAGGAI

Haggai is the second of our books. This short work of only two chapters contains four dated addresses by the prophet. The dates in the book all come from the second year of the reign of Darius, the Persian king—the year 520 B.C. By this time, the Jews had returned to Jerusalem from exile. They had begun to rebuild the Temple, but work had ceased as we recall from the Book of Ezra.

Most of the prophetic work of Haggai centers on attempts to get the Temple reconstruction under way. In his first speech in Chapter 1 the prophet chides the people for being overly concerned for their own welfare to the complete disregard of rebuilding the Temple. Haggai encourages Zerubbabel, who is in charge of the rebuilding work. This encouragement is the theme of Haggai's second speech in Haggai 2:1-9.

In the third speech of the prophet— Haggai 2:10-19—Haggai reminds the people that their living conditions improved after they laid the foundation of the Temple. His final oracle in Haggai 2:20-23 predicts that God is about to shake the earth and overthrow nations. When God does this, Zerubbabel will be God's chosen. Read Haggai 2:20-23.

Read Haggai 1:1-11, and answer these questions.

a. What excuse did the people give for not rebuilding the Temple yet? (1:2)

b. Why had the people expected much and received little? (1:4)

ZECHARIAH 1:1–6:8

The third book in this lesson is the Book of Zechariah. According to the date given in the opening verse, Zechariah was a contemporary of Haggai. However, the Book of Zechariah is as difficult to understand as Haggai is easy. Much of the content of Zechariah is made up of symbolic visions and apocalyptic imagery that make it difficult for us to understand. The images and visions of the book probably made good sense to the prophet's first audience; but for us today, the references are not very clear.

In the first six chapters of the book, Zechariah reports eight visions. The first of these, in Zechariah 1:7-17, is that of the four horsemen. The second vision (1:18-21) is of four horns and four smiths. The third (2:1-5) is of the man with a measuring line. The fourth (3:1-10) is the accusation of Joshua, the high priest. The fifth vision, in 4:1-14, is of two olive trees standing beside a golden lampstand. The sixth vision (5:1-4) is of a flying scroll with curses written upon it. In 5:5-11 we read about the seventh vision, which is a woman in a basket. The final vision, in 6:1-8, is of four chariots.

What can we make of these eight visions? The visions have to do with the coming new age for the Jewish community, which involves God's judgment of the world. The prophet stresses several points as characteristic of the new age. First, the nations who have oppressed Judah will be oppressed. Second, Jerusalem will be restored. Third, two men in the Jewish community will play significant roles and are described as the two anointed ones of God. These men are Zerubbabel, the prince, and Joshua, the high priest.

To become familiar with Zechariah's visions, read the passages below. Then describe each vision in a short phrase.

a. (1:8)

b. (1:18)

c. (2:1)

d. (3:1)

e. (4:2-3)

f. (5:1)

g. (5:7)

h. (6:1-3)

ZECHARIAH 6:9–14:21

Zechariah 6:9-15 gives an account of the crowning of Joshua. Scholars have long wondered why Zerubbabel is not also mentioned in this text. One explanation suggests that Zerubbabel, as a member of the house of David and a potential claimant to

Charles Shaw

Zechariah 6:1-8

the throne, was removed from authority or perhaps even killed by the Persians.

After the visions in the first six chapters, we have two chapters of preaching about the restoration of Judah and Jerusalem. Read Zechariah 8:4-8.

When we turn to Chapter 9 of Zechariah, we seem to begin reading a new book. Notice that this chapter is entitled "An Oracle." Also, Chapter 9 is in poetry form while the earlier chapters are in prose. Another section begins with Chapter 12 where we find another title. The name of the prophet Zechariah does not appear in Chapters 9 to 14. These facts possibly suggest that the present Book of Zechariah was originally three books, which have now been combined.

Much of Chapters 9 to 14 deals with expectations about coming times. Here let us single out only two passages for attention. In Chapter 13 the writer condemns prophets and prophecy. In the future people will be ashamed of either being called a prophet or of having a child who is a prophet. Read Zechariah 13:2-6. We do not know why the community became so suspicious of prophecy and prophets.

Chapter 9 describes future events. One passage speaks of a king of peace who comes to Jerusalem. Many Christians are familiar with this passage because the New Testament uses it to speak about Jesus' entry into Jerusalem on Palm Sunday. Read Zechariah 9:9-10.

Some Christians believe that the personal return of Christ in glory is depicted in Chapter 14 of Zechariah. Read 14:3-5, and answer the following questions.

a. Where will God stand on that day?

b. What will happen to the Mount of Olives?

c. On that day, who is coming with the Lord God?

MALACHI

Malachi, the final book for this lesson, is also the final book of the Old Testament. We know little about the prophet named Malachi whose name means "my servant." We do know he prophesied around 500 to 450 B.C. In his prophecy, Malachi makes a plea for sincere worship.

Throughout its four chapters, the book reflects what might be called a dialogue form. Malachi makes a statement, the hearers protest, and then Malachi answers or refutes their protest. The writer of the book stresses obedience to God and the Law by all members of the community. He calls upon priests to offer pure sacrifices. He condemns divorce and stresses the offering of tithes. Read Malachi 2:13-16.

The book also speaks of the messenger of God who will come in the future. The last two verses of Malachi identify this messenger as Elijah. These verses, and an understanding of John the Baptist as the new Elijah, provide one point of connection between the Old and New Testaments.

Malachi 3:6-12 speaks of the principle of tithing. Read this passage, and answer the following questions.

a. How are the children of Jacob robbing God?

b. What type of test does God invite?

c. What does God promise to do for those who will bring the full tithe to God?

SUMMARY

Like the last lesson, this study includes some of the lesser-known Old Testament literature. Try to remember at least one fact about each of these four prophetic books.

(1) Zephaniah prophesied during the reign of King Josiah in Judah.
(2) Haggai encouraged the people who had returned from Exile to rebuild the Jerusalem Temple.
(3) Zechariah was a contemporary of Haggai whose prophecy was mainly in the form of visions.
(4) Malachi spoke of God's judgment using a question-and-answer method.

QUESTIONS FOR DISCUSSION

1. God acts to eradicate idolatry in Israel and Judah because the promise to bless all nations through Abraham's seed is threatened. Also, God is holy, and sin deserves and demands just punishment. So judgment appears predominant and primary in prophecy. The instruments of that judgment are the foreign nations, yet they too are guilty before God. So the oracles against the nations appear.

God's mercy and commitment to the covenant with the people of Israel, however, require a future for the people. Thus, the restoration of a purified remnant completes the pattern. Discuss how this pattern may reflect on the justice and mercy of God.

2. Twice in Zephaniah humility is emphasized (Zephaniah 2:3 and 3:11-13). Similar ideas are expressed in Psalm 138:6, Isaiah 57:15, Proverbs 3:34, James 4:6, and elsewhere in the Bible. Why is humility such an important characteristic? Discuss also its opposite: pride and haughtiness. Give examples from your own experience or reading that illustrate these two human characteristics. Do you find it more difficult to be proud or to be humble? Why?

3. Malachi 3:1 and 4:5-6 express ideas about the coming of the day of the Lord. These verses were a prophetic warning and encouragement to Malachi's audience. Later these words were recognized as a messianic prophecy. Elijah, who had been dead for centuries when Malachi wrote, was depicted as the forerunner of the Messiah. Jesus identified John the Baptist as the fulfillment of this prophecy. (See Matthew 11:14.) Using this example discuss the problem of interpreting prophecies too literally. How can we decide which interpretation of any passage is correct?

DAILY READINGS FOR MATTHEW, MARK, AND LUKE

Day 1: Matthew 1:1-17
Day 2: Matthew 5:1-12
Day 3: Matthew 13:1-17
Day 4: Mark 4:1-20
Day 5: Mark 16:1-8
Day 6: Luke 2:1-20
Day 7: Luke 24:36-53

Review 4 Sheet

1. Who is the earliest prophet from whom we have a book, and during which century did he prophesy?

2. Who are the three major Old Testament prophets?

3. What is the historical background of each of Isaiah's three parts?

4. During what period in Israel's history did Jeremiah prophesy?

5. Which major Old Testament prophet was active among the exiles in Babylon?

6. Which Old Testament book is considered to be apocalyptic literature?

7. Who does the Book of Daniel indicate is its audience? What background do most scholars assign to the book?

8. Who are the twelve Minor Prophets? List as many as you can.

9. Which prophetic book illustrates the relationship between God and Israel using marriage as an example?

10. Which prophet is especially noted for his preaching in favor of social justice?

(Answers are on page 183.)

THE GOSPELS

INTRODUCTION

Practically everything we know about the life of Jesus we learn from the four Gospels. The first three, Matthew, Mark, and Luke, are called *synoptic* ("with the same eye") because many of the same events are recorded in them. The Fourth Gospel, John, has a different literary flavor and adds details and emphases missing in the Synoptics.

These four works are not biographies. They are biographical sketches that deal primarily with Jesus' ministry of approximately three and one-half years. They climax in Jesus' death, burial, and resurrection. Christians were fascinated with the personal life of Jesus in the early period of the church. Some persons were not satisfied with the canonical Gospels.

Apocryphal gospels were also produced in the early centuries, emphasizing the childhood of Jesus, because the Bible is silent on that period. But the church soon rejected these other works.

BEFORE THE FOUR GOSPELS

The preface of Luke's Gospel tells us about the process by which the Gospels were written. Some of the words of Jesus and accounts of his deeds were kept alive orally by his devout followers. Luke emphasizes that he talked with eyewitnesses (1:1-4). Since there was no scribe to record the words of Jesus, our knowledge of what he said depends on the memories of the witnesses and the faithfulness with which the words were passed down until they were written. However, the problem of accuracy is not as large as it may at first appear. In almost every instance a number of people heard and witnessed each saying and event.

Jesus spoke Aramaic, but the oldest copies of the Gospels are written in Greek. Thus the sayings of Jesus were translated into Greek, although here and there an Aramaic word was left untranslated. One example is *Abba,* meaning "father." A tradition from the second century states that Matthew wrote his Gospel originally in Aramaic, but the only copies we have now are in Greek. These sayings of Jesus and recollections of his deeds became the raw material that went into our Gospels.

SIMILARITIES IN THE FOUR GOSPELS

Remarkably, the four Gospels have much in common. The four pictures the Gospels provide are consistent. All four tell about the ministry of John the Baptist, the controversies that Jesus confronted with his opponents, the feeding of the five thousand, Jesus' walking on the water, the anointing of Jesus by a woman, the cleansing of the Temple, the triumphal entry into Jerusalem, and the Resurrection. The four mention twelve disciples, the multitudes who witness the miracles, and Jesus' teaching in stories, sermons, and debates.

DIFFERENCES IN THE FOUR GOSPELS

All the Gospel writers intend to tell their readers what they consider to be the most important information about Jesus. The four writers probably wrote to four different social groups. So the various audiences and purposes of the writers explain the differences in the accounts.

Mark was probably the earliest Gospel. The writer was at one time a companion of Paul on his first missionary journey and is said to have been an associate of the apostle Peter. The book was likely written for Gentiles living in Rome, to show that Jesus was the Messiah, and to encourage Christians suffering from persecution in Rome. Because of Mark's close association with Peter, it may be that the apostle dictated the account to Mark.

Matthew was writing largely for Jewish Christians. He included more details on Jesus' life than Mark. He emphasized that Christianity is the fulfillment of Old Testament prophecy and the Jewish Law. Matthew was a former publican who became a disciple of the Lord.

Luke was a Greek physician. Perhaps he was converted by Paul, who took Luke with him on many of his missionary journeys (Acts 21:15-18). Luke wrote the Gospel and the Book of Acts as companion accounts. Both books were addressed to a certain Theophilus, perhaps a Roman official. The books may have been written to convince the Roman Empire that Christianity was not a subversive sect. They emphasize that the gospel message is for Gentiles as well as Jews and is universal.

The Gospel of John was the last written of the four. It was written around A.D. 90 by the aging disciple. John had been with Jesus from the beginning of Jesus' ministry. His Gospel is more theological and philosophical than the other three. This tendency may reflect the interest in speculations about Jesus on the part of his audience. John shows that Jesus is the eternal Word of God and the power of God. Seven signs and seven sayings confirm who Jesus is. The book is written that the readers may believe that Jesus is the Christ, the Son of God. (See John 20:30-31.)

MATTHEW
MARK
LUKE

Mosaic showing the Church of the Apostles, a first-century synagogue-church

With this lesson we move into the New Testament. Our subjects are the first three Gospels—Matthew, Mark, and Luke. These Gospels are called the Synoptic Gospels. The term *synoptic* comes from a Greek word *synopsis,* which means "common perspective." Matthew, Mark, and Luke are called the Synoptic Gospels because they share a similar perspective on the life and teachings of Jesus. All three Gospels use a common outline for Jesus' ministry. All three differ from the Gospel of John.

Although Matthew, Mark, and Luke are very similar, many differences exist among the three. In order to gain some insight into why these three Gospels agree in many respects and differ in others, let us take a closer look at the introduction to the Gospel of Luke in Luke 1:1-4.

In these verses the writer of Luke tells us a number of things about the origin of his book. First of all others before him have written narratives or gospels about Jesus. Second, Luke knows and relies on these earlier narrative accounts. Third, these earlier accounts were compiled from the traditions passed along by eyewitnesses and ministers of the word. Fourth, Luke declares that he wants to present the narratives about Jesus in an orderly account. He plans to give the material in what he considers to be the best order, although an order that differs from that of other writers.

We can discern two general principles about the origin of the Gospels from these opening verses of Luke. First of all some of the writers of the Gospels depended on earlier narratives or gospels. So the first three Gospels have a literary relationship. This relationship explains their similarities and common perspectives. In the second place, the Gospel writers went their own ways in shaping the materials for their own purposes. Their varied purposes explain their differences.

Throughout the history of the church Christian thinkers have tried to determine the literary relationship among Matthew, Mark, and Luke. Most scholars have concluded that Mark was the earliest Gospel and that the writers of both Matthew and Luke used Mark in writing their books.

Matthew and Luke differ from Mark in one major respect. These two Gospels contain many of Jesus' teachings that do not appear in Mark. Most of the best-known parables and sayings of Jesus are not found in Mark. However, both Matthew and Luke contain many of these teachings. This fact could mean either that Luke or Matthew depended on the other or that both depended on a common source not used by Mark. Most biblical students today conclude that Matthew and Luke used a collection of the teachings of Jesus, a collection that did not survive as an independent work. This collection is commonly called "Q," the first letter of the German word *Quelle,* which means "source."

MATTHEW 1:1-17

Let us now examine each of these three Gospels individually. We will start with Matthew. Matthew begins with two introductory chapters on the ancestry and birth of Jesus. We find the list of Jesus' ancestors in the first seventeen verses of the book.

Matthew 1:1-17 gives us the genealogy of Jesus. Most of the names are of men, but several women are also referred to. Read these verses, and list below as many references to women as you can find.

MATTHEW 1:18-13:58

An account of Jesus' birth follows this list of ancestors. Matthew's account of Jesus' birth has several special features. Matthew gives special attention to Joseph. An angel of the Lord appears to Joseph in a dream, telling him that Mary his betrothed is with child by the Holy Spirit. Read Matthew 1:18-21.

Matthew's story assumes that Bethlehem is the home of the Holy Family. Wise men visit the birthplace after seeing the star. Joseph takes his family to Egypt after being warned in a dream to flee. King Herod slaughters all children "in and around Bethlehem" who are two years old or less. After Herod's death, Joseph takes his family to Nazareth in Galilee rather than returning to Judea.

Matthew understands all the events associated with Jesus' birth as fulfillments of Old Testament prophecies. The first two chapters alone quote four Old Testament passages. This emphasis on Jesus as the fulfillment of Old Testament prophecy continues throughout the Gospel.

In his desire to show God's promises to Israel fulfilled through Jesus to the church, Matthew pictures Jesus as a figure of great authority—a new Moses passing down a new law. Matthew begins developing this theme as early as the birth story, in which foreign kings come to honor the newborn child. Matthew organizes his material to emphasize Jesus' authority.

The most noteworthy feature about the Gospel of Matthew is the fact that the writer collects the sayings and teachings of Jesus into five major speeches. In Chapters 5 to 7 we have the Sermon on the Mount, in which Jesus speaks of the nature and character of life in the Kingdom. The narratives in Chapters 8 and 9 follow this speech. The second speech is in Chapter 10 where Jesus discusses the nature of mission work in the world. Narratives follow in Chapters 11 and 12. Chapter 13 contains a

Charles Shaw

Jesus teaching

collection of Jesus' parables on the Kingdom.

Matthew 5:1-12 contains the Beatitudes, a part of the Sermon on the Mount. Each Beatitude begins with the word *Blessed*. Write down the kind of people that are blessed in each beatitude.

a. (5:3)

b. (5:4)

c. (5:5)

d. (5:6)

e. (5:7)

f. (5:8)

g. (5:9)

h. (5:10)

MATTHEW 14–28

Chapters 14 through 17 are narratives. The fourth speech follows in Chapter 18 where Jesus discusses life in community and the relationship of members to one another. The fifth speech is in Chapters 24 through 25 where Jesus denounces the Jewish leaders and talks about the events of the last days. In these five speeches, Matthew presents the words of Jesus as the authoritative voice of God's son. In the remainder of the Gospel, Matthew reports appearances of the risen Christ and concludes with Jesus' final commission to the eleven disciples.

MARK 1–9

Let us now turn to the beginning of the Gospel of Mark. Mark opens with an account of the preaching and activity of John the Baptist. The Gospel writer views John as the messenger that the Old Testament speaks of as coming before the time of final salvation. John not only fulfills the Old Testament prophecy, he proclaims the coming of Jesus. Mark 1:9-11 reports John's baptism of Jesus. A voice from heaven declares Jesus to be God's beloved son. Read Mark 1:9-11.

The reader of Mark is therefore left with no doubt about the identity of Jesus. He is the fulfillment of Old Testament hopes and is the Son of God.

After a brief reference to Jesus' temptations in the wilderness, Mark tells us that John is arrested and that Jesus then begins his preaching career in Galilee. Mark 1:15 gives us Mark's summary of the basic preaching of Jesus: "The time is fulfilled, and the kingdom of God has come near; repent, and believe in the good news." Jesus preaches that the age of salvation is near. People should prepare for the Kingdom through repentance and belief in the good news.

The rest of Mark 1 and Chapters 2 through 9 describe Jesus' activity and preaching in Galilee and the surrounding regions. Mark focuses on the mighty acts of Jesus—his healings, casting out of demons, stilling the storms, and feeding the multitudes. Very little of Jesus' teaching appears, although Chapter 4—which contains several parables—is an exception.

Mark 5:1-20 contains a typical story of Jesus casting out demons. After reading the story, answer the following questions in your own words.

a. When the wretched man meets Jesus, he cries out to him. What impression do his words leave on the reader of the story? (5:6-7)

b. In what forms was the control of the man by the unclean spirit indicated? (5:3-5)

c. How could an onlooker have known that the man had in fact been healed by the words of Jesus? (5:15)

d. Jesus told the healed man to "tell them how much the Lord has done for you." How do we know that the healed man understood who the Lord was? (5:20)

MARK 10–16

In the first nine chapters Mark stresses the growing hostility toward Jesus. For Mark the shadow of suffering and persecution falls quickly over Jesus' career. Here we see a special characteristic of Mark's portrait of Jesus—Jesus is the suffering one. Mark shows Jesus teaching his disciples that suffering and humiliation will be their fate as well. Mark 10 tells the story of Jesus' journey to Jerusalem accompanied by his disciples.

At the beginning of Chapter 11 Jesus and his followers arrive in Jerusalem on what we today call Palm Sunday. The account of Jesus' ministry in Jerusalem, his suffering, passion, death, and resurrection make up the remainder of the book. The final chapter of Mark—Chapter 16—tells of the women's visit to Jesus' tomb.

One of the interesting and perhaps surprising things about the Gospel of Mark is that we do not know for sure how the book ended. The oldest copies of the book end with Mark 16:8, which states that the women "said nothing to anyone, for they were afraid." Other ancient manuscripts have twelve additional verses. These appear as verses 9 to 20 in many translations. Still other ancient texts add two short verses after verse 8.

Today most scholars believe the Gospel ended with verse 8. Persons in the early church felt that this ending was not satisfactory, and thus they added various conclusions to the Gospel. If Mark originally ended with verse 8 of Chapter 16, then it would be the only Gospel that contains no accounts of Jesus' resurrection appearances.

LUKE

When we turn to Luke we encounter a Gospel that is more like Matthew than it is like Mark. Both Luke and Matthew contain many teachings and parables of Jesus. Again, Luke presents the material in a distinctive arrangement and with special emphases. Chapters 1 and 2 present the accounts of the births of John the

Baptist and Jesus. In both accounts the mothers receive special attention. Luke uses poetic hymns rather than Old Testament quotations.

In the account of Jesus' birth Luke stresses the appearance of the angel to Mary, the trip to Bethlehem from Nazareth, and the appearance of the angels to the shepherds, who then visit the Christ Child. Luke does not refer to the star, the wise men, or Herod's persecution. Luke's account of Jesus' birth indicates some of Luke's major emphases: concern for women, interest in common people, and the universal significance of Jesus.

Read the familiar story of Jesus' birth in Luke 2:1-20, and answer these questions.

a. Where in this story do you see evidence of Luke's special concern for women?

b. Where do you see evidence of Luke's concern for common people?

c. How does Luke emphasize the universality of Jesus in this story?

LUKE 6–18

Throughout his Gospel, Luke includes sayings and teachings of Jesus that not only parallel Matthew but differ as well. In Luke 6 Jesus preaches his Sermon on the Plain—a sermon that parallels part of Matthew's Sermon on the Mount. Read Luke 6:20-22.

In Luke 9:51–18:34 we have a collection of special material found only in Luke's Gospel. In Luke, Jesus shares all these teachings and sayings during his journey to

Jerusalem. That journey took only one chapter in Mark. This special section in Luke contains much of the most familiar material in the New Testament. It includes such stories as the prodigal son, the lost sheep, and the lost coin.

The parable of the widow and the judge in Luke 18:1-8 appears only in Luke. After reading it, answer the questions below.

a. What did Jesus intend to teach through this parable?

b. In what way was the judge similar to God? dissimilar to God?

c. What is the relationship between Jesus' words in verse 1 and verse 8?

SUMMARY

Thus we see that Matthew, Mark, and Luke contain similar material about Jesus. But each Gospel writer gives special form to Jesus' story. To fulfill his own purposes, each writer emphasizes certain aspects about Jesus' life and ministry.

A few words summarize the perspective of each of the Gospel writers.

(1) For Matthew, Jesus is the fulfillment of Old Testament prophecy.
(2) Mark focuses on the mighty acts of Jesus more than on his teachings.
(3) Luke emphasizes Jesus' concern for women, interest in the common people, and universal significance of Jesus.

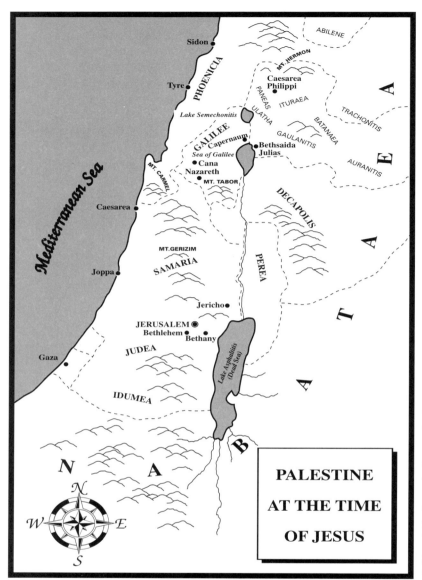

PALESTINE AT THE TIME OF JESUS

day, and his reign is destined for eternity. What evidence do you see of this kingdom?

2. The temptations of Jesus are recorded in two of the Synoptic Gospels: Matthew 4:1-11 and Luke 4:1-13. Read these passages, then discuss with the group how the temptations illustrate the humanity of Jesus. Consider how Jesus' response to temptation can serve as an example to us. How do you respond to temptation in your life?

3. The Gospel of Mark portrays Jesus as the suffering servant. Read the Servant Songs in the Book of Isaiah: 42:1-4; 49:1-6; 50:4-11; and 52:13–53:12. What parallels do you see between Isaiah's suffering servant and Jesus? What does Jesus' suffering mean to us?

4. A variety of literature is found in the Gospels: parables, sermons, and biographical sketches. Which of these types of literature has been most helpful in your life? Be prepared to share your answers with the class members.

QUESTIONS FOR DISCUSSION

1. Matthew begins his Gospel by identifying Jesus as the Messiah (Christ). He then specifically mentions Abraham and David as Jesus' ancestors. Read Genesis 12:1-3 and 2 Samuel 7:18-26 as a review. Why do you think he mentioned these two Old Testament leaders in particular?

Matthew's Gospel closes on the note that salvation through Christ is open to all who will accept it. The kingdom of Jesus Christ is not of this world. But he does rule to this

DAILY READINGS FOR JOHN

Day 1: John 1:1-18
Day 2: John 1:19-34
Day 3: John 3:1-21
Day 4: John 4:7-26
Day 5: John 6:1-15
Day 6: John 17:1-26
Day 7: John 21:5-25

JOHN

**Hadrian's Arch, possibly at the entrance to the Antonia Fortress
where Jesus was brought before Pilate**

© 1983 Biblical Archaeology Society

In this lesson we study the Fourth Gospel, the Gospel of John. We learned in our last lesson that Matthew, Mark, and Luke—the Synoptic Gospels—have many similarities. But since the days of the early church, Christians have noticed how much the Gospel of John differs from the Synoptics. In the Synoptics, Jesus' ministry takes place primarily in Galilee; in John it is chiefly in Judea and Jerusalem. In the Synoptics, Jesus' ministry lasts for only a short time; in John it lasts for over three years since the Gospel refers to three different Passovers. In the Synoptics, Jesus'

preaching focuses primarily on the kingdom of God; in John he preaches about himself and the significance of his ministry.

In the Synoptics, Jesus teaches in short, pithy sayings, in parables, and through conversations in everyday situations. In John, Jesus teaches in long discourses and dialogues. In the Synoptics, Jesus begins his ministry after the arrest of John the Baptist; in John, Jesus carries on a ministry that competes with the Baptist, and he recruits his first followers from John's followers. In the Synoptics, Jesus' miracles are works of compassion, which benefit the needy; in

John, they are primarily signs that point to Jesus' true identity.

Many of the events reported about Jesus in the Synoptics do not appear in John, which contains many episodes not found in the Synoptics. Among those unique to John are the account of the marriage in Cana of Galilee, Jesus' meeting with the woman at the well in Samaria, and the raising of Lazarus.

In many ways the Gospel of John is more an interpretation of who Jesus was than a straightforward report of Jesus' ministry. John is much more philosophical in nature than the Synoptics. Early church tradition, from the second century on, associated the Gospel of John with the disciple, John the son of Zebedee, and its place of origin with the city of Ephesus. The differences between the Synoptic Gospels and John show how the traditions about the interpretations of Jesus developed differently in various centers of Christianity.

The central characteristic of the Gospel of John is its stress on Jesus as the heaven-sent Son of God and divine savior of all who believe in him. The writer summarizes his purpose in John 20:31: "that you may come to believe that Jesus is the Messiah, the Son of God, and that through believing you may have life in his name."

In examining the Gospel of John, we can divide it into four main parts. First, we have a prologue in the first eighteen verses of the book. The second part runs through Chapter 12. Here Jesus reveals himself to the world in sign and word. The third part, Chapters 13 through 20, contains Jesus' special revelation of himself to the disciples. This part also contains the account of Jesus' trial, death, and resurrection. The fourth and final part is the epilogue in Chapter 21.

JOHN 1:1-18

In the prologue in John 1:1-18 John presents Jesus as the incarnation of the eternal word of God. This interpretation of Jesus is one of the most exalted views in the New Testament. Mark associates Jesus' divine sonship with his baptism. Matthew and Luke relate his sonship to his birth. In John, Jesus is the eternal son of God who existed with the Father before creation. The book opens like the Book of Genesis, with a reference to the beginning, to the time before the creation of the world. These opening verses stress two points in particular. First of all, John presents the Word as existing with God eternally and as having shared in the creation of all things. Read John 1:1-3.

The second point these opening verses stress is that the eternal word is now flesh in Jesus who is the light of the world. He reveals the glory of the Father to humanity. Read John 1:4-8.

Read the remainder of the prologue to John (1:9-18), and follow the directions below.

1. Summarize the main idea or ideas of verses 9-13.

2. Summarize the main idea or ideas of verses 14-18.

JOHN 1:19–12:50

We might call the second major section of the Gospel—John 1:19–12:50—the revelation of Jesus to the world. This section tries to demonstrate how Jesus makes himself known, is rejected by many, but is believed in by some.

This section opens with a presentation by John the Baptist and his testimony to Jesus. John makes it clear that he is only "the voice of one crying in the wilderness." When Jesus appears, John does not hesitate to declare who Jesus is. Read John 1:29-31.

Loaves and fishes mosaic in an early church beside the Sea of Galilee

Several of John's disciples follow Jesus and become the core of Jesus' circle of disciples.

Beginning with Chapter 2 the writer of John presents a number of Jesus' miracles, which he calls "signs." Interwoven with the narratives about Jesus' signs are discourses and sermons of Jesus. In John 2:1-11 we read about Jesus' first sign. Here he changes water to wine at the marriage in Cana. The water symbolizes the old life of Judaism. Its change into wine symbolizes the new life given by Jesus.

Read the witness of John to Jesus again, and answer these questions.

a. When he saw Jesus, what title did John give him? (1:29)

b. What did John mean when he said that Jesus was "before me"? (Rereading John 1:1-8 will help you answer this question.)

c. By what sign was John to recognize the one who was the Son of God? (1:33)

JOHN 3–10

Following the story of the wedding at Cana, John reports Jesus' cleansing of the Temple. The Synoptics place this act in the last week of Jesus' life. John places this episode early in Jesus' ministry to show that Jesus' way supplants the old order of Temple worship. Jesus makes this clear in John 2:19 when he says, "Destroy this temple, and in three days I will raise it up." In verse 21 the Gospel writer notes that Jesus is referring to his resurrected body.

In Chapter 3 we read the account of Nicodemus's nighttime meeting with Jesus. Jesus emphasizes the need to be born again. Read John 3:1-6.

This story illustrates one of the literary characteristics of John's Gospel. Jesus makes a statement; the hearer misunderstands the statement; this misunderstanding allows Jesus to give a long speech on the subject to clarify the issue. This technique appears in several places in the Gospel.

In Chapter 4 Jesus leaves Jerusalem to return to Galilee. Passing through Samaria, he encounters the woman at the well. None of the other Gospels shows Jesus in contact with Samaritans. As in the case of Nicodemus he carries on a long conversation with her. In his conversation at the well Jesus talks about the newness of his way and emphasizes the spiritual dimensions of worship.

Chapter 4 concludes, in verses 46 through 54, with the second of Jesus' signs: the healing of an official's son at Capernaum. The third sign—another healing—follows in Chapter 5. This healing takes place in Jerusalem at the pool of Bethzatha. There Jesus heals a man who has been ill for thirty-eight years. Jesus heals on the sabbath. The Jewish opposition to such healing on the sabbath gives Jesus the occasion to speak of his authority and the continuing work of the Father through him. Read John 5:15-18.

We find the fourth and fifth signs in Chapter 6. The fourth sign is the feeding of the five thousand in 6:1-14. The fifth sign is Jesus' walking on the water, in 6:16-21.

Speeches by Jesus follow the fourth and fifth signs. Jesus speaks of himself as the bread of life in John 6:25-65. In Chapters 7 and 8 Jesus again speaks with Jewish leaders in Jerusalem about himself as the one sent by God—the light of the world.

The sixth sign occurs in John 9:1-17. Jesus heals a man born blind. The healed man then bears witness to Jesus. In verse 34 we read that the Jews cast him out of the synagogue. Jesus' speech about his being the door to the sheepfold, as well as the good shepherd, follows in Chapter 10.

Jesus' changing the water into wine is the first of his signs in the Gospel of John. Read the verses below, and list other signs of Jesus.

a. (4:46-54)

b. (5:1-9)

c. (6:1-14)

d. (6:16-21)

e. (9:1-17)

f. (11:1-44)

JOHN 11–19

The seventh and final sign in the revelation of Jesus to the world is the story of the raising of Lazarus in Chapter 11. This episode raises such opposition from the Jewish leaders that they set out to put Jesus

Steps to the Pool of Siloam, Jerusalem

Spirit to support them after his departure. In Chapter 17 Jesus prays to the Father that the disciples might abide in him and in unity with one another.

With Chapter 18 we begin the narrative of Jesus' arrest, trial, crucifixion, and resurrection. This narrative continues through Chapter 19. In many ways, the narrative in John agrees in detail with that found in the Synoptics. John differs from the other Gospels on one point. The day of Jesus' crucifixion is one day earlier than it is in the Synoptics. Jesus' crucifixion is on Thursday —the same time that the lambs are slaughtered for Passover. Again John stresses a theme raised early in the book: Jesus as the Lamb of God who takes away the sin of the world.

In John 17, we find Jesus' high priestly prayer. Skim over this chapter, and answer the four questions below.

a. In verses 1-5, for whom does Jesus pray?

b. What is the main prayer concern that Jesus has for his disciples in verses 16-17?

to death. The Gospel writer thus shows how one of the points of his prologue reaches its fulfillment: "He came to what was his own, and his own people did not accept him." The people's response to the raising of Lazarus gives Jesus the opportunity to talk about the Resurrection and his return to the Father.

With Chapter 13 we come to the third main section of the Gospel. We might call this section Jesus' revelation to his disciples and his return to the Father. In Chapters 13 through 16 Jesus instructs his disciples at the Last Supper. He washes the disciples' feet, and he asks them to have faith in him and to keep the commandments.

Jesus promises them a Counselor or

c. For whom does Jesus pray in verses 20-26?

d. What is the main prayer concern that Jesus has for all believers in verses 20-26?

JOHN 20–21

After John reports appearances of the risen Jesus in Chapter 20, the writer seems to conclude the book in 20:30-31. Read these verses.

Jesus healing

However, John follows this conclusion with an epilogue in Chapter 21. We are not sure whether this ending was written by the writer of the first twenty chapters or was added by a later writer. This epilogue tells of Jesus' appearance to his disciples in Galilee and reports the story of the miraculous catch of fish. It also shows a special interest in Simon Peter and "the disciple whom Jesus loved." Jesus commissions Peter to fulfill his task of feeding the sheep. A second conclusion to the book comes in the last two verses.

SUMMARY

In summary we may say that the Gospel of John presents Jesus as the Son of God sent by the Father to show people, through his death and resurrection, the way to eternal life.

Five familiar parts of this book are listed here.

(1) The prologue to the Gospel (John 1)
(2) The wedding at Cana (John 2)
(3) The woman at the well (John 4)
(4) The raising of Lazarus (John 11)
(5) The narrative of Jesus' death and resurrection (John 18–19)

QUESTIONS FOR DISCUSSION

1. John the Baptist's disciples heard these words of John 1:29: "Here is the Lamb of God who takes away the sin of the world!" They knew and believed in the Scriptures (Old Testament). The idea of the Lamb of God is connected with the sacrificial system of the Old Testament. (See Leviticus 4:32-35; Isaiah 53:4-12.) God accepted the death of an animal as a substitute for the death of a person who had sinned. Sin puts every individual under the sentence of death. So when a person sinned again, another sacrifice was required for that person. What might these words have meant to John the Baptist's audience? What do they mean to us today?

2. The message of the Fourth Gospel is summarized in John 3:16. Can you recite this verse from memory? Try to put this verse into your own words. What do you think John means by the words *eternal life*? What does this concept mean to you? Read John 5:19-47. What does this passage say about the meaning of eternal life?

3. The series of "signs" (miracles) are a feature of John's Gospel. Discuss the functions of ordinary signs, such as road signs. How do the signs in John function?

4. The Gospel of John is rich with significant sayings. One of these is connected with the appearance of Jesus to Thomas. Read John 20:24-29. In your opinion, what is the most important verse in this passage? Discuss with the group why these words are important to Christians today.

DAILY READINGS FOR ACTS

ACTS

Simon Peter's house, Capernaum

This lesson's subject is the Book of Acts. Let us begin by noting that the Book of Acts is not an independent work. It is the second half of a two-volume work. Originally the Gospel of Luke and the Book of Acts were one work. The writer introduces the second half of his work in Acts 1:1-5 just as he did in the Gospel. In this introduction, the writer gives a short summary of the Gospel of Luke and anticipates the contents of the Book of Acts.

Read Acts 1:1-5, and answer the following questions.

a. To whom does the writer address these verses?

b. What does the writer say was the subject of the first book?

c. For how many days did Jesus appear to his disciples?

d. What promise did Jesus make to his disciples?

ACTS 1

The Gospel of Luke and the Acts of the Apostles originally circulated as a single work. In the fourth century, the Council of Toledo permanently divided Luke and Acts into two separate works. It placed the Gospel of Luke with the other Synoptic Gospels. The Council placed the Book of Acts after John.

The present placement of Acts serves two purposes. On the one hand, Acts shows how the work of Jesus continued in the life of the church. Thus it is a good follow-up of the Gospel material. On the other hand as a history of the early church it describes the growth and spread of Christianity. Thus it provides a context within which we can read and understand the remaining New Testament documents, that is, the Letters.

Acts 1:8—a saying of Jesus—provides a clue to the general outline of the Book of Acts. Read Acts 1:8.

Acts describes how the early church receives power. The church then witnesses to the faith, first in Jerusalem, then in Judea and Samaria, and finally to the end of the earth.

Chapter 1 narrates two events. First, the writer reports the ascension of Jesus after forty days of appearances following his resurrection. The account of the Ascension concludes with a promise in verse 11: "This Jesus, who has been taken up from you into heaven, will come in the same way as you saw him go into heaven."

The second event concerns the election of a successor to Judas. The requirements for the successor are spelled out in verses 21 and 22. Read Acts 1:21-22.

The believers propose two candidates. They select by lot so God can determine the outcome. The lot falls with Matthias.

Read Acts 1:6-11 to learn more about the ascension of Jesus. Answer these questions.

a. The disciples wished to know when Jesus would "restore the kingdom to Israel." Why did he not give them a set time?

b. Why was the promise of the coming of the Holy Spirit important?

c. Luke included the Ascension in his account not only to record the past but also to look to the future. Based on this account

what do you think the return of Christ will be like?

d. In your own words tell what the Ascension signaled to the disciples who witnessed it.

ACTS 2–4

Chapter 2 records the coming of the Holy Spirit on the Day of Pentecost. Pentecost is the Greek name for the Jewish Feast of Weeks. The name means "fifty." The festival is so named because it falls on the fiftieth day after the celebration of the barley sheaf during Passover. In the Jewish faith it celebrates the giving of the law at Mount Sinai.

When the Holy Spirit descends upon the early disciples, they speak in tongues. The writer understands this speaking in tongues as the disciples' sudden ability to address the pilgrims in the city in languages that the disciples could not speak previously. Some of those who witnessed the disciples' behavior believe they are drunk.

Peter, after assuring the people that the disciples are not drunk since it is only nine in the morning, explains their behavior. The disciples' possession of the Spirit is the fulfillment of the Old Testament promise in the prophetic Book of Joel. In the last days God's Spirit will be poured out upon all flesh.

Then Peter proceeds to preach about Jesus as the fulfillment of Old Testament expectation. Here we have an account of the first Christian sermon. In this sermon Peter makes the following points. First, Jesus' mighty works, wonders, and signs are the way God attested to Jesus' ministry. Second, Jesus was crucified in accordance with the plan and foreknowledge of God— although at the hands of lawless men. Third, God raised Jesus from the dead and exalted him to God's right hand. To support

Ship mosaic in early Christian church

1.

2.

3.

b. To what four activities did the first converts devote themselves?

1.

2.

3.

4.

c. The early Christians practiced "togetherness." Indicate three ways in which they shared.

1.

2.

3.

his proclamation Peter quotes Old Testament passages from the books of Psalms, Isaiah, and Joel. Finally, Peter asks his hearers to repent and be baptized.

According to Acts 2:41 about 3,000 persons convert to the new faith on the Day of Pentecost. Thus Acts views the Day of Pentecost as the day of the church's birth. The writer then describes the general activity of the followers of Jesus. Read Acts 2:43-47.

In Chapters 3 through 7 the Book of Acts tells how the church establishes itself in Jerusalem and describes some of the problems encountered by the new faith. In Chapter 3 Peter and John heal a lame man on their way to worship in the Temple. The people's response to the healing gives Peter an opportunity to preach. He denounces the audience for their lack of faith and calls on them to repent and accept Jesus as the foretold Messiah. The preaching of the disciples leads to their arrest. In Chapter 4 the rulers, elders, and scribes give them a hearing. They then threaten and release them.

Acts 2:37-47 records the result of the first sermon given by Peter. Read these verses, and answer the following questions.

a. When the people were cut to the heart, Peter gave them two commands and a promise. List these three things here.

ACTS 5:1–9:30

The writer of Acts carefully reports that the early churches share all things in common. Read Acts 4:34-35, which talks about this practice.

Chapter 5 reports how Ananias and his wife, Sapphira, lie about their property sales and withhold money from the community. Scripture tells us that both die when confronted with the seriousness of their deed. The rest of the chapter tells of further trouble with the Jewish authorities, the arrest of the apostles, their hearing and beating by the Sanhedrin, and their release. But the Christians persist in their ways as the closing verse of Chapter 5 tells us: "Every day in the temple and at home they did not cease to teach and proclaim Jesus as the Messiah."

In Chapter 6 we encounter one of the earliest internal problems in the church. The Greek-speaking Christians, or Hellenists, felt they were being neglected in the distribution of the common goods. To meet the needs of this group the disciples select seven members who were to be responsible for the welfare of the Hellenists.

One of those selected is Stephen. Chapter 7 gives his speech before the Sanhedrin. His attack on the Council for their hardness of heart and their unwillingness to see Jesus as the Messiah enrages the leaders. They cast Stephen out of the city and stone him. Thus Stephen becomes the first Christian martyr. One of those present and consenting to his death is Saul—later known as Paul.

As a result of the persecution that arose against the church, the early Christians scattered. In Chapters 8 and following, the writer shows how this persecution and scattering leads to the spread of Christianity. Chapter 8 tells how Philip preaches the gospel in Samaria. The first part of Chapter 9 reports Saul's conversion on the road to Damascus, on his travels to persecute the church.

In Chapter 8 we read of the spread of the gospel from Jerusalem to Samaria. Read Acts 8:1-8, and answer these questions.

a. Why did the church begin to move out from Jerusalem? (verse 1)

b. What did those who were scattered do? (verse 4)

c. The Samaritans paid heed to Philip for two reasons. List those reasons below. (verse 6)

1.

2.

d. How did the people respond to Philip's words and works? (verse 8)

ACTS 9:31–21:16

Before discussing the further work of Peter, the writer summarizes in Acts 9:31: "Meanwhile the church throughout Judea, Galilee, and Samaria had peace and was built up. Living in the fear of the Lord and in the comfort of the Holy Spirit, it increased in numbers."

Peter's work in Lydia, Joppa, and Caesarea is the subject of Acts 9:32–11:18. In these chapters the church develops practices that differ from Judaism. In a vision God tells Peter that food God has cleansed is acceptable for eating. Also, the church admits noncircumcised Gentiles into the fellowship. Both of these decisions distinguish Christianity from Judaism.

The spread of the church into Gentile lands becomes the topic of Acts in 11:19 and dominates the rest of the book. The disciples establish a church in Antioch, and here for the first time the members call themselves Christians. In Chapter 12 we learn that the persecution of the church in Jerusalem—this time under Herod Agrippa, the grandson of Herod the Great—leads to further spread of the faith.

Paul's first missionary journey to Cyprus and southern Galatia—in today's Turkey—is the topic of Chapters 13 and 14. The growing number of Gentiles in the church leads to the Jerusalem conference of leaders in Chapter 15. This conference decides to place only limited requirements on Gentiles. The conference members advise the Gentiles to "abstain from what has been sacrificed to idols and from blood and from what is strangled and from fornication."

The discussion of Paul's second missionary journey, in lands around the Aegean, is reported in Acts 15:36–18:22. Paul's third missionary trip is the subject of Chapters 19, 20, and the first half of 21.

Paul's first missionary journey to Cyprus and southern Galatia is the subject of Acts 13 and 14. Read each of the verses listed here, write the name of each place Paul visited, and trace Paul's journey on the map on page 141. (See completed map on page 184.)

a. (13:1)

b. (13:5)

c. (13:6)

d. (13:14)

e. (13:51)

f. (14:6)

g. (14:25)

h. (14:26)

ACTS 21:17–28:31

The remainder of the book tells how Paul eventually comes to Rome. In Jerusalem some Jews from Asia seize him, causing a riot. The tribune arrests Paul for his own safety. Paul defends his faith before the Sanhedrin, then before Felix the governor of Judea. After being imprisoned for over two years Paul appeals his case to Caesar, a right he has as a Roman citizen. After enduring storm and shipwreck at sea and snakebite on land, Paul arrives in Rome. The book closes with Paul in Rome awaiting his trial before Caesar, but preaching the gospel unhindered.

SUMMARY

The Book of Acts gives us stories of the early heroes of the faith. It shows how their witnessing to the faith and the persecution of the faithful led to the growth of the church and to the development of a worldwide mission.

Five major events found in the Book of Acts are listed below.

(1) The ascension of Jesus into heaven (Acts 1)
(2) The appointment of another disciple to take the place of Judas (Acts 1)
(3) The Day of Pentecost and Peter's sermon (Acts 2)
(4) Paul's conversion while on the road to Damascus (Acts 9)
(5) Paul's three missionary journeys (Acts 13–21)

QUESTIONS FOR DISCUSSION

1. The Book of Acts shows how the early church began in Jerusalem and then moved into all parts of the world. The following are key verses that indicate the geographical progression of the early church: 8:5 (Samaria), 8:40 (the seacoast), 9:10 (Damascus), 11:19 (Antioch and Cyprus),

13:13 (Perga and Pamphylia), 16:11 (Samothrace and Neapolis), and 28:16 (Rome). Think about the contents of the Book of Acts. How does this book reflect the development described above?

2. Peter and Paul are two major figures in the apostolic church. In Chapters 1–12, Peter witnesses to Jewish audiences, saying, "Repent." (For example, see Acts 2:26-38.) Later we see Paul witnessing to Gentiles saying, "Believe." (For example, see Acts 16:30-31.) Discuss the difference between their points of view. Which approach to witnessing for Christ is better for today? Do you see yourself as a witness for Christ? Why or why not?

3. Acts 2:40 and 2:47 seem to be somewhat contradictory. Compare these two verses and discuss how we should understand them. What does the word *salvation* mean to you?

4. In Acts 5:41 it is written that as the apostles left the presence of the council, "they rejoiced that they were considered worthy to suffer dishonor for the sake of the name." Read also Acts 4:13-31. Discuss how the early Christians faced persecution with faith. Note parts of the world in which Christians are suffering persecution even now. Can we rejoice today when we suffer for Christ? What is the relationship between your suffering and your faith?

DAILY READINGS FOR ROMANS

Day 1: Romans 1:1-17
Day 2: Romans 2:17-29
Day 3: Romans 4:1-12
Day 4: Romans 7:7-20
Day 5: Romans 9:1-13
Day 6: Romans 12:9-21
Day 7: Romans 16:17-27

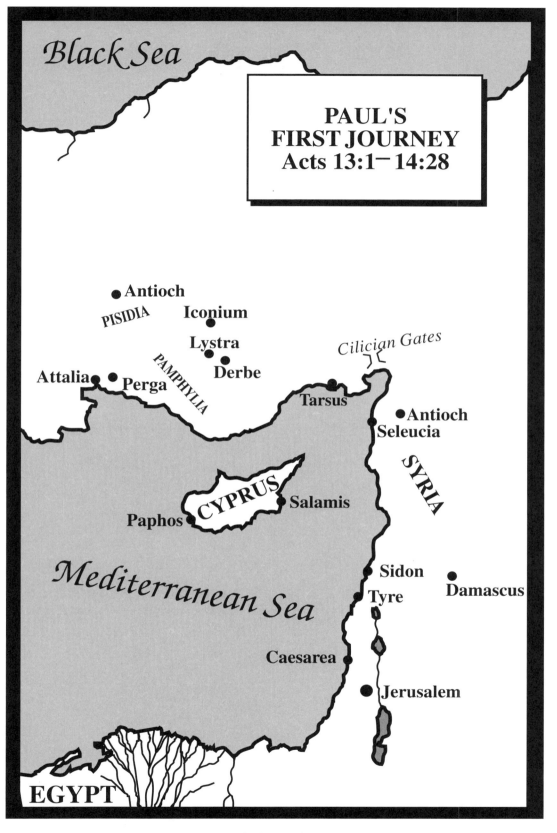

Black Sea

PAUL'S
FIRST JOURNEY
Acts 13:1 – 14:28

Antioch
PISIDIA   Iconium
Lystra
Derbe
Attalia   Perga
PAMPHYLIA
Cilician Gates
Tarsus
Antioch
Seleucia
SYRIA
CYPRUS   Salamis
Paphos
Mediterranean Sea
Sidon
Tyre   Damascus
Caesarea
Jerusalem
EGYPT

Review 5 Sheet

1. Of the three Synoptic Gospels, which one do most scholars consider to be the earliest?

2. Which Gospel writer is especially interested in Jesus' life and ministry as a fulfillment of Old Testament prophecy?

3. Which Gospel writer focuses on the mighty acts of Jesus (healings, casting out of demons, stilling the storms, and feeding the multitudes)?

4. Which Gospel originally contained no post-Resurrection appearances by Jesus?

5. Which Gospel writer emphasizes a concern for women, an interest in common people, and the universal significance of Jesus?

6. In which Gospel is Jesus presented as the Incarnation of the eternal word of God?

7. The Gospel of John presents seven miracles of Jesus, which are called signs. List as many of these signs as you can.

8. What is the significance of the Pentecost event in Acts?

9. What is the most important insight of Peter's vision about the clean and unclean animals?

(Answers are on page 183.)

THE LETTERS

INTRODUCTION

Twenty-one of the twenty-seven New Testament books are epistles. In the Old Testament we have a few letters, such as that which Jeremiah sent to the people in exile (Chapter 29). But these Old Testament letters are incorporated into larger works. The New Testament epistles are letters that stand by themselves.

The letters can be separated into groups in several ways. The letters to Timothy, Titus, Philemon, and Third John are personal letters from the writers to various individuals. These letters are more intimate and specific than the epistles that are addressed to congregations. Probably all the New Testament letters were dictated to scribes. They may have been reread and corrected before the final drafts were finally written on papyrus. Then they were placed in the hands of a messenger to carry to the recipients. The Roman postal service did not carry personal letters.

Another way to group the letters is by writer. Thirteen are under Paul's name, although the actual authorship of some of them is questioned by some scholars. Hebrew is anonymous, one is by James, two by Peter, three by John, and one by Jude. Sometimes the letters by Paul are called *Pauline,* in contrast to the others that are called the *General Epistles.*

THE DATING OF THE LETTERS

All the letters were written from about A.D. 50 to 100. Opinions may vary, but generally the order of writing is Galatians, First and Second Thessalonians, First Corinthians, Philippians, Second Corinthians, and Romans, all in the decade from about 50 to 60. Then follow Ephesians, Colossians, Philemon, First Timothy, Titus, Second Timothy, James, First Peter (the date of Second Peter is unknown), and possibly Hebrews, all before A.D. 70. Jude may have been written about A.D. 80, and John's three letters date in the last decade of the first century.

The letters are particularly valuable because they are the oldest Christian writings we have. Paul's earliest letters pre-date the earliest Gospel (Mark) by at least a few years. Also, Paul wrote other letters (see 1 Corinthians 5:9 and Colossians 4:16); but those that survived were particularly treasured, copied, and circulated by the early Christian communities. This whole process was a part of the activity of the Holy Spirit in the life of the church, we believe.

THE FORM OF THE LETTERS

Archaeology has shown us that the New Testament letters follow the normal form of letters in the Hellenistic world of that time. Only the greetings and endings of the biblical letters show differences in form. The general pattern is (1) salutation; (2) identification of writer; (3) body of the letter, usually divided into theological statements followed by exhortations and practical advice; (4) closing remarks, prayers, requests, and benedictions.

THE CONTENT OF THE LETTERS

Naturally, with a large group of diverse letters we cannot expect uniformity of content. However, these letters do contain teaching about God and the Lord with instruction on the Christian life and conduct. They also respond to problems that the early church faced.

Some basic ideas expressed in the letters are these:

(1) The relationships between God, Christ, and persons and their salvation. The letters express the same ideas on these subjects as those we find in the teachings of Jesus in the Gospels. God is the loving Father who sent his son into the world as the Christ that people might be saved. Christ—crucified, buried, risen, and ascended—is Lord. The world is corrupt and evil. We cannot save ourselves, but by faith in and obedience to Christ an individual can be saved. That person should then, as a part of the body of Christ (the church), live to the praise of God's glory.

(2) While Christ is both at the right hand of God and also inhabiting the church, he will return visibly and in glory at the end of the age. This is the Christian hope, to be with him in glory.

(3) The church is collectively the called-out people of God. Christ loves the church and is in the church through the indwelling presence of the Holy Spirit. As individuals, Christians should live as slaves of Christ. They are redeemed by his blood and are examples of moral, upright persons in an immoral and unrighteous social situation.

(4) The affairs of congregations of Christians should be handled decently and in order with appropriate leaders who love and shepherd the flock of God. Their worship, too, should be done decently and in order. But the Holy Spirit's activity and power in the worship experience should not be hindered.

Christians today recognize in the letters the testimony and instruction of the Apostles. The letters are a basic guide of faith and practice.

ROMANS

© 1995 Biblical Archaeology Society

Ruins of an early Christian church

So far in our study of the New Testament, we have examined the four Gospels and the Book of Acts. The Gospels tell us about the founder of the Christian movement, and Acts tells us about the history of the movement.

The remaining New Testament material is primarily letters, or epistles. Letters are usually written to specific people, addressing specific situations. Many of the New Testament letters attempt to deal with issues and problems that arose in local churches. So, as we study these letters, we will consider them in light of the problems and issues the letters address.

Of all Paul's writings, the Letter to the Romans is the best organized and the most general. It is not the earliest of his writings, but it is the longest. Romans sets out his understanding of Christianity in its fullest form.

Paul writes his letter to the Romans from the city of Corinth, near the end of his last missionary journey. The apostle has two main issues on his mind when he writes to the church in Rome—a church he did not found, in a city he has not visited. First of all, Paul has collected an offering from his various churches. This offering is to go to the church in Jerusalem, which is suffering from hard times primarily because of a great drought and famine in the area. Paul wants this offering to express the unity of the church, the unity between Gentile and Jewish Christians. He is apprehensive about his trip to Jerusalem, and he asks the Romans to pray that he be delivered from unbelievers in Judea.

Paul also wants to carry the gospel to the western part of the Roman Empire, especially to Spain. He wants the church in Rome to support his missionary work.

Paul discusses both the collection and his planned work in Spain in Romans 15:14-32. He explains to the Romans that he has done all that he needs to do in the eastern Mediterranean area. Read Romans 15:23-25.

So Paul writes to the Romans to explain his understanding of Christianity and to encourage the Roman church's cooperation in his western missionary program.

ROMANS 1:1-15

The letter opens in verses 1 to 15 with an introduction. Paul greets his readers and makes an opening statement. Read Romans 1:1-6.

Paul's introduction follows the common form in the world of his day. Unlike our letters where the writer identifies himself or herself at the end, Paul identifies himself in the opening words. He then summarizes some of the essential elements of the Christian faith.

Romans 1:1-7 is a part of the important introduction of the letter. These verses serve as a salutation. After reading this section, answer the following questions.

a. By what characteristics does Paul identify himself to the Christians in Rome? (1:1)

1.

2.

3.

b. Summarize in your own words what Paul says about Jesus in verses 3 and 4.

c. To what are the Christians in Rome called? (1:6-7)

1. (1:6)

2. (1:7)

d. What was Paul's desire for the Christians in Rome? (1:7)

ROMANS 1:16–3:20

After this summary Paul mentions the recipients of his letter and pronounces a blessing upon them. Finally he talks a bit about his coming to Rome and his desire to preach the gospel to those in Rome.

Beginning with Romans 1:16 and continuing through Romans 5:21, Paul discusses the nature of the Christian gospel and

Christian faith. Read Romans 1:16-17. These verses summarize the theme of Paul's letter.

Paul stresses the gospel as the means of salvation. Salvation comes by faith, and salvation comes first to the Jew and then to the Greek. Salvation comes through God's righteousness.

In his discussion of the gospel Paul first tries to show that all persons—Jew and Greek—stand under the wrath of God and are in need of salvation. The human predicament is such that a universal need for the gospel exists.

In Romans 1:18–2:29 Paul argues that all people possess a knowledge of God and are therefore accountable for their behavior and life. Creation itself testifies to the power of God. The world of nature reveals a knowledge of God. However, humanity has not lived by this knowledge. Persons worship and serve the creature and creation rather than the Creator. As Paul states in verses 22 through 23, "Claiming to be wise, they became fools; and they exchanged the glory of the immortal God for images resembling a mortal human being or birds or four-footed animals or reptiles."

Because of the religion and worship of the people of his day, God has given them over to their lusts, passions, improper conduct, and base minds. Their distortion of God's knowledge has its own consequences.

Paul also argues that humanity has a knowledge of God that comes through conscience. The law that is written on the heart will accuse and judge those who do not live by it. Even the Gentile can know God through two sources—the world of creation and the human conscience.

Beginning with Romans 2:7 Paul confronts the Jew who has knowledge of God through the law of Moses. The Jew is better off than the Gentile because the Jew has the law; but in the end, the Jew also stands condemned by the law. Thus Paul concludes in

Romans 3:9 that "all, both Jews and Greeks, are under the power of sin."

Romans 1:16-17 is an important summary of the theme of the letter. For what two reasons was Paul not ashamed of the gospel?

a. (1:16)

b. (1:17)

ROMANS 3:21–4:25

Against this background of human need, Paul states that God's justice and righteousness make salvation available to all through faith in Jesus Christ. Read Romans 3:21-24. These four verses summarize Paul's point.

For Paul salvation is through faith and not through human achievement or obedience to the law. In Chapter 4 he gives the example of Abraham. Abraham, Paul says, lived years before the law was given. Even before he was circumcised Abraham accepted the promises of God on faith. God reckoned this faith to Abraham as righteousness. Thus all persons receive righteousness through faith. And all persons—Gentile and Jew—who live by faith are descendants of Abraham.

Romans 3:21-26 explains faith as the means of salvation. Read these verses, and answer the following questions.

a. What is the condition of all individuals before God?

b. How can a sinful person be justified before God?

ROMANS 5–11

With Chapter 5 Paul turns to the nature of the Christian life and the freedom it brings to people under the gospel. This discussion continues to the end of Chapter 8. Salvation brings peace and reconciliation with God. The redeemed are now part of a new creation, a new humanity. Christ is a second Adam, and Christians are citizens of a new age. The Christian lives in a new freedom—the freedom of the Spirit—which is also freedom from sin and death. Throughout this section Paul speaks of salvation as a past experience, a present reality, and also a future hope. Thus he can advise his readers that they are dead to sin and at the same time warn them not to let sin reign over them.

In Chapters 9 to 11 Paul speaks about the failure of his own people—the Jews—to believe in Christ. Paul refuses to believe that the Jews are no longer the chosen people of God. Instead he argues that God is bringing Gentiles to faith because Israel was unfaithful and also in order to make the Jews jealous. He holds out the hope that after the full number of Gentiles have come into the faith, Israel will be saved. In spite of his desire to answer the question of Israel's hardness of heart, Paul ends this section by simply saying that all things are in God's hand. Read Romans 11:33-36.

Chapter 8 describes the Christian life in the Spirit. Skim the chapter, noting the verses listed below, for the answers to the following questions.

a. From what has the law of the Spirit of life set us free? (8:2)

b. On what do those who live according to the Spirit set their minds? (8:5)

c. To what does the Spirit bear witness with our spirit? (8:16)

d. How does the Spirit help us in our weakness? (8:26-27)

ROMANS 12–16

In Chapters 12, 13, 14, and the first part of Chapter 15, Paul offers ethical advice to the Romans on a number of issues. This advice ranges from relationships within the church, to relations with the government, to questions of clean and unclean food.

The last half of Chapter 15, which we mentioned earlier, talks about the collection for the Jerusalem church and Paul's visit to Rome. The final chapter, Chapter 16, contains a number of personal matters. Paul sends special greetings to persons in the church at Rome. He commends Phoebe, a deaconess, to the congregation. Paul closes with a benediction. Read Romans 16:25-27.

In the Letter to the Romans, Paul gives his clearest statement on the gospel as he understands it. He strongly emphasizes that we are all sinners—saved by faith, not by works or the law.

Romans 12:1 begins an important section of practical teaching. Read the verse, and explain in your own words what spiritual worship is.

Charles Shaw

"All foods are clean."

Romans 14:20

SUMMARY

Three main parts of the Letter to the Romans that are important to remember are listed here.

(1) Paul's introduction of himself and the essential elements of the Christian faith (Romans 1)
(2) Paul's explanation of Abraham as one who was justified by his faith (Romans 4)
(3) Paul's discussion of the failure of the Jews to believe in Christ (Romans 9–11)

QUESTIONS FOR DISCUSSION

1. The New Testament letters are best studied in light of the problems and issues they address. What problems and issues does Paul's Letter to the Romans address? If you were to write a similar letter today, what problems and issues would you address in that letter?

2. In Romans 1:18-23, Paul argues that humankind has not lived by the knowledge of God, but has worshiped the creation rather than the Creator. Persons have "exchanged the glory of the immortal God for images resembling a mortal human being or birds or four-footed animals or reptiles" (verse 23). What kinds of idol worship would Paul accuse us of today?

3. The role of faith in salvation is often emphasized (see Romans 3:21-26 and 5:1-5). But Paul's teaching on baptism (Romans 6:1-14) is usually overlooked. In the early church the symbolism of baptism was that of burial. Early Christians would dress in their finest clothes for baptism, as they would for a funeral. In baptism we identify with the Lord, sharing in his death, burial, and resurrection. New, victorious life in Christ means walking in newness of life because we have died to our former state. We have resurrection power as a result of our death, burial, and resurrection. Read this passage and discuss with the group the symbolism of baptism. What does baptism mean for you? What does it mean for your children? How can a clearer understanding of Paul's teaching here help us to live a victorious Christian life?

4. Romans 13:1-7 teaches us that we should be subject to the governing authorities. As long as the authorities over us do not force us to break God's law, we should obey them. But if the authorities force us to break the Word of the Lord, we should say, "whether it is right in God's sight to listen to you rather than to God, you must judge" (Acts 4:19). After reading these verses, discuss whether we should be subject to the government all the time. Explain your responses.

DAILY READINGS FOR FIRST AND SECOND CORINTHIANS, GALATIANS, EPHESIANS, PHILIPPIANS, AND COLOSSIANS

FIRST CORINTHIANS
SECOND CORINTHIANS
GALATIANS
EPHESIANS
PHILIPPIANS
COLOSSIANS

Mosaic of a small ship from a first-century house in Magdala.

© 1995 Biblical Archaeology Society

In this lesson we will briefly survey six New Testament letters. All of these letters claim Paul as the writer, but modern scholarship has raised questions about whether Paul wrote Ephesians and Colossians. He definitely wrote the other four.

First of all let us look at Paul's letters to the Corinthians. Unlike the situation with the Roman church, Paul is very familiar with the situation in Corinth. Acts 18:1-18 tells how Paul established the church in Corinth. When Paul visited this cosmopolitan and wealthy commercial center in Greece, he stayed there for over a year and a half. After he left, he kept in touch with the church. First Corinthians 5:9-11 refers to an earlier letter Paul wrote the congregation—a letter that is no longer in existence.

FIRST CORINTHIANS

Paul wrote First Corinthians to help the church answer questions and deal with problems that were dividing it. According to 1 Corinthians 7:1 the church had written Paul a letter asking his opinion on several issues. In addition, according to 1 Corinthians 1:11 a group called "Chloe's people" had given Paul an inside report about matters in the church.

FIRST CORINTHIANS 1–6

In First Corinthians, Paul discusses eleven major issues and topics. The church was divided into four factions. Some members stressed the importance of Paul, others Cephas, some Apollos, while others claimed to be followers of Christ. Paul discusses these divisions in Chapters 1 to 4. Paul tries to play down the importance of human figures in the church and stresses the unity of the church in spite of its diversity. Read 1 Corinthians 1:10.

In Chapter 5 Paul talks about immoral behavior. Apparently a Corinthian Christian is living with or is married to his father's wife. The church interprets this action as an expression of Christian freedom, believing that Christians can live outside the law. Paul commands them to kick the man out of the church.

The problem of court cases between Christians is the topic of Chapter 6. Paul recommends that the church handle disputes between members, for the pagan courts cannot be expected to render Christian decisions. Better than all, Paul says, is the willingness to suffer injury at the hand of another member than to go to any form of court.

In Chapters 5–7 of First Corinthians, Paul discusses sexual morality. Read 6:12-20, and answer the following questions.

a. How should Christians think about their bodies? (verse 15)

b. How does sexual immorality differ from every other sin? (verse 18)

c. Polluting our bodies by engaging in sexual immorality is like polluting what holy place? (verse 19)

FIRST CORINTHIANS 7–16

Beginning with Chapter 7 Paul discusses questions that the church has addressed to him. Throughout his discussion of marriage and celibacy, Paul points to the fact that the world is passing away and in its present form is near its end. Therefore, persons should remain in their present condition except to devote their full energies to the Lord's business.

The first two questions concern marriage and celibacy. With regard to marriage Paul recommends that persons accord each other their conjugal rights, as neither controls his or her own body. Each rules over the other's body. Once married, Paul forbids divorce, and here he refers to one of Jesus' sayings. Paul does make an exception in the case of a Christian who marries an unbeliever. If the unbeliever desires a divorce, he or she is to receive one.

On the question of celibacy, or those who are unmarried, Paul does not appeal to any authority. He gives his own opinion. Persons who are currently single should remain so. However, it is better to marry than to give way to immorality. Read Paul's discussion in 1 Corinthians 7:8-9.

The sixth problem Paul elaborates on is the issue of eating meat sacrificed to idols. Chapters 8, 9, and 10 deal with this issue. During Paul's day, the sacrificial animals dedicated to foreign gods were afterward sold in the marketplace for a cheap price. Many members bought and ate this meat—

not only because it was cheap but because it showed their total disdain for the pagan gods. For some members, eating meat that was used in pagan worship created great problems. Paul recommends that the stronger Christians give up this practice, when necessary for the sake of the weaker members' consciences. Or, as Paul writes, "If food is a cause of their falling, I will never eat meat, so that I may not cause one of them to fall."

The role of women in worship is the topic of 1 Corinthians 11:2-16. Women can pray and prophesy in church only if they cover their heads. Such a covering or veil indicates dependence or subordination. Here Paul reflects the typical understanding of the Old Testament in his day. Man is made in the image of God, but woman is made from man and therefore subordinate.

Paul discusses the abuse of the Lord's Supper observance in 1 Corinthians 11:17-34. He recommends order and respect while stressing unity in the body and blood of Jesus. He condemns the Corinthians for eating and drinking too much at the meal, as well as for eating in isolated groups.

Paul informs them about spiritual gifts in Chapters 12, 13, and 14. According to Paul the greatest spiritual gift is love. While Paul appreciates all the gifts in the church—including speaking in tongues—he admonishes the Corinthians to use their gifts for the benefit of the whole church. The use of spiritual gifts in worship is to be "done decently and in order."

The question of resurrection and life after death is the topic of Chapter 15. Here Paul affirms for the doubting Christians that God will resurrect Christians from the dead just as he resurrected Jesus.

Finally in Chapter 16 Paul mentions the collection that he has been taking up in all the churches. This collection will be sent to the church in Jerusalem. Paul asks them to put aside an offering every Sunday. He will then pick it up and carry it to Jerusalem.

First Corinthians 15 is the great passage on the Resurrection. Read verses 51-58, and answer these questions.

a. What will happen after the last trumpet sounds?

b. If we are alive at the coming of the Lord, how will we be affected?

c. Over what is Jesus Christ victorious?

SECOND CORINTHIANS

We have discussed the Book of First Corinthians in some detail since it allows us to see what problems and issues arose in the church and how Paul tried to answer them. Paul wrote Second Corinthians only after another visit to the church failed to solve the problems there firsthand. He had written at least one other letter to the church.

By the time Paul wrote Second Corinthians, he and the church were again on good terms and the personal attacks on him had quieted down. Much of this letter—Chapters 1 through 7—is Paul's reflection on the Corinthian situation and his troubles with the congregation. He describes his understanding of the ministry of an apostle. He closes this section with the statement: "I rejoice, because I have complete confidence in you."

The special collection for the Jerusalem church is the topic of Chapters 8 and 9. In Chapters 10 to 13 Paul strongly defends his ministry and authority. These chapters do not seem to fit the context very well. Many persons argue that these chapters were actually part of one of Paul's earlier letters, written when he was still at odds with many in the Corinthian congregation.

GALATIANS

Next we turn to Paul's Letter to the Galatians. In this book Paul is anxious to call the Galatians back to his understanding of the gospel. Paul defends himself and his gospel. Read Galatians 1:11-12.

In the first two chapters Paul argues for the divine origin of his gospel, a gospel that he did not receive from human sources. We find the heart of Paul's message in Galatians, as well as the heart of his gospel, in Galatians 2:16: "A person is justified not by the works of the law but through faith in Jesus Christ."

The Galatians had decided that one had to keep the law—especially the law of circumcision—in order to be a Christian. Paul attempts to show that works of the law are not required for salvation, for if justification were through the law, then Christ died to no purpose.

In Chapters 3 and 4 Paul tries to prove the truthfulness of his understanding of the gospel. He does so by first appealing to the experience of the Galatians themselves. Notice his question in Galatians 3:2: "Did you receive the Spirit by doing the works of the law or by believing what you heard?" Then, as in Romans, Paul presents Abraham as the man of faith and shows that Abraham was justified before the law and on the basis of his faith. Through faith all are Abraham's offspring. In discussing this point Paul states that no differences exist within the body of Christ. As Galatians 3:28 tells us: "There is no longer Jew or Greek, there is no longer slave or free, there is no longer male and female; for all of you are one in Christ Jesus."

The final two chapters of the book discuss the freedom that the believer has in Christ. Paul describes it as a freedom to live out of love, being led by the Spirit.

However, Christian freedom does not mean license to do what one wants, but freedom to walk in the Spirit—bearing the fruits of the Spirit.

In his letter to the Galatians Paul speaks of the example of Abraham. Read Galatians 3:6-14, and answer these questions.

a. Why was Abraham considered righteous by God?

b. Who are the descendants of Abraham?

c. From what has Christ redeemed us?

d. What blessing may Gentiles receive through faith?

EPHESIANS

Let us now turn to the Book of Ephesians. The central theme of this work is that of unity. In Chapter 1 Paul stresses the fact that God's plan is to unite all things in Christ. Verses 9 and 10 of this chapter tell us more. Read Ephesians 1:9-10.

Chapter 2 focuses on the fact that Christ breaks down the wall separating Jew and Gentile. The writer makes this specially clear in verse 14: "For he is our peace; in his flesh he has made both groups into one and has broken down the dividing wall, that is, the hostility between us."

In Chapter 3 Paul presents himself as an instrument in making the mystery of the revelation and plan of God understandable to his audience. In Chapters 4 through 6 he urges them to live lives worthy of their high calling.

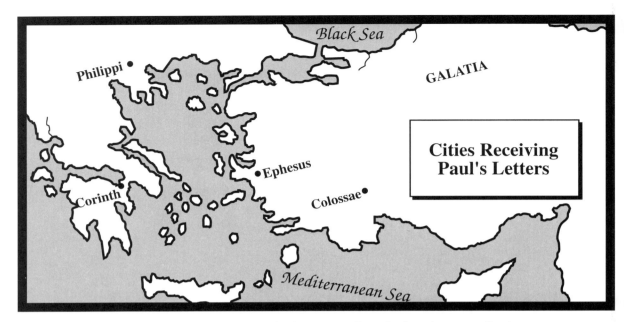

Cities Receiving Paul's Letters

The theme of Ephesians is unity. The basis of that unity is our common salvation. God's purpose and a promise are contained in Ephesians 1:11-14. Read these verses to find the answers to these questions.

a. What is God's purpose for those who hope in Christ? (verse 11-12)

b. What is God's promise in verses 13-14?

PHILIPPIANS

When we turn to the Letter to the Philippians, we encounter one of the letters Paul wrote while in prison. However, we never learn where he is imprisoned—whether in Rome, Caesarea, or some other place. In Philippians 1:12-26 Paul talks about his imprisonment.

In Philippians 2:4-11 Paul describes the humiliation and exaltation of Jesus. We often call this passage the Philippians hymn.

Despite imprisonment Paul says more about joy and rejoicing in this letter than in any other. Throughout the letter he rejoices in the relationships he has had with the church in Philippi and in the assistance they have given him. For Paul joy and contentment go together. In Philippians 4:11-13 he speaks of the nature of his contentment. Read these verses.

COLOSSIANS

Our final book in this lesson is Colossians. In its four short chapters this work stresses the supremacy and sufficiency of Christ. Although this letter, like most of the New Testament letters, mentions many ordinary and practical matters, it also contains one of the noblest views of Christ in the New Testament. It provides much of the thought that finds later expression in the Christian doctrine of the Trinity. Read Colossians 1:15-20.

1. Paul's own profound philosophy of life is expressed in Philippians 1:21. Write it in your own words below.

2. Paul prayed for the Christians in Colossae (Colossians 1:9-14). Read this prayer, and answer these questions. Your answers will help you think about the prayer.

a. Why did Paul pray that the Colossians would be filled with the knowledge of God's will? (verses 9-10)

b. Why did Paul pray that they would be strengthened with all power? (verse 11)

c. Why did Paul assume that the Colossians would give thanks to God? (verse 13)

SUMMARY

Five portions of these letters' literature are important to remember.

(1) Paul's discourse in First Corinthians on spiritual gifts (1 Corinthians 12–14)
(2) Paul's words on love, also in First Corinthians (1 Corinthians 13)
(3) Paul's discussion in Galatians of the true purpose of the law (Galatians 3)
(4) Paul's words in Philippians about his imprisonment (Philippians 1)
(5) Paul's portrayal in Philippians of the humiliation and exaltation of Jesus (Philippians 2)

QUESTIONS FOR DISCUSSION

1. Paul dealt with the problem of court cases between Christians in 1 Corinthians 6. Read 6:1-8 and discuss how a strong application of Paul's teaching might help the cause of Christ in our age. How does disunity within the Christian community make it difficult to apply Paul's teaching today? How should controversies and damages be resolved among Christians?

2. In response to the problem of dissension among church members in Corinth, Paul stresses the unity of the church in spite of its diversity. Begin discussion of this question by defining *theological diversity*. This principle allows for differing views to be expressed with equal validity, as long as they are within the limitations of our Christian heritage. What parallels do you see between Paul's response and the idea of theological diversity?

3. Ephesians 5:21-33 uses marriage as an analogy of the relationship between Christ and the church. This question can open up controversial ideas about male superiority, the rights of women, and the marriage-divorce problem. But the passage has much to say about the marriage relationship itself. Read these verses and discuss how appropriate the ideas are to our modern situation.

4. The Letter to the Colossians contains one of the noblest views of Christ in the Bible. Read Colossians 1:15-23. What attributes does Paul give to Christ in these verses? What would you add to Paul's description? What would you take away?

DAILY READINGS FOR FIRST AND SECOND THESSALONIANS, FIRST AND SECOND TIMOTHY, TITUS, AND PHILEMON

Day 1:   1 Thessalonians 1:1-10
Day 2:   1 Thessalonians 5:1-11
Day 3:   2 Thessalonians 2:1-17
Day 4:   1 Timothy 3:1-16
Day 5:   2 Timothy 4:1-22
Day 6:   Titus 3:1-15
Day 7:   Philemon 1-25

FIRST THESSALONIANS
SECOND THESSALONIANS
FIRST TIMOTHY
SECOND TIMOTHY
TITUS
PHILEMON

Holmes Photography

A modern Macedonian shore

With this lesson we conclude our look at the letters of Paul. First we will look at the two letters written to the church in Thessalonica. These letters are perhaps some of the earliest of Paul's writings. Edward P. Blair describes the first of these letters in an accurate and very telling way. His statement is worth quoting in full.

1 Thessalonians is Paul's most solicitous, affectionate letter. Here the great apostle appears not as a warrior doing battle for the truth (as in Galatians), or as a lawyer arguing a case (as in Romans), or as a fireman rushing to extinguish a devastating blaze (as in 1 and 2 Corinthians). Here he is a tender shepherd of newborn lambs—a pastor—who lovingly feeds, protects, and encourages the young. To use the letter's own figures of speech, Paul is a nurse caring for children, . . . a father gently encouraging his little ones.*

FIRST THESSALONIANS

Paul begins First Thessalonians with a word of thanksgiving that extends through Chapter 3. Paul reminisces about the founding of the church and his later relationship with the congregation. He remarks that the church's faith in God has gone forth everywhere. The church is an example of all the believers in Macedonia and Achaia.

In the last two chapters of First Thessalonians, Paul exhorts the members to grow in the Christian faith and to develop in the new life they have begun. He then raises one matter of faith that troubles the congregation later. This matter is the issue of the resurrection and the return of Jesus. He states that those who have died will be raised to life at the return of the Lord. He gives his opinion on Jesus' return in some detail. Read 1 Thessalonians 4:16-17.

In the first part of Chapter 5 Paul talks further about the return of the Lord. He warns that one cannot be certain of the time since "the Lord will come like a thief in the night." What one can do in anticipation of the day is to live prepared for his coming.

The question of what will happen at Jesus' return seems to be the uppermost concern in the church at Thessalonica. Read 1 Thessalonians 4:13-17, and answer the following questions.

a. When the Lord comes, what will accompany his descent from heaven?

b. What will happen to those who are dead in Christ?

c. What will happen to those who are alive?

SECOND THESSALONIANS

Paul writes a second letter to the Thessalonians to clarify matters about the return of Christ. The congregation has been caught up in this topic, which Paul had raised in his first letter. In 2 Thessalonians 2:2 Paul warns the members "not to be quickly shaken in mind or alarmed, either by spirit or by word or by letter, as though from us, to the effect that the day of the Lord is already here." This verse suggests some of the church's anxiety about the matter. It also indicates that persons were quoting or circulating letters in Paul's name, but the letters were not actually written by him.

In 2 Thessalonians 1:5-12 Paul speaks of the return as a time of great judgment and vengeance upon those who are not obedient to the gospel. Read 2 Thessalonians 1:9-12.

In Chapter 2 Paul writes of developments and events that will precede and signal the coming of Jesus. He speaks of a rebellion that will come and of a "lawless one" who will be revealed. This "lawless one," whom

---

* From *Abingdon Bible Handbook*, by Edward P. Blair (Abingdon Press, 1975), pages 295–96.

the one destined for destruction supports, will oppose and exalt "himself above every so-called god or object of worship, so that he takes his seat in the temple of God, declaring himself to be God." Scholars have tried to decipher Paul's images here. None has met with success, and even Paul says he is speaking about a mystery. He assures his readers that "the lawless one will be revealed, whom the Lord Jesus will destroy with the breath of his mouth, annihilating him by the manifestation of his coming."

In 2 Thessalonians 3 Paul reprimands some members of the church for their idleness. He charges them with "living in idleness and not according to the tradition." He does not say why some are given to idleness, but some may have decided that with the imminent return of Jesus, working made no sense. Paul uses himself and other disciples as examples of persons to be imitated. They had worked with toil and labor, night and day. Finally, he reminds them of the command he gave while he was with them: "Anyone unwilling to work should not eat."

Paul concludes Second Thessalonians by telling them that he writes this letter in his own hand. He did the same thing in the Galatians letter. Usually Paul dictated his letters, and a scribe wrote them down.

Second Thessalonians also contains a discussion of what will happen when Christ returns. Read 2 Thessalonians 2:3-12, and answer these questions.

a. What does Paul say must happen before the coming of Christ? (verse 3)

b. What will the lawless one do? (verse 4)

c. What will happen to the lawless one? (verse 8)

d. Who will be condemned? (verse 12)

FIRST AND SECOND TIMOTHY, TITUS

Persons often refer to the letters of First and Second Timothy and Titus as the Pastoral Epistles. They are so designated because the letters are primarily concerned with the life and work of pastors and ministers. They read more like ministers' manuals than letters.

In modern times scholars have raised questions about whether Paul wrote these letters. The reasons for doubting Paul's authorship are numerous. Words and ideas appear here that are not found in Paul's other writings. The letters refer to events about which we have no other information. For example, Titus 1:5 refers to a mission of Paul and Titus on Crete. We have no other information about such a mission. Some scholars doubt Paul's authorship of the Pastorals because the organization in the church seems more developed here than in Paul's other writings.

No one can say for certain whether Paul wrote the Pastorals. Perhaps disciples of Paul wrote these letters. Or, perhaps notes written by Paul to Timothy and Titus were later expanded to give the Pastorals their present form and content.

The Pastorals reflect three basic interests. These interests are concern with preserving the true faith of the believers, repudiation of false or unacceptable faith and life, and instructions about officials and their functions in the church.

Charles Shaw

2 Timothy 2:3-6

FIRST TIMOTHY

In 1 Timothy 1 the writer warns Timothy against persons who are more concerned with myths, endless genealogies, and speculations, than with divine training in the faith. The writer then charges Timothy to be a faithful minister of the gospel so that he can live in good conscience and not shipwreck his faith.

Chapter 2 and the first thirteen verses of Chapter 3 discuss matters of worship and qualifications of good church leaders. The writer encourages intercessory prayer for persons in high positions, advises women to be submissive and live modestly, and outlines the qualities of a good bishop and a good deacon.

With 1 Timothy 3:14 the letter returns to describing Timothy's responsibility for teaching the Christian faith and life. The writer admonishes him to "let no one despise your youth, but set the believers an example in speech and conduct, in love, in faith, in purity." After describing the role of widows and elders in the church in Chapter 5, the writer again stresses the nature of true ministry in Chapter 6. He also warns against false teachers who are often dominated by a love for money.

In 1 Timothy 4:11-16 to Timothy is urged to faithful service. After reading this passage, answer the following questions.

a. How is Timothy to be a good example to believers?

b. To what public responsibilities is Timothy to attend?

c. Why is Timothy to take heed especially of his life and teaching?

SECOND TIMOTHY

The Second Letter to Timothy sounds almost like a last will and testament. Second Timothy 4:6-8 speaks of the writer's interpretation of his approaching hour of death: "I am already being poured out as a libation, and the time of my departure has come. I have fought the good fight, I have finished the race, I have kept the faith."

Second Timothy begins with personal reflections on the maternal line of Timothy's family. Writing in Paul's name, the writer tells the young minister not to be ashamed of either testifying to the Lord or to Paul. Paul remains unashamed of the gospel, but mentions many Christians who have turned away from him, shamed by his chains. Second Timothy 2:1-13 calls Timothy to accept suffering as a good soldier, confident that God will not deny him. The rest of Chapter 2 warns the young minister to avoid disputing about words. Rather, he is to make himself a vessel fit for noble use.

In Chapter 3 the writer warns Timothy that stressful times will come in the last day. Persons will become lovers of self and inhumane to others, while the outward form of religion will be very popular. Again the writer holds up the pattern of Paul as a model to be imitated. Chapter 4 opens with a charge to Timothy. Read 2 Timothy 4:2-5 aloud. These verses closely resemble an ordination charge.

Read 2 Timothy 2:20-26, and answer the following questions.

a. How can one be a vessel for special use?

b. How should a young person handle youthful passions?

c. How should a Christian deal with opponents?

TITUS

The final Pastoral Epistle is the Letter to Titus. Paul frequently refers to Titus in his letters. Titus was a Gentile who was converted to Christianity and often accompanied Paul. Like the books of First and Second Timothy, this letter offers instruction for a younger minister. Chapter 1 deals with the qualifications and appointment of elders in the church. Chapter 2 advises Titus about the proper approach to various groups in the church: older men, older women, younger men, and slaves. The final chapter offers ethical advice on the art of living in the light of the faith.

PHILEMON

The final letter in this lesson is the Letter to Philemon. Paul wrote it while awaiting trial in Rome. There a runaway slave came under Paul's influence and was converted to Christianity. Paul sent the slave back to his master with this letter.

In the Letter to Philemon, Paul does not attack the institution of slavery, but he does ask Philemon to receive Onesimus back as someone more than a slave: "no longer as a slave but more than a slave. a beloved brother—especially to me but how much more to you, both in the flesh and in the Lord" (verse 16). For Paul, the common bond of Christians transcends the master-slave relationship. Read Philemon 17-20.

Persons often wonder why this short letter of personal correspondence came to be in the Bible. The early church claimed a bishop named Onesimus. One scholar has suggested that this was none other than the slave of Philemon. In this theory, Onesimus collected the letters of Paul from various churches and included the one to his master, Philemon, which described the connection between Paul and Onesimus.

Read Philemon 8-20, and answer these questions.

a. How does Paul feel toward the runaway slave Onesimus? (verse 10)

b. Paul did not keep Onesimus with him, even though Onesimus was very useful to him. Why did Paul send the slave back to Philemon? (verse 14)

c. How does Paul want Philemon to receive Onesimus? (verses 16-17)

d. What is the relationship between Paul and Philemon, as Paul understands it? (verse 20)

SUMMARY

Four main parts of this literature are important to remember.

(1) Paul's discussion in First Thessalonians about the Resurrection and the return of Christ (1 Thessalonians 4–5)
(2) Paul's words in Second Thessalonians about the events just before the coming of Christ (2 Thessalonians 2)
(3) The advice in First Timothy about worship and good church leadership (1 Timothy 2–3)
(4) The ethical advice to Titus about how to live a life of faith (Titus 3)

QUESTIONS FOR DISCUSSION

1. The members of the church in Thessalonica were evidently concerned about the events surrounding the second coming of Jesus. Are we as concerned about this event as the Thessalonians were?

Why or why not? Think about this event as Paul describes it to the Thessalonians. Do you picture the Second Coming in a similar way? If not, how does your view differ from the picture Paul portrays?

2. Think about the advice given to Timothy on the appropriate behavior of women. If you need to refresh your memory, read 1 Timothy 2:8-15. Use a commentary to gain more insight on the culture and context of this instruction. How has the church's view of women changed since this letter was written to Timothy? If you could speak with the writer, how would you respond to this advice about women?

3. Titus 2:11-14 provides a model for developing Christian maturity: "a people of his own who are *zealous for good deeds*" (italics added). What attitudes should we be developing toward ourselves in relationship to the world, to our lifestyle, and toward others? How would you characterize Christian maturity? Give examples.

4. We are told in 1 Timothy 6:10 that "the love of money is a root of all kinds of evil." However, many persons think of money as the most important thing in their lives today. Have you read about or do you know of someone who has loved money but is miserable? someone who has fallen into evil? How should Christians deal with the problem of the attraction of money?

DAILY READINGS FOR HEBREWS; JAMES; FIRST AND SECOND PETER; FIRST, SECOND, AND THIRD JOHN; AND JUDE

Day 1: Hebrews 1:1-14
Day 2: James 1:16-27
Day 3: 1 Peter 5:1-14
Day 4: 2 Peter 1:1-21
Day 5: 1 John 4:1-12
Day 6: 2 John 1-13, 3 John
Day 7: Jude 1-16

HEBREWS, JAMES
FIRST PETER
SECOND PETER
FIRST JOHN
SECOND JOHN
THIRD JOHN
JUDE

Mosaic floor in early Christian monastery

In this lessson we will look at eight New Testament epistles. With the exception of the Book of Hebrews, all of these are very short letters. They usually deal with more general issues than the letters of Paul, most of which treat very specific issues. None of these eight letters was written to a specific congregation.

At the conclusion of this lesson you will have studied twenty-one New Testament letters. Write the names of these letters, in their biblical order if possible.

1.

2.

3.

4.

5.

6.

7.

8.

9.

10.

11.

12.

13.

14.

15.

16.

17.

18.

19.

20.

21.

HEBREWS

First of all let us turn to the Book of Hebrews. This work was written anonymously, that is, without any named writer. It was written to people who were thinking about giving up the Christian faith and returning or converting to Judaism. Thus the book is entitled "The Letter to the Hebrews." The recipients of the letter were undergoing persecution in the Roman Empire. The writer speaks of "a hard struggle," "abuse and affliction," and "the plundering of property." The community's suffering has not yet led to martyrdom. The writer reminds the readers in Hebrews 12:4 that "in your struggle against sin you have not yet resisted to the point of shedding your blood."

The intensified persecution of Christians was tempting many to take refuge in Judaism. Judaism, unlike Christianity, was legally recognized and protected in the Roman Empire.

The writer tries to get his readers to remain within the church and to remain faithful to Christ, in spite of the present suffering and persecution. The book presents an involved and elaborate argument to demonstrate the superiority of Christianity over Judaism. It does this by constantly appealing to Old Testament passages that are seen as predictions or declarations about Jesus, his life, death, and redemptive work.

We must remember that the Old Testament was the only Bible of the church at that time. The New Testament as a collection of authoritative writings did not yet exist. In arguing from the Old Testament the writer is appealing to Scripture. Thus the writer uses the sacred writings of one religion to prove the superiority of another religion.

The writer of Hebrews sets out to show that Jesus is superior to the angels and to Moses himself. Some of these arguments may seem a bit strange to us, but we must remember that they were probably matters of very serious debate between the Jewish and Christian communities. The letter opens by contrasting the old ways of revelation with the new revelation through the Son. Read Hebrews 1:1-3.

HEBREWS 2–11

In proving Jesus' superiority in Hebrews 1–4 , the writer stresses that God addresses only Jesus—not the angels nor Moses—as Son. God resurrected and exalted Jesus, who now sits at the right hand of God. God crowned Jesus with glory. We can see a good example of the writer's approach in Hebrews 2:5-8. Read these verses. In this passage, the writer refers to Psalm 8, which he understands to be a description of Jesus and his exalted status—a status not shared by any other.

Throughout Hebrews 4:14–10:18 the writer argues for the superiority of Jesus' priesthood and sacrifice over that of the Jewish levitical priesthood. These chapters depict Jesus as the great high priest who is sinless and also a blameless sacrifice. He functions as priest in the heavenly sanctuary, of which the Jerusalem Temple is only a reflection or model. Jesus' sacrifice—unlike that offered in the Temple—does not have to be repeated, but is a sacrifice offered once and for all. At the right hand of God, Jesus constantly intercedes for Christians, unlike the Jewish high priest who only enters the Holy of Holies once a year to intercede for the people.

In Hebrews 10:19–19:29 the writer tells his readers that because of God's revelation in Christ, they must hold all the more firmly to faith. Failure to do so brings fearful judgment. Chapter 11 describes the ancient heroes of faith and calls upon the readers to imitate these heroes and live by faith.

Read Hebrews 10:1-10, and answer the following questions.

a. According to Hebrews 10:1, why couldn't the law make those who approach perfect?

b. According to Hebrews 10:7, why did Christ come into the world?

c. By whose will are we sanctified through the offering of the body of Jesus? (Hebrews 10:10)

HEBREWS 12–13

The writer challenges those who are persecuted and who are tempted to give up the faith to imitate Jesus and thus share in his suffering and eventually in his victory and triumph. Perhaps no passage summarizes this view better than Hebrews 12:1-2. Read these two verses.

The final chapter, Chapter 13, gives some practical advice while challenging the readers to live in imitation of Jesus with their eyes on the ultimate goal of the Christian pilgrimage. Read Hebrews 13:12-14.

The next seven letters discuss general issues and are addressed to the church in a general way. They are often called the catholic Epistles. These books bear the names of their writers or supposed writers.

JAMES

Now let us look at the Letter of James. Although the writer only speaks of himself as "James, a servant of God and of the Lord Jesus Christ," church tradition assumes that the letter was written by James, the brother of Jesus. Nothing in the letter itself suggests

Hebrews 10:12

Charles Shaw

or claims that the book was written by a brother of Jesus.

The book offers practical advice and wisdom on the art of living the life of Christian faith. In this regard it is similar to Jesus' Sermon on the Mount or the Old Testament Book of Proverbs.

Much of the letter is written in the imperative mood. The book's one hundred eight verses contain about sixty imperatives that admonish and exhort the reader. Unlike Hebrews the book does not have a central subject that it explores in depth. It moves from one topic to another.

One central emphasis that runs throughout the book is the stress laid on the need to express the Christian life in deeds and works. This emphasis is seen most clearly in James 1:22-25.

For the writer, "religion that is pure and undefiled before God, the Father, is this: to care for orphans and widows in their distress, and to keep oneself unstained by the

world." In Chapter 2 the writer compares faith without works to faith with works and concludes that "faith without works is also dead."

Read James 1:2-4 and 1:12-15 on trials and temptations. Then answer these questions.

a. Why does James have such a positive outlook about meeting trials?

b. Why can we not say that "I am tempted by God"?

c. How then are we tempted?

Preaching the gospel

Charles Shaw

reminds the readers that God does not calculate time in human terms (2 Peter 3:8).

Read 2 Peter 3:8-13 on Christ's return, and answer the following questions.

a. According to verse 9, why does the Lord delay his return?

b. How will the day of the Lord come?

c. In Noah's time the earth was destroyed by a flood. How will the earth be destroyed in the day of the Lord?

FIRST AND SECOND PETER

Two New Testament letters bear the name of Peter. Like the Book of Hebrews, First Peter was written to encourage Christians who were suffering persecution. The writer makes several points in offering hope to the readers. First, he reminds them that they possess "an inheritance that is imperishable, undefiled, and unfading." Therefore they can endure the present sufferings and even view them as a good. Second, the writer stresses that "the end of all things is near," and therefore, the suffering will soon end. Finally, we see a theme that characterizes much of the early Christians' understanding of their persecution; namely, that Christian suffering is a sharing in the suffering of Christ. Such suffering is to be welcomed rather than avoided. Read 1 Peter 4:12-14.

When we turn to Second Peter a new issue emerges: the delay in Jesus' return. False teachers and scoffers are challenging the idea of the return. Second Peter answers that God remains faithful to the promise and that the delay in the return is simply God's desire to prolong the time people have for becoming Christians. The writer

FIRST, SECOND, AND THIRD JOHN

The three short epistles of First, Second, and Third John were written to strengthen members in the faith and to warn against certain heretical teachings. For the writer, true believers are those who not only confess faith in Christ but also those who obey his commandments and love one another. In 1 John 2 the writer warns the readers against false leaders—called antichrists— who lead Christians astray. One of the heretical views these epistles denounce is what later came to be called Docetism. Docetists taught that Christ was not really human; he only appeared to be human. First John 4:1-3 shows how the writer warns against this view. Read these verses.

JUDE

Our final book for this lesson is the one-chapter Letter of Jude. This work, like several of the letters in this lesson, warns the readers against false teachers. The letter does not discuss the content of their teaching so much as to characterize them as immoral, covetous, loudmouthed, and flattering.

1. Read 1 John 4:1-16, and answer these questions.

a. How can we know which spirit (prophet) is of God rather than the antichrist?

b. How can we know if a spirit (prophet) is of the antichrist rather than of God?

2. Read Jude 17-19. How will scoffers in the last time cause problems?

SUMMARY

These eight letters, which we have quickly surveyed, show how problems and issues developed in the early church. These problems and issues included persecution and suffering, the rise of heretical views, the clash of differing ideas, and the delay of the Second Coming. All of the letters attempt to defend what Jude calls "the faith that was once for all entrusted to the saints."

Five important parts of these letters are listed here.

(1) The argument in the Letter to the Hebrews for the superiority of Jesus over Moses and the angels (Hebrews 1–4)
(2) The list in Hebrews of the ancient heroes of the faith (Hebrews 11)
(3) The concern in Second Peter of the delay of Jesus' return (2 Peter 3)
(4) The warning in First John about antichrists, or false leaders (1 John 2)

(5) The further warnings in the Letter of Jude about these false leaders (Jude)

QUESTIONS FOR DISCUSSION

1. Chapter 11 of Hebrews lists great people of faith. After reading the chapter, discuss whose faith impresses you most. How does God challenge us by such examples of faith? What persons do you know who are examples of faith? What qualities make them examples for others?

2. Take a look at 1 Peter 2:4-10, noting particularly verse 9. (See also Exodus 19:5-6.) Where in our study have you confronted this idea before? These words were applied by the writer to Christians in the early church. How do they apply to us today? How does the idea of the priesthood of all believers affect our understanding, for example, of the role of women in the church today? Do you consider yourself to be among the priesthood of all believers? Why or why not?

3. The problem of false teachers (also called *antichrists* or *false leaders*) is frequently addressed in the letters we studied today. (See 2 Peter 2:1-3; 1 John 2:18-27; 4:1-3; and Jude 5-16. If these letters were being written in our time, what false leaders would the writers be warning us against? Be prepared to explain your answers.

DAILY READINGS FOR REVELATION
Day 1:   Revelation 1:1-20
Day 2:   Revelation 2:1-11
Day 3:   Revelation 4:1-11
Day 4:   Revelation 13:1-18
Day 5:   Revelation 15:1-8
Day 6:   Revelation 21:1-14
Day 7:   Revelation 22:1-21

REVELATION

Mosaic of grapevines from early Christian monastery

© 1995 Biblical Archaeology Society

The final book in our survey of the Bible is the last book of the New Testament: the Revelation to John. The book's title— Revelation—comes from the opening word of the book. In Greek, this term is *apocalypse,* a word that has become a part of everyday speech in modern times. The word *apocalypse* means "a revealing" or "a making known." We have come to associate the word *apocalypse* with ideas of the end of time. Revelation does have the end of time as a central theme.

The Revelation to John is the second apocalyptic book in the Protestant Bible. The other is the Old Testament book of Daniel. Although our Bible contains only two books entirely of this type, Jews and Christians wrote many books in which they revealed hidden mysteries or the future course of history. The century before Christ and the century afterward were very productive times for such works. Several apocalyptic or revelation books from this period have survived. Among them are the books of Enoch, Baruch, and some of the Dead Sea Scrolls. The apocalyptic book of Second Esdras is part of the Catholic Bible but is not found in Protestant versions. Other biblical books contain apocalyptic segments, such as portions of Ezekiel and Mark.

Before we examine the Revelation to

John, let us mention a few things about apocalyptic literature. In apocalyptic literature a person has visions or is taken on a heavenly journey. In these visions or on this journey the mysteries of life or the future are made known. These mysteries are not presented obviously but are made known in symbols or images. These symbols or images are interpreted to the person by an angel or some heavenly figure.

In Revelation the writer—who calls himself John—has visions. He tells us that he had visions on the Lord's day while on the island called Patmos. The Romans used this island, which lies off the coast of modern Turkey, as a place of exile for political troublemakers. John tells us he was sent to Patmos "because of the word of God and the testimony of Jesus." We are not sure of the identity of John, the writer, since many persons in the early church had this name.

REVELATION 1–3

John sets out to make known what was revealed to him. In the opening verses of the book he stresses the fact that what has been made known is "what must soon take place." John warns that "the hour of [God's] judgment has come." Read Revelation 1:1-3.

Persons write apocalyptic literature believing that the end of the world is near and that the triumph of God over the forces of evil is imminent. These writers want to make known the events between their day and the end. For John the second coming of Christ was near at hand Read Revelation 1:7.

After the introduction we can divide the Revelation into two sections. The first section contains letters to seven churches in Asia Minor. We find these letters in Chapters 2 and 3.

Several issues arise in these letters. The churches are suffering persecution and undergoing stress and trial. Christians are dying and suffering martyrdom for the faith. However, some of the Christians are giving up their faith or are being tempted to do so. Some of the churches are listening to false teachers. In Revelation 2:20 John refers to "that woman Jezebel, who calls herself a prophet and is teaching and beguiling my servants to practice fornication and to eat food sacrificed to idols."

In John's letters to the seven churches God challenges the members to remain faithful even in persecution and martyrdom. John views the churches' conditions as a battle between God and Satan. Finally, Chapter 3 promises a speedy end to the ordeal, with the promise of reward for those who remain faithful and punishment for those who are unfaithful. Read Revelation 3:19-22.

John's letters to the seven churches in Asia are found in Revelation 2 and 3. Read the verses listed here, and write the names of these seven churches.

a. (2:1)

b. (2:8)

c. (2:12)

d. (2:18)

e. (3:1)

Revelation 5

f. (3:7)

g. (3:14)

REVELATION 4–5

The second main section of the book begins with Chapter 4 and contains the visions of John, which reveal the church's final triumph. The writer tells us that he is taken to the heavenly world. Read the opening verse of Chapter 4.

John then describes his vision of God seated on the throne, surrounded by twenty-four elders. Seven flaming torches and four creatures that have the forms of a lion, an ox, a human, and an eagle are also present. God holds a scroll that is written inside and out, sealed with seven seals. The scroll contains the mysteries of things to come.

In Chapter 5 the writer introduces Jesus, whom he describes as "the Lion of the tribe of Judah, the Root of David." John depicts Jesus as a slain lamb, with seven horns and seven eyes. Only the Lamb is worthy to open the seals on the scroll and make known its mysteries.

1. In Chapter 4 John has a vision of the throne of God in heaven. He sees twenty-four elders and four strange creatures. They sing praises to God in antiphonal fashion. Write the words of praise each group sings:

The four creatures:

The elders:

2. In Chapter 5 the creatures and the elders together sing praises to the Lamb. Then angels take up a part of their praise. Write the praise of angels in verse 12.

REVELATION 6–11

Chapters 6, 7, and 8 contain the account of the breaking of the seals. As the Lamb breaks each seal, some tribulation is loosed. With the first four seals, John sees what have been called the four horsemen of the apocalypse. They represent war, anarchy, famine, and death. With the breaking of the fifth and sixth seals, John sees the souls of martyred saints and disasters in the natural world—earthquakes and darkness. Before the opening of the final seal, the writer describes an angel of God who places a divine seal on the foreheads of the faithful. They number 144,000 or 12,000 from each of the twelve tribes of Israel. These thousands are joined by a vast throng who shout their praise of God and the Lamb. This multitude are the saved who are delivered from the tribulations.

In Revelation 8:1 the Lamb breaks the final seal, and silence falls upon the heavenly world.

Revelation 8:2 introduces seven angels, each of whom has a trumpet. When they blow these trumpets, disaster strikes the

Revelation 14:14

earth. Chapters 8 through 11 report the sounding of the trumpets and the distress accompanying it.

Chapters 6, 7, and 8 contain the account of the breaking of the seals. When the Lamb breaks the seventh seal (Revelation 8:1-5), the blowing of the seven trumpets by angels begins. The seventh trumpet provides the conclusion in 11:15-18. Read this section, and write what the loud voices in heaven said when the trumpet was blown.

REVELATION 12–20

Chapter 12 begins another group of heavenly visions. Here we encounter the figures of the woman, the dragon, and the child. War breaks out in heaven, and Michael and his angels throw Satan out of heaven. On earth, he pursues the woman, who perhaps represents the church. Because of his successful pursuit, the dragon, that is, Satan, wages war on the woman's other offspring—"those who keep the commandments of God and hold the testimony of Jesus."

Chapter 13 describes two beasts—one from the sea and one from the earth. John tells us that the second beast's number is 666. The emperor at the time of the writing is Nero. Each Hebrew letter has a numeri-cal value. If one spells out the name Nero Caesar in Hebrew, the value of the letters equals 666. Read Revelation 13:16-18.

The visions in Chapter 14 and the account of the seven bowls containing the wrath of God in Chapters 15 and 16 lead to the vision of the fall of Babylon, which begins in Chapter 17. John describes Babylon as sitting on seven mountains and as a harlot and a persecutor. No doubt this description is John's understanding of Rome, which was persecuting the church. John identifies the present persecutor of the church in Revelation 17:10—the Emperor Domitian who ruled from A.D. 81 to 96. During his reign, a systematic persecution of Christians began.

The fall of Babylon in Chapter 18 is the prelude to the final triumph of the Lamb, which Chapters 19 and 20 describe. With the triumph of Christ an angel binds Satan for a thousand years and throws him into a pit. After this John depicts the first resurrection from the dead. The faithful who are resurrected will reign with Christ for a millennium, or a thousand years. After this Satan is loosed again. He is defeated a second time and cast into a lake of fire and sulphur to be tormented forever. The general resurrection and the final judgment then follow.

Revelation 20:11-15 describes the great white throne of judgment. Read this section, and answer these questions.

a. How is the awesomeness of the judge depicted?

b. Books were opened in this vision. One was the "book of life." What was written in it?

c. What was written in the other books?

REVELATION 21–22

The concluding two chapters, Revelation 21–22, tell about the new heaven and the new earth. A new Jerusalem will descend from heaven. John describes the city as an ideal, pure place. Read Revelation 21:1-8, 21-27.

The Revelation concludes by stating that its words are true and with the warning that no one should add to or take away from its contents. John gives the promise of Jesus, "Surely I am coming soon."

Revelation 21–22 describes the new heaven and the new earth. Read 21:1-4, and find the answers to the questions below.

a. In the new creation where will God dwell?

b. Express in your own words the picture of God and God's relationship to the people that this passage presents.

SUMMARY

In summary we can say that the writer of the Revelation to John, using all the symbols and imagery of the apocalyptic thought of his day, wrote to Christians who were suffering great persecution. He wrote to encourage their faithfulness, promising them that God was still supreme and that very shortly Christ and the church would triumph. Satan would be destroyed, and the intended creation would come to be.

Five main parts of Revelation that are important to remember are listed here.

(1) John's letters to the seven churches in Asia (Revelation 2–3)
(2) John's vision of God seated on a throne (Revelation 4)

(3) The breaking of the seven seals on the scroll (Revelation 6–8)
(4) John's vision of the beast from the earth and the beast from the sea (Revelation 13)
(5) John's vision of the New Jerusalem (Revelation 21–22)

QUESTIONS FOR DISCUSSION

1. Revelation 2–3 contains the letters to the seven churches. These chapters include several warnings to these churches and a few praises. Note particularly, 2:2-7, 10, 14-15, 19-20, and 3:1, 4-5, 8, 12, 15, 19-21. Imagine that John was writing to your church. What do you think he would find that would be praiseworthy? What would he condemn?

2. Writers of apocalyptic literature such as Revelation often used symbols. Persons cannot understand the real meaning of apocalyptic visions unless they have a "key" to the meaning of the symbols. Remember that the writer of Daniel was writing during a time of persecution and did not want his work to be understood by the wrong people. The same is true for the writer of Revelation. Why do you think John wrote his visions in such symbolic language? What effect does this practice have on later attempts to understand the biblical message?

3. In recent years Revelation has received considerable attention from those who see John's visions coming to fruition in our times. Perhaps you or someone else in the group is familiar with some of these recent interpretations of Revelation. What value do you see in applying John's visions to our times. What are the dangers in such an application?

4. Revelation closes with an invitation and a benediction (22:16-21). Read these verses. Do you feel that this is an appropriate ending to the book? Why or why not? How do you think that the persecuted and anxious Christians in John's day would have received these final words?

Review 6 Sheet

1. Which New Testament letter sets out Paul's understanding of Christianity in the fullest form?

2. In Paul's mind does salvation come through human achievement, faith, or obedience to the law?

3. For Paul what Old Testament figure is the best example of one who was justified by faith?

4. According to Paul what is the greatest spiritual gift?

5. According to Paul what unified Jew and Greek, male and female, slave and free?

6. Which New Testament letter provides the background for the Christian doctrine of the Trinity?

7. What three New Testament letters are concerned with the life and work of pastors and ministers?

8. Which letter is written from Paul to another individual on behalf of a slave?

9. Which letter was written to persons thinking about giving up the Christian faith and returning or converting to Judaism?

10. What kind of persons do the letters of First John and Jude warn against?

11. The New Testament contains seven letters that are often called the catholic Epistles. List as many of these letters as you can.

12. What kind of literature is the Book of Revelation, and what is its purpose?

13. What is the symbolism of the Lamb?

(Answers are on page 183.)

HOW TO TEACH
BOOKS OF THE BIBLE

BOOKS OF THE BIBLE is a study for adults of all ages who want to be better informed about the contents of the Bible. BOOKS OF THE BIBLE includes illustrative drawings, photographs, maps, and other information that will shed light on the Scripture that is being discussed.

SPECIAL FEATURES OF THIS BIBLE STUDY

• BOOKS OF THE BIBLE emphasizes the content of the biblical books. Most persons are familiar with some of the Bible stories and with some parts of the Bible more than other parts. After completing this study, class members will be able to locate these Bible stories and will have a good general knowledge of what is in the Bible.

• BOOKS OF THE BIBLE uses the Bible itself. During each class session, group members will explore the appropriate books in the Bible. Class members will learn about all sixty-six books of the Bible in the order in which they appear. At the end of the study persons will have paged through the whole Bible, from Genesis to Revelation.

• BOOKS OF THE BIBLE contains a pronunciation guide for use while teaching or participating in the class sessions. How many times have you stumbled over a biblical name or avoided discussing a person or place because you could not pronounce the word? While you are using this Bible study, you will find pronunciations of biblical names and places readily available on pages 179–181.

• BOOKS OF THE BIBLE contains six "Review Sheets." These are for use by class members either individually or during the class sessions. Answers to these review questions are given on pages 182–183.

• BOOKS OF THE BIBLE contains six articles that give general, introductory information on major portions of Scripture. These introductions are found on pages 7, 29, 61, 79, 121, and 143. As the teacher of BOOKS OF THE BIBLE you will want to present this information to class members at appropriate times throughout the study.

ORGANIZING THE CLASS SESSIONS

BOOKS OF THE BIBLE takes six months, or two quarters, or twenty-six weeks to complete. Although this study is designed primarily with the Sunday morning church school setting in mind, it would also be appropriate for a weekly Bible study class. Each lesson will take approximately forty-five minutes to complete. However, should your group decide to meet for longer than forty-five minutes, each lesson contains enough material to be easily adapted to longer sessions.

Begin preparing for each session by looking over the workbook questions, as well as by reading the content in the each lesson.

BOOKS OF THE BIBLE also contains a number of discussion questions at the end of each lesson. You may want to read these questions before leading the discussion in each lesson.

ASSEMBLING YOUR MATERIALS

You will need these items to conduct each session.
(1) BOOKS OF THE BIBLE
(2) A Bible—you may choose any translation; the answers in this book are

from the New Revised Standard Version.

(3) Maps of Palestine and the Middle East in Bible times (Some maps are printed with the lessons.)

HOW TO ADAPT
BOOKS OF THE BIBLE

You may want to adapt BOOKS OF THE BIBLE in a number of ways and for a variety of settings. One possible setting would be a youth Bible study or a church school class. Here are some suggestions to help you.

The class members may want to take occasional breaks during the study. Twenty-six sessions is a long study of one topic using the same format during each session. To avoid a sense of boredom among class members, you might break up the study by skipping a week here and there and studying something else. Convenient stopping places would be where the review sheets are located. If you are using BOOKS OF THE BIBLE in youth classes, you might vary the approach using roleplays or other activities especially appropriate for youth.

The class members may want to study only a certain portion or portions of Scripture. Perhaps the group is scheduled to meet for fewer than twenty-six sessions. Or, perhaps class members are not interested in studying the whole Bible. Again, segments of Scripture that would be appropriate for short-term study are located between the review sheets.

If the group is scheduled to meet for fewer than twenty-six sessions, you might ask class members to choose a certain number of books that they would most like to study. This method would insure that class members are able to study what interests them most.

Perhaps class members will want to spend more than one session on each lesson. Each lesson in BOOKS OF THE BIBLE contains plenty of information, and some groups may want to spread the content over two or more sessions. Groups that choose this approach should be aware that they will not be studying a "summary" or "survey."

Perhaps the class session will be held in a room that does not have tables and chairs. You might consider meeting in the sanctuary of your church, where persons could use the pews to balance workbooks and Bibles.

Without tables, using workbooks is difficult but not impossible. You might have students pull extra chairs in front of the chairs they are sitting in. Or, perhaps someone in the group would volunteer to make a plywood lapboard for each student.

Perhaps you intend to use BOOKS OF THE BIBLE in a setting other than the Sunday morning church school. This study would be appropriate for church school teacher training, a pastor's Bible study, individual Bible study, or many other settings.

THE TEACHER AS DISCUSSION LEADER

As the teacher of BOOKS OF THE BIBLE, your main responsibility during each class period will be to lead the class discussion. The amount of time available for discussion will vary from group to group. The workbook will take about twenty to twenty-five minutes to complete. Use the remaining time to discuss the workbook and the discussion questions.

Some teachers are apprehensive about leading a discussion. In many ways, it is easier to lecture than it is to lead a class discussion. But remember that the class members will probably benefit more from the sessions when they actively participate in a discussion of the material.

Leading a discussion is a skill that any teacher can master with a little practice. And keep in mind—especially if your class members are not used to discussion—that they will also be learning through practice. Here are some pointers on how to lead interesting and thought-provoking discussions in your study group.[1]

Preparing for a Discussion

1. Focus on the subject that will be discussed and on the goal you want to achieve through that discussion.
2. Prepare by collecting information and data that you will need; jot down these ideas, facts, and questions so you will have them when you need them.
3. Begin organizing your ideas; stop often to review your work. Keep in mind the climate within the group—attitudes, feelings, eagerness to participate and learn.
4. Consider possible alternative group procedures. Be prepared for the unexpected.
5. Think through several ways to bring the discussion to a close, having reached your goal.

Establishing a Climate for Learning

The teacher's readiness and preparation quickly establishes a climate in which the group can proceed and its members learn and grow. The anxiety and fear of an unprepared teacher are contagious, but so are the positive vibrations coming from a teacher prepared to move into a learning enterprise.

An attitude of shared ownership is also basic. Group members need to perceive themselves as part of the learning experience. Persons establish ownership by working on goals, sharing concerns, and accepting major responsibility for learning.

Here are several ways the teacher can foster a positive climate for learning and growth.

1. *Readiness*: A teacher who is always fully prepared can promote, in turn, the group's readiness to learn.
2. *Exploration*: When the teacher encourages group members to freely explore new ideas, persons will know they are in a group whose primary function is learning.
3. *Exposure*: A teacher who is open, honest, and willing to reveal himself or herself to the group, will encourage students to discuss their feelings and opinions.
4. *Confidentiality*: A teacher can create a climate for learning when he or she respects the confidentiality of group members and encourages the group members to respect one another's confidentiality.
5. *Acceptance*: When a teacher shows a high degree of acceptance, students can likewise accept one another honestly.

Keeping the Discussion Going

Most discussion group settings will require the teacher's response in some way. At times his or her decision will be the appropriate one; at other times the teacher will misunderstand the situation. During an evaluation period, or after the session, the teacher may get some valuable feedback from group members. Ask for such feedback!

You, as the teacher, are responsible for establishing discussion boundaries. For example, most groups have a limited and designated block of time together and need some guidelines for getting into the subject.

Establishing boundaries means giving the group three things: a central focus, a specific assignment, and a time limit. Each of these will vary in degree, and the teacher is responsible for keeping them in balance to meet the needs of the group.

To establish *central focus*, be simple and direct about the major theme. *Specific assignments* may be, for example, listing questions or ideas on a chalkboard or a large sheet of paper. *Time limit* means something like, "For ten minutes let's discuss this question."

Assume that your group will follow instructions. You will instill self-confidence in group members when you assume that they can discuss the assignment. Some class members may hesitate, but simply wait for them. Most of them will move on.

Persons appreciate, and have the right to expect, some form of guidance from the teacher. The teacher, in turn, has spent time studying and planning. Creative guidance is far removed from rigid control.

Establishing boundaries, or offering guidelines, is different from controlling. Controlling is a negative experience when members do not feel free to express their opinions. Control denies freedom and ownership. Establishing boundaries also means encouraging the shy person and discouraging the excessive talker.

The idea of establishing boundaries for a group may look good on paper. But in the middle of a discussion or at some slack period when one person jumps off the track, what does the teacher do? How does a teacher determine whether the discussion has gotten out of bounds? And when does a teacher permit the discussion to change direction or get out of bounds?

When a person or persons attempt to change the subject or direction of the discussion, think about these questions:

1. Is the newly introduced subject or comment related to the present subject? What is the relationship between the two subjects?
2. Do we have enough time to pursue and integrate this new material?
3. Is this newly introduced subject coming up later in this or another lesson?
4. Why is the person introducing this subject or making this comment now?
   - Is the person tired or bored?
   - Is the person making a bid for power and influence?
   - Does the person have a sincere interest or personal need to get into this topic?
   - What nonverbal response does the group seem to be giving?
   - How do I perceive the group responding to the person?
   - Can I refer the person to reading material or private conversation rather than taking up group time?

Dealing With Conflict

What if conflict or strong disagreement arises in your group? What do you do? Think about the effective and ineffective ways you have dealt with conflict in the past.

Group conflict may come from one of several sources. One common source of conflict involves personality clashes. Any group is certain to contain at least two persons whose personalities clash. If you break your class into smaller groups for discussion, be sure these persons are in separate groups.

Another common source of group conflict is subject matter. The Bible can be a very controversial subject. Remember the difference between discussion or disagreement, and conflict. As a teacher you will have to decide when to encourage discussion and when to discourage conflict that is destructive to the group process.

Group conflict may also come from a general atmosphere conducive to expression of ideas and opinions. Try to discourage persons in your group from being judgmental toward others and their ideas. Keep reminding class members that each person is entitled to his or her own opinions and that no one opinion is more valid than another.

Closing the Discussion

Most discussions are intended to be incomplete. Rarely is a discussion designed to end with a nice, neat answer. Perhaps the greatest gift a teacher can give is allowing group members to leave in a stage of incompleteness and continued search. Often the stirring of the mind and spirit is an indication that some real work is going on.

As teacher, do not be afraid of a disturbing or incomplete closing. Trust your group. They are adults. They may not be nearly as disturbed as you are. As a teacher, you may feel that the class members will not come back. However, if you have prepared for and led a fruitful discussion, you will make a positive impact on the class members. They will be back.

Often the close of a discussion calls for a summary or conclusion. Here are some ways you might do this:

1. Let each person, or several persons, offer at least one or two meaningful ideas that have come from the discussion. Ask the persons to do this in a sentence or two; avoid letting them make speeches.
2. List some points, observations, or conclusions on paper or the chalkboard.
3. As teacher, you can make a summary statement.

Leave a discussion as open-ended as possible. Trying to wrap up everything in a conclusion is frustrating. *Close but do not conclude.* Also, time spent concluding is of less value than group discussion time. You might ask each person to sit quietly for sixty seconds and think of one or two new thoughts.

---

[1] Adapted from *How to Lead a Discussion*, by Travis Woodward. A Skill Training Package, copyright © 1975 by Graded Press.

GUIDE TO PRONUNCIATION

Aaron: AIR-uhn
Abdon: AB-duhn
Abednego: uh-BED-ni-goh
Abiathar: uh-BIGH-uh-thahr
Abimelech: uh-BIM-uh-lek
Abram: AY-bruhm
Absalom: AB-suh-luhm
Achaia: uh-KAY-yuh
Achan: AY-kan
Achish: AY-kish
Adar: AY-dahr
Adonijah: ad-uh-NIGH-juh
Aegean: uh-JEE-uhn
Agur: AY-guhr
Ahab: AY-hab
Ahasuerus: uh-hash-yoo-ER-uhs
Ahaz: AY-haz
Ahijah: uh-HIGH-juh
Ai: igh
Amalekites: uh-MAL-uh-kightz
Amariah: am-uh-RIGH-uh
Amittai: uh-MIT-igh
Ammonites: AM-uh-nightz
Amnon: AM-non
Amon: AM-uhn
Amorites: AM-uh-rightz
Ananias: an-uh-NIGH-uhs
Anathoth: AN-uh-thoth
Antioch: AN-tee-ok
Antiochus: an-TIGH-uh-kuhs
Apocalypse: uh-POK-uh-lips
Apocalyptic: uh-pok-uh-LIP-tik
Apocrypha: uh-POK-ruh-fuh
Apollos: uh-POL-uhs
Artaxerxes: ahr-tuh-ZUHRK-seez

Baal: BAY-uhl
Babel: BAY-buhl
Balaam: BAY-luhm
Balak: BAY-lak
Barak: BAIR-ak
Baruch: BAIR-uhk
Bashan: BAY-shuhn
Belshazzar: bel-SHAZ-uhr

Bemidbar: beh-mid-BAHR
Benaiah: bi-NAY-yuh
Berechiah: ber-uh-KIGH-uh
Bereshith: BER-uh-shith
Bethel: BETH-uhl
Bethzatha: beth-ZAY-thuh
Bildad: BIL-dad
Boaz: BOH-az

Caesarea: ses-uh-REE-uh
Calcol: KAL-kol
Caleb: KAY-luhb
Capernaum: kuh-PUHR-nay-uhm
Cephas: SEE-fuhs
Chaldeans: kal-DEE-uhnz
Chebar: KEE-bahr
Chloe: KLOH-ee
Corinth: KOR-inth
Cushi: KOOSH-igh
Cyprus: SIGH-pruhs
Cyrus: SIGH-ruhs

Dagon: DAY-gon
Darius: duh-RIGH-uhs
Debarim: deh-bahr-EEM
Docetism: DOH-suh-tiz-uhm
Domitian: duh-MISH-uhn

Ebenezer: eb-uh-NEE-zuhr
Edom: EE-duhm
Edomites: EE-duh-mightz
Ehud: EE-huhd
Eleazar: ell-ee-AY-zar
Eli: EE-ligh
Eliada: i-LIGH-uh-duh
Elihu: i-LIGH-hoo
Elijah: i-LIGH-juh
Elimelech: i-LIM-uh-lek
Eliphaz: EL-i-faz
Elisha: i-LIGH-shuh
Elkanah: el-KAY-nuh
Elon: EE-lon
Enoch: EE-nuhk
Ephah: EE-fuh

Ephesus: EF-uh-suhs
Ephod: EE-fod
Ephraim: EE-fray-im
Ephrathah: EF-ruh-thuh
Esdras: EZ-druhs
Ethan: EE-thuhn
Ezrahite: EZ-ruh-hite

Galatia: guh-LAY-shuh
Gaza: GAY-zuh
Gedaliah: ged-uh-LIGH-uh
Genealogy: jee-nee-AL-uh-jee
Gera: GEE-ruh
Gibeah: GIB-ee-uh
Gibeon: GIB-ee-uhn
Gilgal: GIL-gal
Gog: gog
Gomer: GOH-muhr
Gomorrah: guh-MOR-uh
Goshen: GOH-shuhn

Habakkuk: huh-BAK-uhk
Hachilah: huh-KIGH-luh
Hadad: HAY-dad
Hadoram: huh-DOR-uhm
Hagar: HAY-gahr
Haman: HAY-muhn
Hamitic: huh-MIT-ik
Hanani: huh-NAY-nigh
Haran: HAIR-uhn
Hazor: HAY-zor
Hebron: HEE-bruhn
Heman: HEE-muhn
Hezekiah: hez-uh-KIGH-uh
Hilkiah: hil-KIGH-uh
Hiram: HIGH-ruhm
Homer: HOH-muhr
Hor: hor

Ibzan: IB-zahn
Iconium: igh-KOH-nee-uhm
Iddo: ID-oh
Ishbaal: ISH-bay-uhl
Ishmael: ISH-may-uhl
Issachar: IS-uh-kahr

Jair: JAY-uhr
Japheth: JAY-fith
Jebusite: JEB-yoo-site

Jehoahaz: ji-HOH-uh-haz
Jehoiada: ji-HOI-uh-duh
Jehoiakim: ji-HOI-uh-kim
Jephthah: JEF-thuh
Jeroboam: jer-uh-BOH-uhm
Jeshua: JESH-yoo-uh
Jezebel: JEZ-uh-bel
Jezreel: JEZ-ree-uhl
Joab: JOH-ab
Joash: JOH-ash
Joppa: JOP-uh
Josiah: joh-SIGH-uh
Jotham: JOH-thuhm

Kadesh-barnea: kay-dish-BAHR-nee-uh
Kiriath-jearim: kihr-ee-ath-JEE-uh-rim
Korah: KOR-uh

Laodicea: lay-od-i-SEE-uh
Leah: LEE-uh
Lemuel: LEM-yoo-uhl
Lethech: LEE-thik
Levitical: li-VIT-i-kuhl
Lydda: LID-uh
Lystra: LIS-truh

Macedonia: mas-uh-DOH-nee-uh
Magog: MAY-gog
Mahol: MAY-hol
Manasseh: muh-NAS-uh
Mashal: MAY-shuhl
Matthias: muh-THIGH-uhs
Megiddo: mi-GID-oh
Melchizedek: mel-KIZ-uh-dek
Mene: MEE-nee
Mephibosheth: mi-FIB-oh-sheth
Meshach: MEE-shak
Mesopotamia: mes-uh-puh-TAY-mee-uh
Midian: MID-ee-uhn
Miriam: MIHR-ee-uhm
Mizpah: MIZ-puh
Moab: MOH-ab
Mordecai: MOR-duh-kigh
Moresheth: MOR-uh-sheth

Nabal: NAY-buhl
Naboth: NAY-both
Nahum: NAY-huhm
Naphtali: NAF-tuh-ligh

Nazirites: NAZ-uh-rightz
Nebat: NEE-bat
Nebo: NEE-boh
Nebuchadnezzar: neb-uh-kuhd-NEZ-uhr
Negeb: NEG-eb
Nero: NIHR-oh
Nineveh: NIN-uh-vuh

Obadiah: oh-buh-DIGH-uh
Og: og
Onesimus: oh-NES-uh-muhs
Othniel: OTH-nee-uhl

Paphos: PAY-fos
Parsin: PAHR-sin
Pashhur: PASH-huhr
Pastorals: PAS-tuhr-uhls
Patmos: PAT-muhs
Patriachal: pay-tree-AHR-kuhl
Pentateuch: PEN-tuh-tyook
Peres: PEE-res
Perga: PUHR-guh
Pergamum: PUHR-guh-muhm
Pethuel: pi-THYOO-uhl
Philemon: figh-LEE-muhn
Philistines: fi-LIS-teenz
Phoebe: FEE-bee
Phoenician: fi-NISH-uhn
Polytheism: POL-ee-thee-iz-uhm
Purim: PYOO-rim

Rahab: RAY-hab
Ramah: RAY-muhth
Rehoboam: ree-huh-BOH-uhm
Rei: REE-igh
Rezon: REE-zuhn

Sadducees: SAD-joo-seez
Salamis: SAL-uh-mis
Samaria: suh-MAIR-ee-uh
Sanhedrin: san-HEE-druhn
Sapphira: suh-FIGH-ruh
Sardis: SAHR-dis
Semites: SEM-ightz
Septuagint: SEP-too-uh-jint
Seraphim: SER-uh-fim
Shadrach: SHAD-rak
Shamgar: SHAM-gahr
Shechem: SHEK-uhm

Shekel: SHEK-uhl
Sheshbazzar: shesh-BAZ-uhr
Shiloh: SHIGH-loh
Shimei: SHIM-ee-igh
Shinar: SHIGH-nahr
Sidon: SIGH-duhn
Sihon: SIGH-hon
Siloam: sigh-LOH-uhm
Simeon: SIM-ee-uhn
Sinai: SIGH-nigh
Sisera: SIS-uh-ruh
Smyrna: SMUHR-nuh
Synoptic: sin-OP-tik

Tamar: TAY-mahr
Tarshish: TAHR-shish
Tekel: TEK-uhl
Tekoa: tuh-KOH-uh
Tel-abib: tel-uh-BEEB
Teraphim: TER-uh-fim
Thaddaeus: THAD-ee-uhs
Theophilus: thih-AHF-ih-luhs
Thessalonica: thes-uh-luh-NIGH-kuh
Thyatira: thigh-uh-TIGH-ruh
Tola: TOH-luh
Torah: TOH-ruh
Tyre: tire

Uriah: yoo-RIGH-uh
Uz: uhz
Uzziah: uh-ZIGH-uh

Xerxes: ZUHRK-seez

Yahweh: YAH-weh

Zadok: ZAY-dok
Zebedee: ZEBH-uh-dee
Zebulun: ZEB-yuh-luhn
Zedekiah: zed-uh-KIGH-uh
Zelophehad: zuh-LOH-fuh-had
Zephaniah: zef-uh-NIGH-uh
Zerubbabel: zuh-RUHB-uh-buhl
Zeruiah: zuh-roo-IGH-yuh
Zophar: ZOH-fahr

ANSWERS TO REVIEW SHEET 1

1. Part one, Chapters 1–11, describes the Creation and early history of humankind. Part two, Chapters 12–50, contains narratives about Israel's ancestors (Abraham, Isaac, Jacob), and Jacob's sons.

2. The five major characters are Adam, Eve, Cain, Abel, and Noah.

3. God asks Abraham to sacrifice his son, Isaac.

4. Abraham's two sons are Isaac and Ishmael.

5. Isaac's sons are Jacob and Esau.

6. Their twelve sons are Judah, Reuben, Benjamin, Joseph, Issachar, Zebulun, Dan, Asher, Naphtali, Gad, Simeon, and Levi.

7. Exodus tells the story of the Israelites' liberation from Egyptian oppression.

8. God says to Moses, "I AM WHO I AM."

9. The Hebrews wander in the wilderness.

10. They build the Tabernacle.

11. The laws cover such topics as worship, cleanness and uncleanness, sacrifices, the priesthood, and festivals.

12. The Hebrews go to the land of Canaan. They cross the Jordan River.

13. Joshua succeeds Moses.

ANSWERS TO REVIEW SHEET 2

1. The Former Prophets are Joshua, Judges, First Samuel, Second Samuel, First Kings, and Second Kings.

2. God commissions Joshua to lead the people across the Jordan River and into the Promised Land.

3. Joshua renews the covenant between the people and God.

4. When a strong leader is present, the people are faithful to God. When the leader dies, the people forsake God. God sends enemies to oppress the people. The people repent, and God sends another leader to rescue them.

5. The book's main character, Ruth, was a Moabite who became an Israelite through marriage.

6. Samuel, Saul, and David are portrayed.

7. The Philistines are Israel's main opponents.

8. Solomon succeeds David as king.

9. The Divided Kingdoms are Israel, in the north, and Judah, in the south.

10. Assyria defeats the Northern Kingdom.

11. Babylonia defeats the Southern Kingdom.

12. First and Second Chronicles cover the same historical period that First and Second Kings narrate.

13. These Jews had to rebuild the Jerusalem Temple.

14. Ezra and Nehemiah tell this story.

15. The festival of Purim is connected with the Book of Esther.

ANSWERS TO REVIEW SHEET 3

1. Job, Proverbs, and Ecclesiastes are Wisdom Literature.

2. Chapters 1, 2, and 42 are prose; the remainder of the book is poetry.

3. The Book of Job raises the question of why innocent persons suffer.

4. Job confesses that he is of little account when measured against the mysteries of God's creation.

5. The Hebrew Psalter includes hymns of praise, individual laments, individual psalms of thanksgiving, Zion psalms, communal psalms of thanksgiving, and communal laments.

6. Proverbs contains long poems praising the pursuit of wisdom and short proverbs that give insights into life.

7. The writer says that there is nothing new under the sun. Everything is vanity.

8. Song of Solomon is love poetry describing courtship, love, and human intimacy.

ANSWERS TO REVIEW SHEET 4

1. *Amos is the earliest writing prophet. He prophesied during the eighth century B.C.*

2. *The Major Prophets are Isaiah, Jeremiah, and Ezekiel.*

3. • *Chapters 1–39 deal with the threat of impending defeat by the Assyrians.*
   • *Chapters 40–55 discuss the imminent return from Babylonian Exile.*
   • *Chapters 56–66 describe the situation in Jerusalem after the exiles have returned and God's future transformation of the world.*

4. *Jeremiah prophesied during the destruction of Judah and Jerusalem. He also prophesied to the exiles during the Babylonian Captivity.*

5. *Ezekiel was active among the exiles in Babylon and prophesied to them.*

6. *The Book of Daniel is apocalyptic literature.*

7. *The book says that it is written to the Babylonian exiles. Most scholars assign Daniel to the period of persecution of Jewish religion during the reign of Antiochus IV (second century B.C.).*

8. *Hosea, Joel, Amos, Obadiah, Jonah, Micah, Nahum, Habakkuk, Zephaniah, Haggai, Zechariah, and Malachi are the twelve Minor Prophets.*

9. *Hosea illustrates God's relationship to Israel in terms of a marriage.*

10. *Amos is known for preaching in favor of social justice.*

ANSWERS TO REVIEW SHEET 5

1. *Most scholars consider Mark to be the earliest Gospel.*

2. *The writer of Matthew has this special emphasis.*

3. *The writer of Mark focuses on the mighty acts of Jesus.*

4. *Mark originally contained no post-Resurrection appearances by Jesus.*

5. *The Gospel of Luke has these special emphases.*

6. *The Gospel of John presents Jesus in this way.*

7. *Changing water into wine at the wedding in Cana*
   Healing of the official's son at Capernaum
   Healing of the sick man on the sabbath
   Feeding of the five thousand
   Walking on the water
   Healing of the man born blind
   Raising of Lazarus

8. *During the festival of Pentecost, the Holy Spirit empowered the disciples as Jesus had promised. It is considered the "birthday" of the church.*

9. *Peter realized that God was telling him to extend his ministry to* all *persons, not just the Jews.*

ANSWERS TO REVIEW SHEET 6

1. *The letter to the Romans is the fullest discussion of Paul's concept of Christianity.*

2. *In Paul's view, salvation comes through faith.*

3. *Abraham is the best example.*

4. *The greatest spiritual gift is love.*

5. *All are one in Christ Jesus.*

6. *The Letter to the Colossians provides this background.*

7. *The Pastoral Epistles have this concern. They are First Timothy, Second Timothy, and Titus.*

8. *The Letter to Philemon is written by Paul to Philemon regarding his slave, Onesimus.*

9. *Hebrews was written to these Christians.*

10. *First John and Jude warn against antichrists, or false leaders.*

11. *The catholic Epistles are James, First Peter, Second Peter, First John, Second John, Third John, and Jude.*

12. *Revelation is apocalyptic literature. Its purpose is to address a persecuted community with words of hope and ultimate victory.*

13. *The Lamb symbolizes the risen, and now victorious, crucified Christ.*

Completed map. See page 141.